Sew, Serge, Press

Sew, Serge, Press

SPEED TAILORING IN
THE ULTIMATE SEWING CENTER

Jan Saunders

Chilton Book Company • Radnor, Pennsylvania

Designed by Arlene Putterman
Manufactured in the United States of America
Needleart on the cover designed and stitched by Margaret Cusack

Library of Congress Cataloging in Publication Data

Saunders, Janice S.
     Sew, serge, press: speed tailoring in the ultimate sewing center
     Jan Saunders.
          p.   cm.—(Creative machine arts)
     Bibliography: p. 204
     Includes index.
     ISBN 0-8019-7878-5
     1. Machine sewing.   2. Tailoring.   3. Tailoring (Women's)
     I. Title.   II. Series: Creative machine arts series.
     TT713.S24   1989   88-43309
     646.2′044—dc20   CIP

1 2 3 4 5 6 7 8 9 0   8 7 6 5 4 3 2 1 0 9

*Stacy Industries, whose products are recommended throughout this
book, ceased business as we went to press. Many stores will still have
Stacy interfacings in stock. Or you may contact the Pellon Company, which will continue to make several Stacy products available,
for further information (see Sources of Supply for address).*

Contents

Foreword

Those of us who are self-taught in sewing rely on people like Jan Saunders, who have the equivalent of a classical training in home economics, to teach us the latest and smartest techniques.

I've been a fan of Jan's since the publication of her Illustrated Speed Sewing, which revealed a deep understanding of the sewing machine and its nuances. Now Chilton and I are proud to add another classic to her body of work. I especially enjoyed her step-by-step approach to speed-tailoring a blazer, so that as you learn in each chapter how to interface, make welt pockets, line a jacket, etc., you are actually constructing something useful.

My husband liked the nitty-gritty on pressing with the new presses because several years ago I gave him one for his birthday. He likes to iron a week's worth of shirts while he watches Monday Night Football. Now he also knows how to clean his beloved press, thanks to Jan.

You will undoubtedly have your own favorite parts of Jan's book—perhaps the up-to-date serger techniques or the profiles of sewing celebrities and writers, or the customized machine settings for different techniques.

Whether you already sew in your own Ultimate Sewing Center or merely fantasize about it, Jan's book will update your skills. Happy sewing!

Robbie Fanning

Series Editor, Creative Machine Arts,
and co-author, Complete Book of Machine Embroidery

Preface

My folks couldn't afford to dress me like all the preppie kids in junior high school. Besides, I was too tall and gangly to fit many ready-made clothes. Luckily, I learned how to sew. I would bring a dress or outfit home on Mom's charge, study the style and fabric—even the buttons—then take it back to the store. I'd scour the fabric stores for the same style pattern, the right fabric and buttons, and I'd look over the belts and accessories to be sure my knockoff was the image of the ready-to-wear original.

I also took great pains to make my creations with the same top-stitching, the same contrasting cuffs and collar, the same shaped belt loops as the original. As my sense of style and sewing skills improved, I chose more complicated patterns. It was fun, challenging, and no one ever asked me if I made my clothes.

When it was cool to be different, I created psychedelic "art to wear" with ready-to-wear style, but my creations fit and were made a lot better than the store-bought variety.

Today I use the same eye for detail in my tailoring projects. But it didn't come without failure and experimentation.

I wrote this book as a way to share my successes and failures with you. I have worked in the industry since college and have had the great pleasure of learning about new sewing technology, from notions to sewing machines, almost before the items hit the market. With this book, I hope to save you time by recommending fast, professional techniques and products I like, and to share my failures so you don't make the same mistakes.

The material presented here comes from many sources. Some of the tips I learned from sewing friends and teachers; others are bits and pieces from favorite sewing publications. The rest are from years in front of my sewing machine, serger, and press—*my* Ultimate Sewing Center . . . my escape, my therapy, and a source of immediate gratification I must share with you.

Jan Saunders
Columbus, Ohio

Acknowledgments

I am grateful to the following companies and people for supplying materials that helped me research and write this book: Bernina of America, Betty Bennet and John Montieth of Redlands Sewing Center, Bobbie Carr of the Fabric Carr, David Coffin, Colony Cleaners, Clotilde, Inc., Crown Textile Company, Mary Dion for her willingness to share her knowledge of pressing, Dublin Cleaners, Elna, Inc., the many folks at Fabric Farms, Karyl Garbow, Sue Hausmann, Hi-Steam Corporation, Walt Hunt of Wheeler's Sewing Center in Santa Ana, California, Linda Losneck, Grace Johnson, June Tailor, Inc., Margaret Komives, Nancy's Notions, Ltd., Pellon Corporation, Stacy Industries, Inc., the Singer Company, Joe Rimelspach for use of his photographic equipment, Sussman Automatic Steam Products Corporation, and Viking White Sewing, Inc.

Thanks to all the sewing celebrities profiled in this book, who graciously shared their personal stories with me.

I also thank my artist, Tracie Korol, for coming through with such fine work.

Robbie Fanning gave kind words and encouragement and lent her creative mind and skilled hand to make this book the best it can be.

Finally, thanks and gratitude to my husband, John Moser, for being my cheerleader, photographer, and the family homemaker while I wrote this book.

Introduction

In this book I describe tailoring and other couture touches possible on all types of sewing machines. I have included information on the proper uses of fusible interfacings to achieve hand-tailored results in half the time it takes to pad-stitch a lapel. You will also find new product tips and tricks, a speedy welt pocket application, handpicked zipper application by machine, topstitching variations, and much more. Basic serger techniques are also included, so that you can sew as quickly and efficiently as possible.

Until recently, we've been spoiled by easy-care fabrics. When natural fibers regained popularity, some of us had forgotton how to use pressing equipment properly on ready-to-wear clothes and for home sewing.

The pressing information in this book is collected from dry cleaning and pressing professionals and covers both the hand iron and commercial or home press. There are tips for using other pressing tools, such as a puff iron, professional steam iron, tailor's ham, point turner, and tailor board—all of which can help beautify your handmade originals. For those who have forgotten the proper way to press a shirt, skirt, or slacks, Chapter 12 is a refresher course on using the press or hand iron.

Sprinkled throughout this book are profiles of well-known sewing celebrities, who tell how they got started on their sewing careers and offer tips on how they organize workspace. I think you'll find their stories fun and interesting.

Sew, Serge, Press is designed to supplement your pattern instructions. For example, when you read a section in the pattern instructions that explains how to complete a welt pocket, look up "welt pocket" in the index of this book and turn to the appropriate page. Regardless of the age or brand of your sewing machine, this book can show you a better way to sew a welt pocket. The machine settings, including the best stitch to use, the presser foot, and stitch length and width, are listed, and step-by-step instructions are written in an easy-to-understand way. You can write in your own machine settings, too, in the spaces provided.

I've found the best way to learn anything is to do it myself. As you read through the book, I'll show you how to construct and speed-tailor a blazer with me, so you can try each technique for yourself. If you work steadily as you read, you'll finish the book and have a new blazer, too.

To perfect the techniques presented here, try the suggested stitches and settings, record them for your machine in the space provided, then make a sample of each. I keep notes and swatches from sewing seminars and fashion shows and sketch ideas from ready-to-wear in a stenographer's notebook (it fits well in my purse). This way, if I'm looking for something special to put on a suit pocket or an interesting way of topstitching, or if I'm making a blouse and want a particular collar treatment, I simply look in my notebook for ideas. Once I've decided on a treatment, I test it, fine-tune it, make a sample, and write any special instructions to myself. The perfected sample and notes go into a large three-ring binder with plastic pocket pages for my permanent record. Even though I think I'll never forget the settings, I find this record saves a lot of time when I use the technique again. You may want to make a similar notebook as you practice these techniques.

If you own a serger, you probably know some of the virtues of professionally finishing your projects. In this book, you will also find serging shortcuts, with suggested tension settings. Again, record settings for your serger next to mine, and make a swatch for your notebook.

When your pattern instructions tell you to press a particular area, turn to the appropriate page in this book and refresh your memory on the proper method and preferred equipment to use.

When you become proficient in using your sewing machine, serger, and pressing equipment, you'll see your fabric stockpile begin to dwindle, and your wardrobe take on a sophisticated new look.

Chapter 1

Let's Get Organized: Setting Up the Ultimate Sewing Center

When I got married, I brought more sewing paraphernalia into our home than clothing and furniture combined. I had zippers in one place, buttons scattered in other places, fabric shoved into boxes, bags, and suitcases, and pressing equipment I had never used (the movers discovered it under the bed). With all this, I was still rushing off to the fabric store for thread, zippers, and buttons, even though I knew I had what I needed . . . somewhere.

The ideas in this chapter are what I used to get my own house (and sewing room) in order. You may think it a bit compulsive. But if your work area looks like mine after a few hours of sewing, you'll thank yourself for spending some time organizing and inventorying your sewing supplies. This system works for me, and I hope it will work for you. Think of it as an idea smorgasbord: use what you like and leave the rest.

INVENTORYING FABRIC

If your fabric stockpile keeps growing, it's probably time to get your fabric organized or, at least, manageable.

First, pull out all your fabric from drawers, closets, boxes, and bags and take a look at it. Surely some of it would be better off given to a charity, sold at a neighbor's garage sale, or given to a friend. I know my tastes have changed over the years, and since I have found a palate of colors that best suits me, I have been able to contain my fabric to a few drawers in the cutting table.

Organize fabric by season (linens together, wools together, etc.). To help with your wardrobe planning, put blouse weights that work with a particular suiting in close proximity. Linings, interfacings, swim wear, dress weights, sweater, and craft materials should all have easily accessible, but separate, homes.

While taking inventory of your fashion fabric, cut 2″ × 2″ (5 cm × 5 cm) swatches of each. Staple swatches on a 3″ × 5″ (7.5 cm × 12.5 cm) card, and note the width and yardage on hand. If you have lining to match, swatch and staple it to the same card, noting yardage (Fig. 1.1). To help in wardrobe planning, take the cards shopping with you, and add only those fabrics to your inventory that coordinate with what you already have. Store cards in a recipe file, by fabric category.

HINT: Until I reorganized my fabric, my interfacing was crammed into a large shopping bag. I never knew what type or weight was in the bottom of the bag. Then I noticed interfacing is generally wrapped in a plastic instruction sheet. I thought, Why not make a plastic bag

out of the instruction sheet by zigzagging or stapling the edges together? This way, the instructions are there for reference, and the extra scraps are neatly folded and put in the bag for future use (Fig. 1.2).

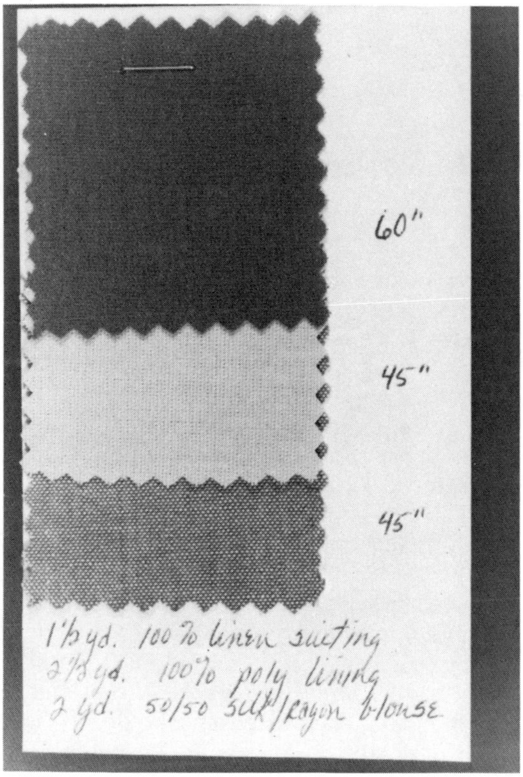

Inventory your buttons, zippers, trims, laces, and elastic by putting them in large Ziploc® bags or see-through shoe boxes. This way, you can check your inventory before making a trip to the fabric store.

It's not as difficult as it seems to get rid of outdated or outgrown patterns. Organize them by garment category (dresses, suits, blouses, etc.). I found three-tiered wire baskets at a discount store which hold about 100 patterns each (Fig. 1.3). One tier holds top patterns; the next, dresses and suits; the other, pants and skirt patterns. When I need a new outfit, or want to make that favorite pair of pants again, I don't have to riffle through all the other patterns to find the one for the job.

CUTTING AREA

Your cutting area can be as simple as a cardboard cutting board on a bed or dining room table, or as fancy as a cutting table designed specially for the area or room you sew in.

Some cutting tables fold down from the wall, then fold back up, out of the way, when not in use. The top of my cutting table is made of heavy plywood covered with a formica-type laminate. It rests on two chests of drawers my family was ready to donate to charity. I use the space between the chests for storing a tall wastebasket (Fig. 1.4), which I push fabric and pattern scraps into while cutting. The space could be used just as easily for file cabinets or pattern storage.

If at all possible (alas, I am not so lucky), the cutting table should be placed in the center of the room for easy access to all four sides. If it is also within reach of the sewing machine, you can swing around and use the cutting table as a desk, a place to put cut pattern pieces, or a drawing board.

FIG. 1.1 Staple swatches on an index card, noting width and yardage.

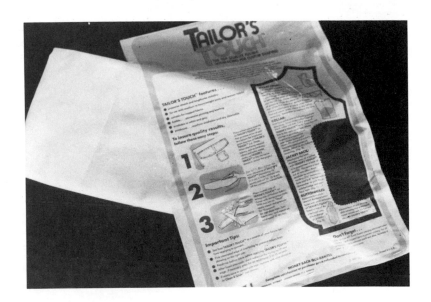

FIG. 1.2 Store extra interfacing in a bag made out of the plastic instruction sheet.

FIG. 1.3 Three-tiered wire basket holds patterns organized by garment category.

LIGHTING AND ADDITIONAL STORAGE

Proper lighting is important and easy to install. A quick trip around the lighting department of your local hardware or discount store will give you some great ideas, such as track lighting, fluorescent lights, or gooseneck lamps that attach to the edge of your tabletop. While you are there, you may want to look for shelving, pegboard, and bulletin board. I used rubber-coated wire shelving at one end of the room to hold project bins (Fig. 1.5). More wire shelving is used as a garment rack for projects in progress. I use a pegboard to hold shears, thread, embroidery hoops, and other sewing odds and ends (Fig. 1.6).

Because I spend so much time in my sewing room, I decorated it in soft, comfortable colors. Music and a phone are close by.

NEAR YOUR SEWING MACHINE

Use a bulletin board or a blank wall over or near your sewing machine to tack up pattern instructions or notes and clippings. A notion caddy to one side of your machine can

FIG. 1.4 Cutting table supported by two chests of drawers.

FIG. 1.5 Rubber-coated wire shelving holds project bins.

hold extra bobbins, pins, threads, and presser feet within convenient reach. Some machines come with an accessory box for this purpose. Finally, tape a large Ziploc bag to your sewing table to hold tissue pattern pieces (Fig. 1.7).

HINT: After removing the tissue pattern piece from the fabric, fold tissue so the name of the pattern piece and the pattern number can be seen through the bag. This way you will not have to fish around and unfold every pattern piece in the bag to find the one you are looking for.

6

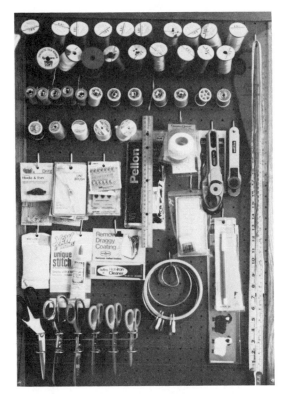

FIG. 1.6 Pegboard holds thread, hoops, and other sewing odds and ends.

PRESSING AREA

Tape or pin another Ziploc® bag to the end of the ironing board or pressing table to store press cloths. Position one or more shelves over the ironing board or pressing table to hold your tailor's ham, sleeve board, pressing mitt, and other pressing essentials. If you don't have room for a shelf, find a large, flat basket or bin to store pressing accessories under the ironing board or pressing table.

HINT: If you use a press for most of your sewing, have a travel iron handy. You will put it to good use with the press and have it to take along on vacation or a business trip.

PUTTING IT ALL TOGETHER

Now that your fabric, patterns, and other sewing paraphernalia are inventoried, let's look at the place where the creativity takes place—your sewing machine.

If your sewing equipment does not include a serger or press, position the ironing board to one side, at the same level as your machine. You may also want to invest in a secretarial chair (I found one at a garage sale for $10.00). This way, you can roll over to the ironing board and press each seam without having to

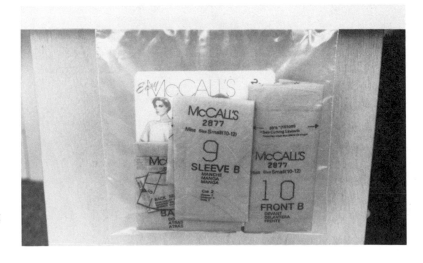

FIG. 1.7 Tape Ziploc bag to sewing table to hold pattern pieces.

Sandra
Betzina

San Francisco, California

How did Sandra Betzina start sewing? All the girls in her school had to take one hour of sewing and one hour of cooking every day for five years. She said she didn't mind because she loved to sew. School is where she learned the basics. But she has taken sewing past the basics.

Sandra's friends are artists and clothing designers, many of whom have lofts or shops in the fashionable areas of San Francisco. Her friends have helped her think creatively with her sewing and have shared many of their professional shortcuts and finishing techniques. She has incorporated them into her latest book and video, *Power Sewing (New Ways to Make Fine Clothes Fast),* and in her syndicated column, "Sew with Flair." (Sandra also represents the American Home Sewing Association on media tours.)

Sandra's sewing room started with the idea of putting a skylight in the unused attic of her home. The idea evolved into a beautiful sewing room, a master bedroom, guest bedroom, and bathroom, adding an additional 1200 square feet of living space to her home, where she and her husband, Dan Webster, are rearing their four children.

The architect designed a 28-foot skylight to run the entire length of the sewing room. An oak counter under the dormer windows holds the sewing machine, with plenty of space underneath for storage. The marble floor, Sandra feels, is great for anyone who sews, because it is easily swept clean. It is

Sandra Betzina

also set in about $1\frac{1}{2}$" (3.8 cm) of concrete, which acts as a thermal mass, collecting the daytime heat through the skylight and releasing it during the chilly San Francisco evenings.

With such an elegant workplace, it's no wonder Sandra devotes two days a week to sewing and writing. Her phone is turned off, and she accepts no calls or engagements during that time. As she puts it: "Sewing is my time alone, which I find creative and therapeutic. It offers a peaceful feeling that provides me with a sense of accomplishment."

get up. With pressing equipment close to the machine, you'll be more likely to press each seam as you go, with better looking, better made projects as a result.

If you are lucky enough to have a serger and/or a press, position your sewing machine in the center, with the serger and press to either side. This way, your Ultimate Sewing Center is set up for speed and efficiency. Simply serge, sew, and press.

Sewing Machine

Since sergers have become so popular, I've heard a lot of people say that all you need to go with your serger is a sewing machine with a zigzag stitch and built-in buttonhole and that there is no need to waste money on a new machine. I also know some who took this advice and aren't enjoying their sewing any more than before they got the serger.

I love to sew. The focal point of my Ultimate Sewing Center is my sewing machine (Fig. 1.8). It is the one piece of equipment I depend on totally for the sewing I do. The model I have is easy to use and versatile. I could have bought a less expensive model that wouldn't do as much, but I wanted a machine for which the only limitation was my imagination.

Don't skimp here. Buy the best machine you can afford. Research different brands rather than buying the first one you see. Chances are you'll have to live with your decision for a long time, so take your time and decide what features are important to you. I look for stitch quality over a broad range of fabrics. Because I like to make gifts and clothing that have a unique yet classic look, decorative potential is also important to me.

If you haven't shopped for a machine in a few years, you may not be aware of the innovations developed since your old standby was manufactured. Even though you may have a particular price range in mind, keep an open mind. Give yourself permission to spend the money on a machine you will enjoy using every day.

Spend some time researching different brands. Visit a number of dealers and ask to see a demonstration on the top-of-the-line and middle-of-the-line machines. Ask for the literature on both, and ask to keep the stitch samples from the demonstration. Keep notes and run a few stitches and a buttonhole or two yourself. Don't plan to see too many demonstrations or machines in one sitting. It may be confusing.

Once you have narrowed down your choices to the two or three best machines for your needs, go back to the dealers with any further questions. Bring your own fabric and ask to see appropriate seam finishes, buttonholes, embroidery stitches—anything important to you.

Buy from a reputable dealer who offers lessons on your machine or in-house service and who makes new educational information available to you. There's nothing worse than buying a machine, then putting it in the closet because you don't know how to use it.

Ask whether the dealer attends regular service clinics and educational meetings conducted by the sewing machine distributors he or she does business with.

Most sewing machine companies have an educational staff that travels from dealer to dealer giving informative seminars. Find out if your dealer is one who schedules events like this for customers, and ask to be put on the mailing list.

Finally, ask for the names of several customers as references. Call and ask how they like the machine and dealing with the retailer. If the dealer is hesitant to provide you with some names, it may be an indication that service leaves something to be desired.

Once you've bought a machine, get to know it thoroughly. Learn its settings and peculiarities. Throughout this book, you will find suggested machine settings as shown below, with space for yours after you've fine-tuned them on a sample:

(continued on page 15)

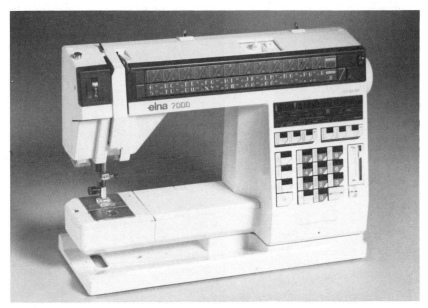

A. Elna 7000.

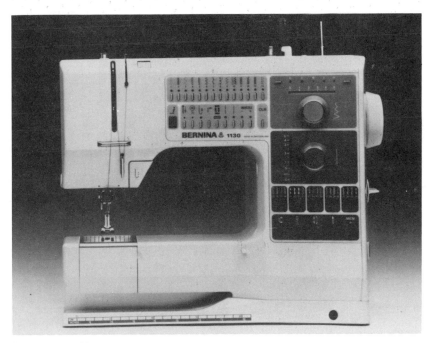

B. Bernina 1130.

FIG. 1.8 The sewing machine gallery. Here are the top-of-the-line sewing machine models from the major companies at press time. Of course, every company has models from basic mechanical models to electronic and computerized models.

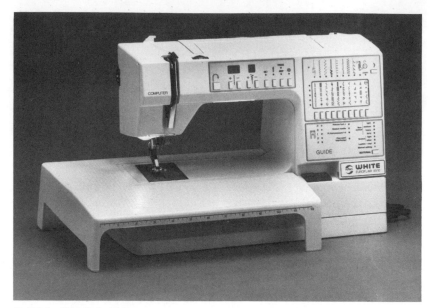

C. White Euroflair 8910.

D. Viking Husqvarna 990.

FIG. 1.8 The sewing machine gallery, *continued*

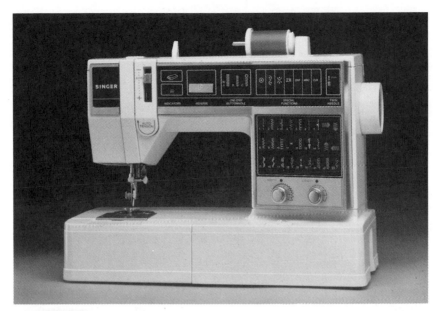

E. Singer 6268.

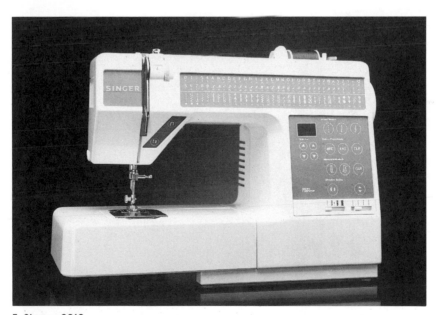

F. Singer 2210.

FIG. 1.8 The sewing machine gallery, *continued*

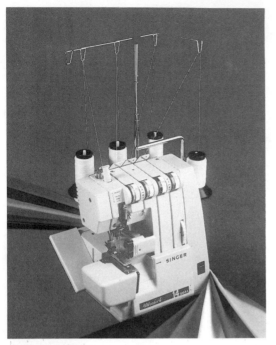

A. Singer 14064.

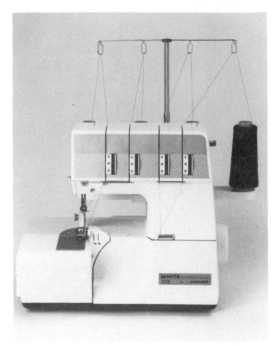

B. White SuperLock 228.

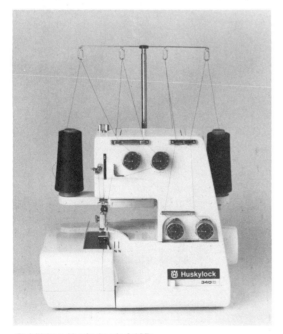

C. Viking Huskylock 340D.

FIG. 1.9 The serger gallery. Here are the top-of-the-line serger models from the major companies at press time. Every company has different models from the basic 2/3-thread to the more advanced 2/3/4 and 5-thread models.

Stitch: multiple zigzag stitch	_____
Stitch width: widest	_____
Stitch length: 1–1.5, or 15 stitches per inch	_____
Foot: standard zigzag foot	_____
Needle position: center	_____

At the right is a place to write in your own machine settings after you have fine-tuned each technique for your machine.

Serger

Sergers are fast becoming a sewing necessity. They have revolutionized home sewing in the same way that microwave ovens have revolutionized food preparation. If you are not familiar with a serger, it is an industrial-looking machine that will sew the seam, overcast the edge, and trim the excess seam allowance off in one step (Fig. 1.9). It works with 2, 3, 4, or 5 threads and loopers rather than bobbins. The loopers "knit" the thread across the seam allowance, while the needle or needles stitch a secure seam.

The serger makes fast work of $\frac{1}{4}''$ (6 mm) seams or can be used to finish raw edges before a garment is constructed with the traditional $\frac{5}{8}''$ (1.5 cm) seam allowance. Depending on the model you have, a serger can be used to create a host of decorative edge finishes that can't be duplicated on your conventional sewing machine.

The serger differs from the conventional sewing machine, which has a stitch selector for changing stitches, in that the stitches are changed by changing the needle or looper tension and the needle plate. At the moment, industry standards do not exist for serger tension settings, so you will have to experiment to achieve desired results. The stitch settings in this book are a general guideline for both needles and loopers. The guidelines listed below will help you set tensions on your own serger. For future reference, record your settings in the spaces provided and keep a notebook of swatches with tension settings for each technique in the book.

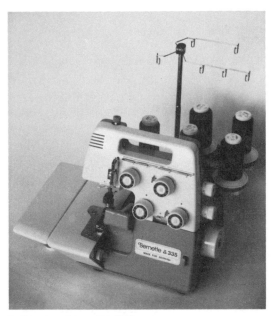

D. Bernina Bernette 335.

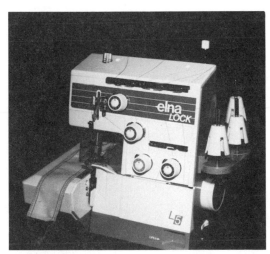

E. Elna Lock L5.

FIG. 1.9 The serger gallery, *continued*

1. Very tight: Tension dial at tightest setting.
2. Tight: Tension dial halfway between tightest setting and normal.
3. Normal: Balanced tension with other looper(s) and needle(s).
4. Loose: Tension dial halfway between normal and loosest setting.
5. Very loose: Tension dial almost to 0 but still with a little tension.

SERGER FURNITURE

I suggested earlier in this chapter that you arrange your sewing equipment with the sewing machine in the middle and the serger and ironing board or press on either side. But what do you put the serger on? I have mine on a flat, portable sewing machine table that enables me to have access to the upper and lower loopers. On the other side I have another such table for the press. The tables are a comfortable height, reasonably priced, and large enough that the equipment can be moved back and out of the way if I need a little more working surface.

Robbie Fanning's sewing area is against one wall in the bedroom, approximately three feet from the bed. Her serger sits on a rolling computer table next to the sewing table. This way, she can move it out into a sewing L, then push it back against the wall, out of the way, when she's finished. Both systems work well, but you may be interested in purchasing furniture specially designed to house your sewing machine and serger. Most of these tables position the serger on the right and the sewing machine on the left. Some are made of wood, others of fiberboard covered with a thick, plastic laminate surface. Some are on wheels, other on metal legs. One model I saw can be purchased as a modular unit so that you can start with a sewing cabinet and later add a serger extension and storage drawers. By the time this book is published, there will undoubtedly be more furniture choices.

Factors to consider before buying a particular system are:

1. Available space in your home.

2. Configuration of the table or cabinet. Will it fit in the corner or against one wall?
3. Budget.
4. Fit—I'm tall and find some sewing tables too short or confining.

Therefore, sit down in a chair like yours at home and sew at the table or cabinet on the dealer's floor. Check for comfort and accessibility. Can you reach the bobbin and loopers easily? Is the needle in front of you, or do you have to lean one way or the other to see where you are sewing? Is your work at the right height? Do you have enough knee space?

Check on price and availability. Some dealers don't stock a full line of cabinets because shipping costs are high and cabinets are easily damaged in shipping. If the store does not carry the model you are interested in and offers to special order it for you, find out what happens if you don't like it. Try not to buy one just by looking at a catalog sheet. Sometimes the real thing looks quite different than what you expected.

Now that we've taken care of housing the serger, let's look at another wonderful piece of equipment for The Ultimate Sewing Center—the press.

Press

The art of pressing is essential to the art of sewing. So says every home economics teacher who ever taught sewing, dressmaking, draping, and tailoring. For that reason, I bought a press for home use, and it's the best tool I've found for pressing ready-to-wear clothes and for my sewing projects.

Because I work so much with natural fibers, I find I'm pressing now more than ever before. There are many other reasons why my press has become an integral part of my Ultimate Sewing Center. Here are just a few.

Until the press was introduced about 10 years ago, I had some unpleasant experiences using fusible products, from interfacings to waistband shapers. In addition, I couldn't get seams and other areas (e.g., front tabs, collars,

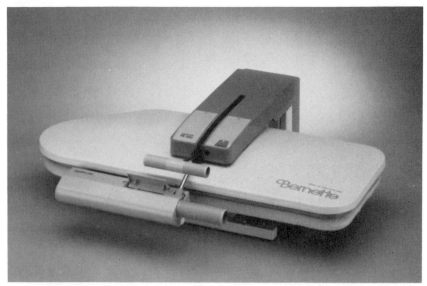

A. Bernette Press.

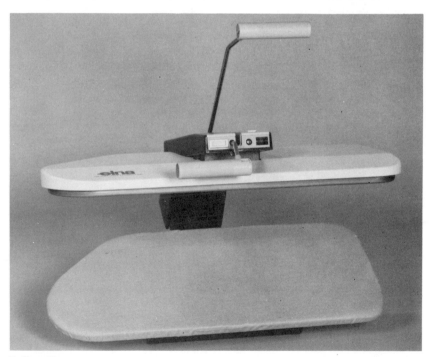

B. Elna Press.

FIG. 1.10 The press gallery. Here are the top-of-the-line press models from the major companies.

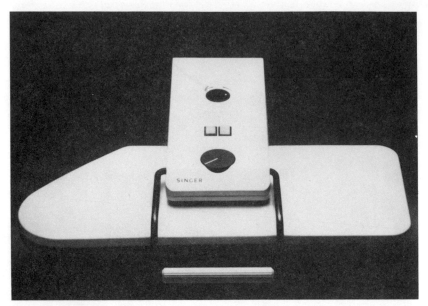

C. Singer Press.

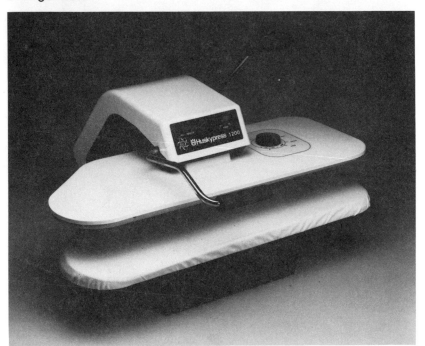

D. Viking Huskypress 1200.

FIG. 1.10   The press gallery, *continued*

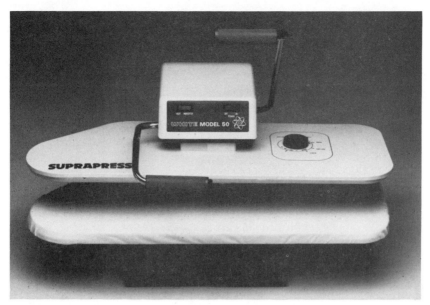

E. White Suprapress.

FIG. 1.10 The press gallery, *continued*

cuffs, and facings) pressed as flat as I wanted. I wasn't able to get the crisp look I wanted for my tailoring projects. The reason? I didn't know how to control the three elements to successful pressing: heat, moisture, and pressure. With the press and other pressing tools, I can control all three (Fig. 1.10).

Generally, presses have a heating shoe and board shaped to fit various parts of the garment (see Chapter 2). Pressing goes faster than with a hand iron because the heating shoe is much larger. For most presses, you need both hands to bring the heating shoe down to the pressing surface, so that you don't inadvertently press your hand. Some presses also have an automatic safety device that warns the user that the press is on and when it has been closed longer than 10 seconds. A buzzer sounds, and the electricity is turned off automatically to prevent scorching. You can use a press standing up or sitting down, and it can be set up just about anywhere.

The most pressure you can exert with a hand iron is about 25 pounds (11.25 kg). Most presses have the capability of pressing with 100 pounds (45 kg) of pressure: great for fusing interfacing and fusible web, using hot-iron transfers, pressing pleats and creases, and pressing out hemlines and wrinkles on fabrics made of natural fibers. Yet you have the option of using less than full pressure to press napped fabrics.

With a press, shine is almost eliminated because you bring the heat to the fabric without moving an iron across it. In fact, I've found I don't need a press cloth as often with the press as with an iron.

Using a press for knits enables you to press without stretching the fabric out of shape. I block needlework and set in pleats by pinning into the padded pressing surface. Some presses have accessories available, such as a sleeve cushion or pressing mitt. These are used to press areas that would crease or mark easily,

19

such as a jacket sleeve, pants inseam, or zipper.

I hope this chapter has helped you clean out and reorganize your sewing room or area. In Chapter 2, I discuss pressing equipment necessary to speed-tailor a garment. Some of it you may already have. Some of it you'll want to add to your inventory immediately. Put the rest on a wish list, for the next holiday so that you'll be sure to get something you can really use.

Pressing Matters

My husband wanted to have a suit made by a tailor rather than buying one off the rack. After he selected the fabric and style, the tailor told him the suit would run $400— and that was in 1976! He was shocked and asked why it was so expensive. The tailor replied, "I make art." Pressing is the art that turns home sewing into couture.

There's a big difference between ironing and pressing. Ironing is moving a hot iron across the fabric in a pushing and sliding motion. It is generally done without a press cloth, and the action of moving the iron over fabric can polish the fibers, creating shine. Pressing, essential to clothing construction, is done by lifting and lowering the iron or press to block an area, smooth a seam allowance open, or flatten edges.

I always thought that to "press as you sew" all you need is a steam iron, press cloth, and tailor's pressing ham. Then I discovered that by adding a few more tools to my inventory of pressing equipment, I could produce garments that looked like the tailor's $400 art. In most cases, I was able to eliminate the costly step of sending finished projects to the cleaners for final pressing.

In this chapter I discuss what you must have, what is even better to have, and what the pros have.

THE MUST HAVES

Tailor's Pressing Ham

The ham is a curved, stuffed cushion used to press curved areas of a garment (Fig. 2.1). A good ham has cotton muslin or drill cloth on one side and wool on the other. The cotton side is used to press cotton, cotton blends, and linens that require higher iron temperatures. The wool side is for tailoring with wool, silk, and wool blends and, if used properly, will minimize shine.

Sleeve Roll

A sleeve roll, or seam roll, is a long narrow tube or cushion with cotton muslin or drill cloth on one side and wool on the other, like

21

the ham (Fig. 2.2). It is used to press seams open in sleeves, pants legs, or anywhere you do not want a crease in a cylindrical shaped area.

You may also use a wooden rolling pin for a sleeve roll. Pressing a seam open against a wooden surface permanently sets the thread and presses seams very flat, which is desirable in some cases. Pressing a seam open or creasing a hemline in fabric made of natural fibers can break the molecule in the fiber. Therefore, when using an uncovered rolling pin, be sure the area to be pressed fits properly. Otherwise you may press a permanent mark in the fabric.

For a sleeve roll that produces a softer looking seam, cover the rolling pin with cotton muslin, drill cloth, or wool, depending on the project.

Press Cloths

Press cloths prevent shine and ensure successful press-as-you-sew results. For heavy fabrics I recommend using a heavy cotton muslin or drill cloth, available at most fabric stores or through mail-order sources. Beeswax and paraffin are sometimes used to finish the press cloth, which helps press sharp creases

A

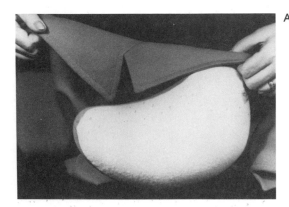

FIG. 2.1 Tailor's ham (*A*) and ham holder (*B*) (photo courtesy of June Tailor).

B

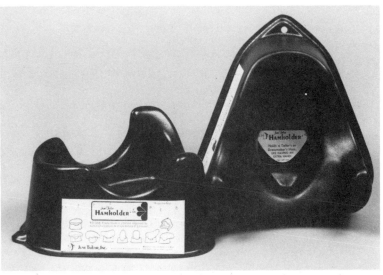

FIG. 2.2 Sleeve roll (photo courtesy of June Tailor).

and pleats (they will not come off on the fabric).

Press cloths work best if they are made of a natural fiber. This way iron or press temperatures can be high, and moisture evaporates easily.

HINT: For a permanent press, all moisture must be pressed out of a fabric.

Specialty press cloths are great for certain jobs and are generally available through mail-order catalogs. June Tailor makes a press cloth for any job (see Sources of Supply). Some press cloths are designed to hold moisture longer, which prevents shine on wools, Ultrasuede®, and other short-napped fabrics. You may prefer to make a wool press cloth. To use it, place napped sides together, and press on the wrong side of cloth.

For velvet, velveteen, and corduroy, prevent crushing the nap by using a bristled press cloth. If you don't sew a lot with these fabrics, make a press cloth from velvet or velveteen. Place napped surfaces together and a terry cloth towel under fabric, between the wrong side of the fashion fabric and the pressing surface. For small areas, you can place the right side of a napped fabric against the bristles of a clean nylon or horsehair hairbrush and press from the wrong side.

Sometimes you need a press cloth you can see through—there are many on the market. In a pinch, though, I have used cheesecloth. To wet, dunk one end of cloth in water, roll it up, and wring it out. The wringing action evenly dampens the rest of the cloth. See-through press cloths are great for positioning interfacing, fusing appliqué pieces, or any other time you need to see what and where you're pressing.

Teflon® pressing sheets also make good press cloths when moisture isn't needed. They were developed so that fusible web could be fused to one side of a piece of fabric without gumming up the iron. They come in different sizes, tolerate high temperatures well, and are see-through.

Steam or Travel Iron

For successful pressing you need *heat, moisture, and pressure*. Therefore your steam iron should be heavy enough to help put adequate pressure on the fabric while you are pressing and fusing. I also have a Teflon-coated shoe cover to protect the sole of the iron from fusible adhesive that may ooze through the press cloth (Fig. 2.3). The Teflon sole cover also prevents shine and, if your iron has large steam holes, prevents marking the fabric.

A travel iron with a sharp tip or angle on the front is also great for pressing small areas. Dry cleaners use a small, narrow iron similar to a travel iron to press seams open and to press narrow pleats and small areas on children's and women's clothing when they finish the garment (see Chapter 12). A good travel iron is a must if you use a press for most of your sewing.

Ironing Board, Sleeve Board, Pad, and Cover

I need an ironing board and sleeve board to run a household and to sew. Both are heavily padded to provide a cushioning effect so that seam allowances won't press through to

23

FIG. 2.3 Iron with Teflon-coated shoe cover to protect it from fusible adhesive and shine.

the right side of the fabric. Both of mine came covered with a washable muslin cover rather than with the more common reflective, silicone-treated cover. Reflective covers are supposed to make ironing go faster, but often they hold in too much heat without letting steam escape. This can be dangerous for delicate fabrics. The 100 percent cotton muslin cover I use on my ironing board is also gridded to help in straightening fabric, pressing hems, and measuring and making front tabs, cuffs, waistbands, and belts (Fig. 2.4). I use the sleeve board for pressing underarm seams, inseams, and small, hard-to-press areas.

Portable Ironing Board

I made a portable ironing board from a cardboard fabric bolt. Many fabric stores throw them away, so next time you're in your favorite store, ask if they'll give you one. To make the board, wrap it with a couple of layers of wool tight around the bolt and slip-stitch. Make a case using wool on one side and cotton muslin or drill cloth on the other. Measure

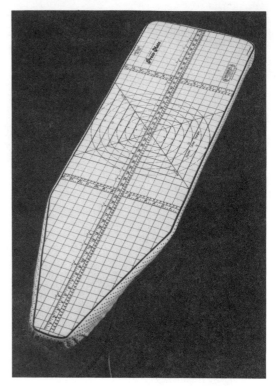

FIG. 2.4 100 percent muslin ironing board cover is gridded for straightening fabric, pressing hems, and measuring front tabs, cuffs, waistbands, and belts (photo courtesy of June Tailor).

the bolt (remember to add seam allowances), then stitch three sides of the case by machine, turn right side out, and press. Slip bolt into the case and slip-stitch the open end closed. This ironing board slips easily into a suitcase or garment bag and is great for touching up most fabrics.

Horsehair Brush

When I visited the dry cleaner, I saw that most of the hand pressing was done from the wrong side. First, seams were pressed open and the fabric was smoothed. To finish pressing, the garment was top pressed with a professional steam press, and the steam was brushed away with a horsehair draftsman's

Gail Brown

Hoquiam, Washington

Gail Brown

"I don't have a sewing room. I sew all over the house, surrounded by things I like and near my children. We have a big house, and I have the luxury of sewing wherever the action is ... because I like to be right in the middle of it. I'm currently redecorating a room, so my sewing machine and I have moved into that room to create."

You may know Gail Brown from reading her articles in *Needlecraft for Today, Sew News, Sewing and Serging Update Newsletters,* or *McCall's Pattern Magazine.* You may also know her from reading one of her books: *Sewing with Sergers, Creative Serging Illustrated, Sew a Beautiful Wedding, Sensational Silk,* the *Instant Interiors* home decorating series, or *The Super Sweater Idea Book.*

Where does she get all this knowledge and expertise? As former marketing director for a knit fabric company, she was involved in all aspects of the knit fabric business and perfected many of the techniques found in her books and articles. She furthered her experience as the communications director of Stretch & Sew Fabrics.

One thing is certain. This University of Washington home economics graduate and mother of two has always been where the action is in home sewing, and continues to be, with two more books to be released in 1989. Look for *Gail Brown's Book of Sewing and Serging Knits* and a compilation of sewing tricks from the Update Newsletters.

brush (available where drafting supplies are sold). Removing moisture in this way keeps the garment pressed and wrinkle-free. It also restores the nap of wools and heavier napped fabrics and helps eliminate shine.

TO GO WITHS

Next time you go shopping, add the following items to the grocery list: white vinegar, aluminum foil, vegetable brush, small funnel or plastic squeeze bottle, and a roll of adding machine tape.

Mix equal parts of white vinegar and water and dampen press cloth to set permanent creases. This mixture will also help press out hemline creases and the center fold on a piece of fabric. Occasionally I have used white vinegar full strength to press out a crease or remove a spot. Be sure to test the mixture or straight white vinegar on a scrap or in a seam allowance first.

If you run out of vinegar, use aluminum foil to set creases and pleats. Place foil between the ironing board and fabric. The heat and steam penetrate the fabric, hit the foil, then bounce back up through it for a permanent crease. This is one of the reasons reflective ironing board covers are popular.

HINT: If you are using a synthetic fabric, test this on a scrap or in a seam allowance first to be sure the fabric can take the heat.

A shallow bowl next to the ironing board or press can hold either water or the white vinegar mixture. The small vegetable brush is used to dip into the bowl and sprinkle the press cloth. This saves running to the sink every five minutes for water.

To prevent ridges from pressing through to the right side, I discovered paper adding machine tape under the seam allowances works just as well as brown paper strips and is much easier to use.

Use the small funnel or plastic squeeze bottle to pour distilled water into the iron without spilling it all over the place.

EVEN BETTER TO HAVE

By making a modest investment in other pressing aids, I've been able to eliminate taking my finished garments to the cleaners for final pressing. The biggest investment has been my press. In this book I often refer to the various parts of the press, so familiarize yourself with the terms in Fig. 2.5 to better understand the procedures. The terms I use are generic. If you own a press, terminology may differ slightly depending on the brand. Feel free to relabel the drawing to fit your own brand.

Not to be confused with the old-fashioned mangle, the press is compact and has the iron and ironing board in one unit. You simply place your fabric on the padded board and press. In Chapter 12 I explain the most efficient way to use it for pressing finished garments.

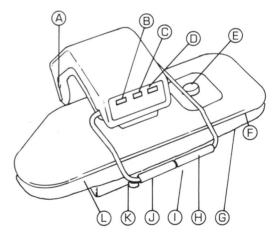

FIG. 2.5 The press. *A*, opening latch; *B*, thermostat; *C*, on/off switch for steam boiler; *D*, main on/off switch; *E*, temperature selection thermostat; *F*, heating shoe; *G*, padded ironing board; *H*, pressure handle; *I*, lock or closing screw to close press for storage; *J*, open/close handle and steam control; *K*, water reservoir; *L*, ironing board cover.

Pressing Cushions

A sleeve cushion, small pressing cushion, and pressing mitt are great for curved and cylindrical areas (Fig. 2.6). Both pressing cushions are available through your local sewing machine dealer. The pressing mitt is available through mail-order catalogs.

The long sleeve cushion is shaped for an adult jacket sleeve and is used to prevent creasing. The curved end is fuller on one edge than the other and it fits perfectly in a jacket sleeve—the fuller edge to the back of the sleeve, flatter edge to the front. I also use the sleeve cushion to press pants inseams open. The cushion adjusts to uneven thicknesses, so I generally don't find it necessary to use paper under the seam allowance to prevent ridges from pressing through to the right side.

The small pressing cushion is used to cushion smaller areas and for quick touch-ups. For pants, the square cushion is placed under the zipper between the pants and the board. When the press is closed, the fabric around the zipper is pressed smooth, because the cushion fills in the uneven areas created by the zipper. This accessory has many other uses, too (see Chapter 12).

I use the pressing mitt like a mini–pressing ham, to help shape and mold areas with the press. You'll see more about this in Chapter 4.

Wooden Yardstick

For perfectly flat, smooth seams I use an unvarnished wooden yardstick (you may have to sand it so it won't snag the fabric). Wood holds steam without too much heat buildup and sets the thread in the stitches. The yardstick slips easily into inseams and works well on other long seams. When pressing seams open, you don't need to cushion the seam allowance with paper because the fabric falls away from the seam allowance when the yardstick is underneath.

Point Turner, Tailor Board

For perfect corners on collars, cuffs, and pockets, use a point turner (Fig. 2.7). The point is sharp enough to push out a point gently but not so sharp as to poke through the fabric.

Pressing from the wrong side, opening seams, and flattening edges work best on unpadded, wooden tools. The tailor board is compact, has inward and outward curves, and has padded accessories for softer treatments (Fig. 2.8). It can be used as a clapper, to press steam into wool without building up too much heat, to block and set a curve, or to press a collar point.

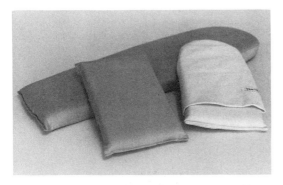

FIG. 2.6 Small pressing cushion, sleeve cushion, and pressing mitt are used with the press for curved and cylindrical areas.

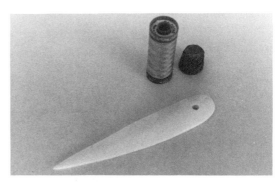

FIG. 2.7 Collar point turner.

FIG. 2.8 Tailor board and pads (photo courtesy of June Tailor).

FIG. 2.9 Adjustable dress form (photo courtesy of Nancy's Notions).

Needle Board or Velvaboard

A needle board looks as if hundreds of needles are stuck upside down in a board. It is used as a pressing surface, not as a press cloth. Needle boards come in a variety of sizes and are available from your fabric store or through mail-order companies. If you work with a lot of napped fabrics, a needle board is a good investment because it reflects steam and is used with a bristled or napped press cloth. Sandwich the fabric between the press cloth and needle board. To prevent shine and to prevent crushing the nap on velvet, velveteen, velour, and corduroy, use even pressure with your iron or press.

Dress Form

I have really enjoyed my dress form because I don't have to get dressed and undressed a dozen times to fit a garment. The one I have is adjustable in the bust, waist, and high hip, which is great for fitting both my fat and thin times (Fig. 2.9). If you sew for other people, you can also adjust it for each customer to avoid costly and time-consuming fitting mistakes.

WHAT THE PROS HAVE

In addition to all the tools listed above, the pros have some additional equipment. You don't have to be a pro to own similar equipment. You just have to want professional results.

Priced between the home steam iron and the press are industrial-type, gravity-feed steam irons with a separate water supply. The two brands most readily available for home sewers are the 4 to 5 pound (2–2.25kg) Hi-Steam Naomoto and Sussman irons (see Sources of Supply) (Fig. 2.10). Rather than filling the iron with water, as with conventional irons,

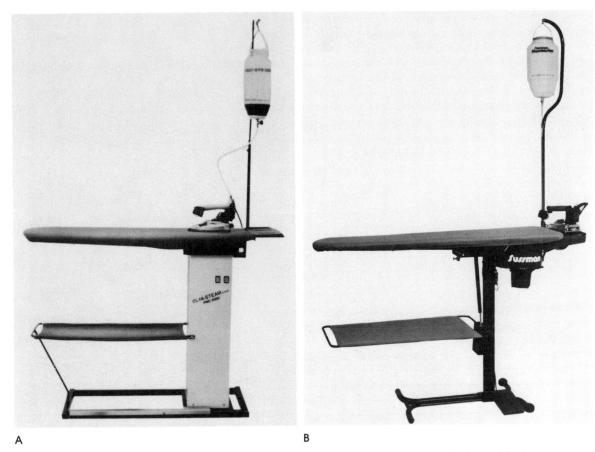

FIG. 2.10 Industrial-type steam irons. *A*, Hi-steam Naomoto iron and vacuum ironing table; *B*, Sussman iron and vacuum ironing table.

you fill a separate water supply that hangs from a pole. Gravity feeds the water into the iron to produce steam. The only drawback to the system is where to hang the water. Both companies offer a portable floor hook for the water supply. Another option is hanging the water supply from a butterfly hook in the ceiling.

Both irons have a Teflon soleplate and extra insulation or protection under the handle to keep your hand cool. These irons are built to last many years and are used by dry cleaners, alterations departments, and dressmakers across the country.

Another product made and distributed by both companies is the ironing table, which is an ironing board with built-in vacuum system. I thought at first that the ironing table was an accessory for the iron until I discovered the table costs more than the iron itself. For a garment to be perfectly pressed and wrinkle-free, all the moisture must be removed from the deepest core of the fiber. The premise behind the vacuum in an ironing table is that the garment is pressed flat with the moisture and pressure from the iron; then the vacuum pulls out the moisture from the fibers to eliminate wrinkling.

If you're interested in a more conventional iron, you might like the lighter weight Rowenta iron (see Sources of Supply) (Fig. 2.11). Like its industrial counterparts, the Rowenta has an extra thick soleplate that keeps the iron hot, even when you are using the steam setting. With the top-of-the-line model, you can use no steam, a burst of steam, or continuous steam. It also has a built-in mist sprayer, which is handy for shirt collars, cuffs, and front tabs.

Another specialty iron is the puff iron, available by mail order (Fig. 2.12). It clamps onto the ironing board or next to the sewing machine and is used to puff shoulders and sleeves. It's great for pressing fancy smocking or for blocking and shaping millinery. It can also be used to puff up napped fabrics and to help contour various parts of a tailored garment.

The proper pressing equipment assures you of professional results only if you use it. In the next chapter, you'll learn how to speed-tailor a garment with fusible interfacings—when and where to use them and how to get professional results with your pressing equipment. To many, using fusibles for tailoring is blasphemy. To me, it's practical. I don't have months to tailor a jacket, and I prefer the results over my unpracticed hand tailoring. Read on to see what I mean.

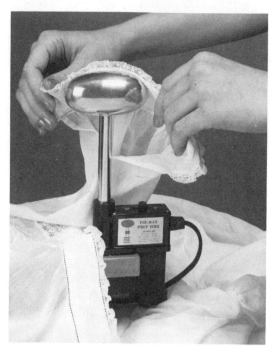

FIG. 2.12 Puff iron (photo courtesy of Nancy's Notions).

To help you better understand the techniques in the book, I am asking you to tailor a jacket along with me. To practice and perfect each technique you will also make stitch samples and put them in a notebook along with notes about your successes and failures. This notebook will be great for future reference.

At the end of each chapter you will find a list of items needed for the following chapter. Below is the list for Chapter 3. Remember, we are going to tailor a blazer together, so don't let this first list overwhelm you.

SUPPLY LIST FOR CHAPTER 3

- Jacket or blazer pattern with waistline dart, patch or welt pockets, collar and lapel, set-in sleeves, lining, and buttonholes
- Wool or linen for the blazer

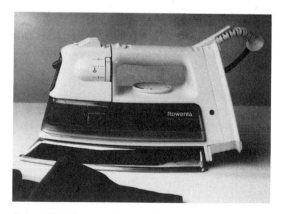

FIG. 2.11 Rowenta steam iron.

- Lining and notions listed on the pattern envelope
- Interfacing swatches from your own stockpile and a swatch each of Armo's fusible hair canvas; Pellon's Pel-Aire™ and Sof-Shape™; Stacy's Suit-Shape® and Tailor's Touch®
- Press cloths, iron or press, and small bowl of water
- Size #70 and #80 (9 and 11) sewing machine needles
- Scissors, shears or rotary cutter and board, pinking shears
- Tape measure, seam guide, pins or pattern weights
- Waxed paper
- Fold-a-Band™ or Fuse-n-Fold™

Chapter 3

Speed Tailoring with Fusibles

In this chapter you'll learn the foundation of tailoring with fusibles and timesaving ideas to get to your sewing machine as fast as possible. Reading this information is helpful, but doing it is even better. Why not make a trip through your fabric stockpile or to the fabric store and speed-tailor a blazer with me? If the volume of the text looks overwhelming, think of it as a long pattern instruction sheet.

Choose a lined jacket or blazer pattern with a waistline dart, patch or welt pockets, collar and lapel, set-in sleeves, and buttonholes. Choose a fabric that has a high natural fiber content and that has no nap (100 percent wool is best; linen is my second favorite). I will help you perfect each technique, so that you end up with a wearable garment and a lot of new knowledge for future projects.

PRESHRINKING

I used to tell sewers to preshrink everything, from fashion fabric to trims, zippers,

lining, and elastic. Then one of my students preshrunk her fusible interfacing and put everything together in the dryer. What a mess!

Now I tell sewers that manufacturers generally preshrink interfacing before it goes on the bolt. I have never had a problem with one of the major brands shrinking because I use a soaking wet press cloth and my press with 100 lbs (45kg) of pressure to fuse interfacing in place. However, I've spoken to many folks who have had a problem with it shrinking. So if you aren't sure, have purchased a bargain interfacing, lost the instructions, or just want to be safe, preshrink it.

To do this, remove the plastic instruction sheet and place interfacing in moderately warm water to soak for about 15 minutes. Remove it and allow it to drain on a dry towel. When most of the water has drained out of it, lay the interfacing out flat and let it air-dry.

Preshrink dry-clean-only fabrics by taking them to the dry cleaners. Or you can preshrink them at home using one of the following methods.

The London Method

Lay fabric flat. Moisten a plush terry cloth towel so it is very damp, not wringing wet. Roll the towel into the fabric and let it sit overnight so the moisture has a chance to absorb into the fabric. Unroll fabric the next day, and either let it air-dry or press it until all the moisture has evaporated.

The Press Method

If you have a press and don't have time for the London method, try this. Set thermostat to the appropriate temperature for your fabric—but no higher than the lowest cotton setting, unless you are preshrinking linen. Unfold your fabric. Starting on one side, place selvage edge even with the straight side of the press so the right side of the fabric is down. Fold fabric into deep pleats, and stack pleats behind the board as shown in Fig. 3.1. Spritz or sprinkle the surface of the fabric so that it is evenly moist, not wet. (If you overdo this, it will take you longer to press the moisture out of the fabric.) Bring the heating shoe down on the fabric and press for about 5 seconds; raise the shoe so steam can escape; press again, 5 seconds at a time, until the fabric is dry.

Continue this process by pulling pleated fabric toward you. Then turn yardage around and finish the unpressed end.

To refold the fabric before cutting out the pattern, turn the press off and let it cool. Fold one end in half (as if the fabric were on the bolt), selvages together, close the press on that end, and fold fabric in half at the other end (Fig. 3.2). The closed press acts as your "helper." If you press sheets or big tablecloths, this is also a great help in folding.

The Wash Method

Although the press method of preshrinking works well with dry-clean-only fabrics, washables should be preshrunk in the manner in which you intend to care for the finished garment. Press them flat before pattern layout.

To make wool or linen machine-washable, wash in cold water. Granted, the fabric will shrink a lot, but sometimes it's necessary. I made a wool shirt for my brother, who is a commercial salmon fisherman in Alaska and can't wear anything that isn't washable. A washable wool was just the ticket. Remember, the fabric shrinks quite a bit, and the amount of shrinkage may vary depending on water

FIG. 3.1 Press method of preshrinking by folding fabric into deep folds and stacking behind the board.

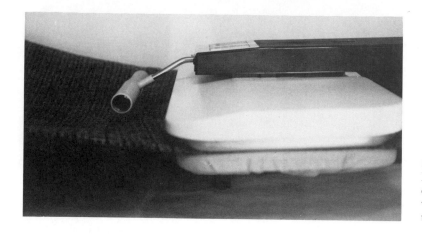

FIG. 3.2 To fold fabric in half for pattern layout, close the press on one end while you fold it evenly on the other.

temperature. So preshrink a swatch to determine how much extra fabric to buy.

WHAT IS INTERFACING?

Interfacing is another piece of fabric used in areas of a garment to give extra body and durability and to increase wear. Interfacing is commonly used in collars, cuffs, front tabs, and waistbands. To speed-tailor a blazer, interfacing is also used on the jacket front and back at the hemlines, and two layers are used on the under collar and front lapel to establish the roll line.

Interfacing falls into two main categories: fusible and sew-in. Fusible interfacing has an adhesive on the wrong side that melts when heated. Sew-in interfacing has no adhesive.

I use fusible rather than sew-in interfacing 95 percent of the time. When fusibles first came out, they were called iron-on interfacings, and they created a stiff, "boardy" appearance. If iron-ons weren't used correctly, they bubbled and came unstuck. Today's fusibles have been vastly improved and are fast and easy to use. They produce a hand I like better than most sew-ins. They are the same fusibles as those used in ready-to-wear.

HINT: Before using an interfacing, test-fuse a 4″ (10 cm) square of it to your fashion fabric to see if you like the result. Try more than one interfacing until you get the desired hand.

I purchase my favorite interfacings 5 yards (4.5 meters) at a time to save unnecessary trips to the fabric store.

Armo, Pellon, and Stacy interfacings are the most widely available; Chart 3.1 should help with your selection.

Before you begin fusing individual pattern pieces, you will need to cut out your pattern and transfer marks from pattern to fabric. In the following section I will help you do so and also will offer suggestions on proper presser feet, needles, and thread for finishing seams as you go.

GETTING STARTED ON YOUR SPEED-TAILORED JACKET

If I can get a jacket laid out, cut, marked, fused, and the raw edges finished in one day, I feel as if I'm about two-thirds of the way finished. You undoubtedly have sewing information from other sources to help with the layout, so I won't take time to go into it in detail here. I will say, though, that matching a plaid or stripe is easier if you use your notches as reference points and trace the plaid or stripe on the pattern tissue.

Roberta Carr

Los Altos, California

Bobbie Carr doesn't have to worry about The Ultimate Sewing Center. She already owns it—the Fabric Carr, her fabric store in Los Altos, California. Adjacent to the store is "The Sewing Room," a full-curriculum sewing school offering a wide range of classes, from basic couture to advanced design.

Educated at the University of Rhode Island and Tobe Coburn School for Fashion Careers, Bobbie brings fashion and sewing together in her classes. She also holds a week-long summer camp in Carmel, California to teach couture techniques. In addition, she publishes a national catalog, "The Fabric Carr Sewing Tools," featuring fine sewing tools, notions, and excellent sewing books. She has recently released a new video on couture techniques.

Bobbie is often seen lecturing at local colleges and universities and has appeared on "Sewing by Satellite." She's recently written articles for *Sew News, Vogue Pattern Magazine,* and *Sew It Seams.* Bobbie says her life is never on an even keel—it's always, "What do we do next? How can we make it better? Who wants to go along?"

Roberta Carr

CHART 3.1 *Interfacing Selection*

Fabric Type	Interfacing Weight	Recommended Interfacing	Fusible or Sew-in	Other Information
Sheer to lightweight fabrics, such as chiffon, georgette, crepe de chine, charmeuse, voile, batiste, gauze, lace, silk broadcloth	Sheer	Self-fabric	S	Matches color and hand
		Organza	S	Available in many colors
		Pellon #906	F	Light, crisp hand
		Bridal illusion, netting, or veiling	S	Adds crispness and won't show through
		Pellon sheer weight #905	S	Nonwoven
Featherweight to mid-weight fabrics, such as gingham, challis, tissue faille, jersey, polyester, silk crepe	Soft	Armo So-Sheer™	F	Nonwoven; white, beige, charcoal
		Pellon KnitShape™	F	Crosswise stretch/lengthwise stability
		Pellon #911FF	F	All-bias gentle support
		Pellon Sheer Blenders™	F	All-bias; charcoal, blue, silver, red
		Stacy Easy-Knit™	F	Crosswise stretch/lengthwise stability
		Stacy SheerFuse™	F	Nonwoven; white, light charcoal, print blender
		Stacy Soft-Fuse™	F	Nonwoven with crosswise stretch
Other featherweight to midweight fabrics: shirtings, broadcloth, oxford, muslin, seersucker, chambray, poplin, pincord, madras, lightweight linen	Firm	Armo PressSoft	S	Woven
		Pellon #910	S	All-bias
		Pellon #911FF	F	White or gray
		Stacy Easy-Shaper™ lightweight	F	25" (63.5cm) wide
	Crisp	Stacy Shirt-Fuse™	F	Crisp nonwoven
		Pellon Shirtailor™	F	Nonwoven; white and charcoal

Fabric	Type	Product		Notes
Skirt, pants, or suiting fabrics, such as gabardine, chino, linen, linen blends, wool and wool-like crepe, duck, cotton and cotton blends, faille, velvet, velveteen	Soft	Armo PressSoft	S	Woven, permanent press
		Pellon KnitShape™	F	Knit; subtle stabilizer
		Pellon Sof-Shape™	F	Tailoring loosely woven light- to midweight fabrics
		Stacy Easy-Knit™	F	Knit; white, beige, black, gray
		Stacy Easy-Shaper™	F	Crosswise stretch/lengthwise stability
		Armo Whisper Weft™	F	White, gray, beige
Other skirt, pants, or suiting fabrics: denim, poplin, flannel, wool, mohair, coating, corduroy	Crisp	Armo Fusible Acro	F	Machine washable hair canvas
		Armo Weft	F	White, gray, beige, black
		Armo Acro	S	Washable hair canvas
		Armo Fino (P-1)	S	Hair canvas for traditional tailoring
		Pellon Pel-Aire	F	Natural, gray
		Stacy Suit-Shape	F	Use for midweight tailoring
		Stacy Tailor's Touch	F	Good one to stockpile for firm tailoring
		Stacy #77 hair canvas	S	Dry-clean only
Fur, fake fur, fleece	Stabilizing	Armo Press Firm	S	Woven, permanent press
		Stacy Sta-Shape	S	Woven, permanent press
		Stacy #77 hair canvas	S	Dry-clean only
		Armo Acro	S	Washable hair canvas
Knits: cotton and cotton blend interlocks, jersey, lightweight sweater knits	Soft	Armo Uni-stretch lightweight	F	Well suited for knits, stretch wovens, and bias
		Pellon KnitShape™	F	Knit; crosswise stretch/lengthwise stability
		Stacy Easy-Knit	F	Knit; crosswise stretch/lengthwise stability
Other knits: double knits, stretch terry, velour, regular weight and heavy sweatshirt fleece	Firm	Pellon Stretch-Ease	F	White charcoal; offers crosswise stretch and recovery

The rotary cutter and board make cutting go faster. I use the large size on straight edges and a smaller one on curves. Use a sharp blade in the cutter. I try to have an extra one on hand in case I run over a pin or am cutting a particularly tough fabric. A good safety practice is to close the blade on the cutter *every* time you set it down. Use the largest board your table can accommodate. For long, straight cuts, guide the cutter against a yardstick or Plexiglas® straight edge. For more intricate cuts, use a pair of sharp dressmaking shears (Fig. 3.3).

Marking

Home sewers ask me how to get the top and undercollars to meet perfectly at the lapels. My answer? Accurate marking. This is one of the rare times I use tailor tacks. The little extra time it takes is well worth it when everything comes together at the lapel (Fig. 3.4).

Other times, I like to mark with a water-erasable or vanishing fabric marker. If you are marking a lot of work at once, use the water-erasable marker. For something you intend to work on immediately, use the vanishing marker. It has air-soluble ink, and the marks stay in the fabric 24–48 hours, depending on the humidity and fiber content of the fabric. (By mistake, a friend of mine took notes from a sewing seminar with her vanishing marker, so we had to run to the copy center immediately before they disappeared)!

Either marker works well on light- to medium-weight fabric. For an accurate mark, rest the point of the marker on the pattern tissue dot for a few seconds so that the ink bleeds through both the tissue and the first and second layers of fabric. For heavier and darker fabrics, push a straight pin through the dots, and mark the pin position with tailor's chalk (vanishing tailor's chalk is available as well). In a pinch I've used the sharp edge of a sliver of soap. Ivory soap doesn't have moisturizer, so it marks well on dark fabrics without leaving a spot. Other markers that work well on dark fabrics are the Chakoner®, Chaco-liner®, or Clo-Chalk® (Fig. 3.5). Each is filled with chalk powder and has a tiny wheel at the bottom that turns and drops a fine line of chalk when you move it across the fabric.

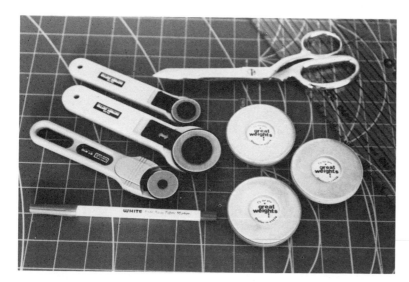

FIG. 3.3 Tools that make cutting go faster are the rotary cutter, board, Plexiglas straight edge, a pair of sharp dressmaking shears, and pattern weights.

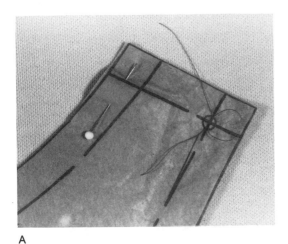

A

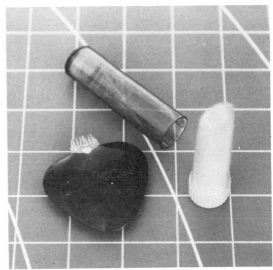

FIG. 3.5 Chakoner and Clo-Chalk markers for dark fabrics.

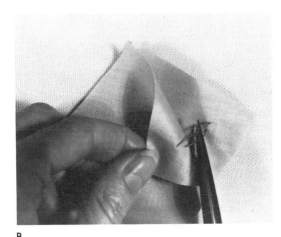

B

FIG. 3.4A and B I use tailor tacks to mark collar and lapel for a perfect match.

How to Fuse

1. Cut interfacing $\frac{1}{2}''$ (1.3 cm) smaller than fabric pattern piece, all the way around. If you will use the pattern more than once, it's worth the time to make separate interfacing patterns. I make mine out of waxed paper.

2. Place fashion fabric on the ironing board or press, wrong side up.

3. Center interfacing on fabric pattern piece, coated side down (wrong sides together). Rub the interfacing against your cheek if you're not sure which side is which. The coated side feels rough. Heat steam or travel iron to cotton setting.

4. Heat-baste interfacing to fashion fabric by pressing lightly with the tip of your iron in several places (Fig. 3.6). This is so the interfacing won't shift when fused (and so you don't inadvertently fuse the interfacing to the press cloth in the next step).

Next come the three ingredients for a successful fuse: heat, moisture, and pressure.

5. *Heat.* Heat your iron or press to the wool setting.

6. *Moisture.* Moisten your press cloth so it is quite damp.

7. *Pressure.* Cover interfacing with press cloth. Lower heating shoe and press for about 10 seconds. Raise the heating shoe, and let the steam escape. Keep press cloth on fabric, then press until fabric is dry. With 100 pounds (45 kg) of pressure, the interfacing is permanently bonded to the fashion fabric and won't bubble after cleaning or washing.

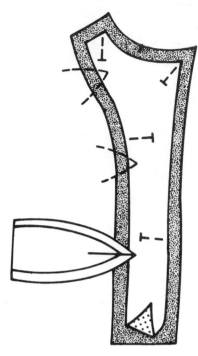

FIG. 3.6 Heat-baste interfacing on fabric, pressing lightly with tip of iron.

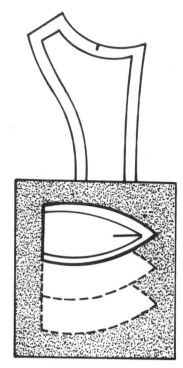

FIG. 3.7 Lower ironing board for better leverage, cover interfacing with press cloth, and press firmly for 15–18 seconds. Move iron to next section, overlapping until piece is fused.

If you don't have a press, lower your ironing board so you have better leverage and can push harder for more pressure. Cover interfacing with press cloth. Press down firmly for 15 to 18 seconds until all moisture has evaporated. Move iron to next section, overlapping until entire piece is fused (Fig. 3.7).

Seam Finishes

Why finish seams on a lined garment when no one will see them? It prevents raveling if something is going to be handled a lot, and it makes you feel better. There are many ways to finish seams, depending on your equipment. Figure 3.8 identifies stitches referred to throughout the book. Look at the stitches on your machine. My terminology is generic and may differ somewhat from what you read in your instruction manual. However, you probably have stitches that are similar.

Most sewing machines have a zigzag stitch,

which I'm sure you've used to overcast an edge. Unless the fabric is firmly woven and fairly heavy, the fabric tunnels, creating a ridge. When this is pressed, it may look as if someone has skied down your side seams. Preventing this is a combination of using the right stitch and the right presser foot for the job. Chart 3.2 is a guide to using the proper presser foot, needle, and thread for finishing seams and throughout construction of your garment.

PRESSER FEET

Look at the presser feet that came with your machine. You have probably used the standard zigzag foot, zipper foot, and buttonhole foot. The presser foot chart in the back of the book may help you use the others. Presser feet are designed for specific purposes and differ from one another on the underside. So dust them off and turn them over. Compare them to the charts in the back of the book.

STITCH LENGTH

The proper stitch length is also important. If the fabric *puckers* as you sew, *shorten the stitch length.* If the fabric *waves* out of shape, *lengthen the stitch length.* This is true for the straight stitch and all others your machine is capable of stitching. It even works for your serger. Why not write this on an index card and post it above or near your sewing machine? It's easy to forget and is *not* a tension problem. The reason? If the fabric puckers, there is not enough thread in the stitch for the fabric to lie flat. Shortening the stitch puts more thread in the seam so the fabric relaxes and lies flat. If the fabric waves out of shape, the stitch is too dense and pushes the fabric out of shape. This is common on cross-grain seams. Also, remember to use a fine needle, fine thread, and a fine stitch on fine fabric; a heavier needle and a long stitch on heavy fabric.

For more intricate stitches such as overlock, double overlock, or super overlock stitch (Fig. 3.8), the feed dogs move forward and backward at the same time the needle moves from side to side, creating the stitch pattern. It is impossible to assign a stitch length to stitches like this, so I will use the word "preset" to describe the stitch length setting for these and other forward and reverse feeding stitches.

NEEDLES AND THREADS

In general, the two most important things to remember are:

1. *Change the needle once per garment.*
2. *If you bought three spools of thread for a dollar, you wasted a dollar.*

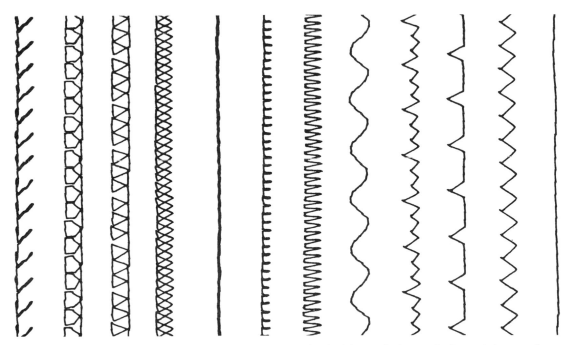

FIG. 3.8 *Left to right,* super stretch stitch, super overlock, double overlock, overlock, straight stretch, picot, interlock, 3-step zigzag, stretch blind hem, blind hem, zigzag, straight stitch.

CHART 3.2 *Needle, Thread, and Presser Foot Guide*

	Type of Fabric	Machine Needle		
		U.S. Size 15 × 1	Eur. Size 130/705	Style
KNITS	**LIGHTWEIGHT**	9	65 H-S	All-purpose
	Tricot	11	70H	
	MEDIUM WEIGHT	11–14	75–90 H-S	Stretch
	Interlock, Qiana, swimsuit fabric, Spandex			
	HEAVYWEIGHT	12–14	80–90 H	All-purpose
	Double knit, velours			
	FAKE FURS and FURLIKE FABRICS	14–16	90–100 H	All-purpose
WOVENS	**VERY SHEER**	8	60 H	All-purpose
	Lace, net, chiffon, voile			
	SHEER	11	70 H	All-purpose
	Qiana, lawn, taffeta, gingham, crepe, organdy			
	MEDIUM	12	80 H	All-purpose
	Wool, linen, piqué, brocade, velvet, velveteen, terry cloth, nylon (outerwear)			
	HEAVY	14	90 H-J	Sharp
	Denim, corduroy, sailcloth, duck			
	EXTRA HEAVY	14–16	90 H-J or 90–110	Sharp or All-purpose
	Canvas, upholstery, awning, drapery fabric			
LEATHER	**VINYLS**	Leather 14–18	NTW 90–110	Wedge-point
	LIGHT TO MEDIUM WEIGHT	Leather 14	NTW 90	Wedge-point
	Leathers and Suedes			
	FURLIKE FABRIC WITH VINYL BACKING	Leather 14–16	NTW 90–100	Wedge-point
	HEAVY	Leather 14–16	NTW 90–100	Wedge-point
	ULTRASUEDE	11	75 H-S	Stretch
DECORATIVE STITCHING	**MACHINE EMBROIDERY**	12–14	80–90 H	All-purpose
	TOPSTITCHING WITH HEAVIER THREAD	14	Topstitching 90	All-purpose large eye
	TWIN NEEDLES	**Dist btwn. needles**	**Size U.S. Eur.**	
		1.6mm	10/70	
		2.0mm	12/80	
		2.5mm	12/80	All-purpose
		2.7mm	12/80	
		3.0mm	14/90	
		4.0mm	14/90	

Thread				Presser Foot
Mercerized Cotton	Cotton-covered Polyester	Polyester	Nylon	
yes	yes	no	yes	Teflon/metal
yes	yes	no	yes	Teflon/metal
yes	yes	yes	no	Teflon/metal
yes	yes	yes	no	Roller foot or even-feed foot
yes	yes	no	yes	Teflon/metal
yes	yes	no	no	Teflon/metal
yes	yes	no	no	Embroidery
yes	yes	yes	no	Teflon/metal
yes	yes	yes	no	Telfon/metal
yes	yes	yes	no	Roller or even-feed foot
yes	yes	yes	no	Roller Teflon foot
yes	yes	yes	no	Roller or even-feed foot
yes	yes	yes	no	Roller or Teflon foot
yes	no	no	no	Varies/Embroidery
no	no	yes	no	Teflon or embroidery foot
				Embroidery/pin tuck foot
yes	yes	no	no	Teflon/metal

I met a woman in California who asked me why her needle was coming unthreaded all the time. I asked her to bring the machine to me, so I could take a look at it: she had worn the needle down to the eye! You guessed it—she had *never* changed her needle. When I asked her if she wanted to buy a package of needles, she said, "No, thank you. All I need is one."

Please remember to change the needle. It prevents skipped stitches and snagging and is the first thing a repair person will do to your machine if you take it in for service. If your machine has a front- or top-loading bobbin, the flat side of the needle goes to the back. If you have a side-loading bobbin, the flat side goes to the right. Make sure the needle is inserted all the way up, and tighten it in with a screwdriver.

For general dressmaking, I prefer an all cotton (size #30 Zwicky) or cotton-covered polyester (Dual Duty). I also use all cotton thread (size #50 Zwicky) or Dual Duty Extra Fine for freehand machine embroidery and special decorative stitching. For topstitching I like 100 percent silk-twist, polyester top-stitching thread, or size #8 pearl cotton (DMC or Coats & Clark). I'm also a nut for specialty threads. I like rayon thread for some embroidery and never overlook the opportunity to use metallic threads, yarns, ribbons, and other intriguing fibers in the bobbin (see Chapters 7 and 10).

For my serger, I like two-ply, 100 percent polyester serger thread or cotton-covered polyester (Coats & Clark) serger thread. Serger thread is finer than thread used on conventional sewing machines, but strong enough to withstand the speed and abuse it takes going through a serger. You can have a fortune tied up in serger thread, so I have four cones of six often-used colors that blend well with most any fabric (black, white, navy blue, gray, tan, red).

In the next section, practice seam finishes on 6″ (15 cm) swatches. Take notes in the space provided and staple finished swatches in your notebook.

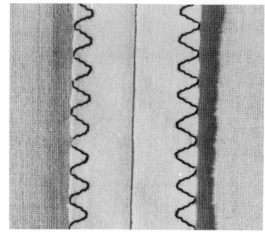

A

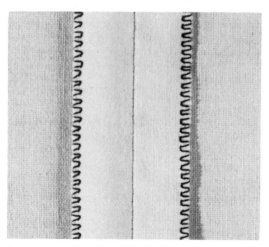

B

FIG. 3.9 Conventional 3-step zigzag (*A*) and interlock (*B*) stitches used as seam finishes for fine fabrics.

Seam Finishes on Fine Fabrics

On the Conventional Machine
Stitch: 3-step zigzag (Fig. 3.9A) ———
Stitch length: 0.8–1, or fine setting ———
Stitch width: widest ———
Foot: standard zigzag (Teflon) ———
Needle: #70/9 ———

Stitch: interlock (Fig. 3.9B) ———
Stitch length: 0.8–1, or fine ———
Stitch width: 4–6 ———
Foot: standard zigzag (Teflon) or
overcast guide ———
Needle: #70/9 ———

1. Place fabric under foot so raw edge is even with the right side of the needle opening in the presser foot. If you are using the overcast guide foot, place raw edge against the guide or blade in the foot.

2. Overcast edge so the needle catches the fabric on the left and swings off the raw edge on the right.

On the Serger

I use my serger to overcast edges on linings and blouse weights. Use a shorter stitch length and narrower stitch width on fine fabrics. Write the normal needle and looper settings for your serger in the space provided at the right. Once tensions have been balanced, stitch a sample and write the settings on it for your notebook. If you remove a needle or change a needle plate to narrow the width, make a note of it, too.

2/3-thread serger

Stitch: 3-thread overlock (Fig. 3.10) ———
Stitch length: 2–3 ———
Stitch width: 2–3.5 ———
Needle tension: normal ———
Looper tension: normal ———
Needle plate: 2 mm ———

3/4-thread serger

Stitch: 3-thread overlock ———
Stitch length: 2–3 ———
Stitch width: 2–3 ———
Right needle tension: normal ———
Upper looper tension: normal ———
Lower looper tension: normal ———
Needle plate: 2 mm ———

3/4/5-thread serger

Stitch: 3-thread overlock ———
Stitch length: 2–3 ———

FIG. 3.10 Serger narrow 3-thread overlock used as seam finish for fine fabrics.

Stitch width: 3 ———
Right overlock needle tension:
normal ———
Upper looper tension: normal ———
Lower looper tension: normal ———
Needle plate: 2 mm ———

Lower cutter, or place edge of fabric just to the left of the blade. Serge to overcast edges on a single layer of fabric so that ravelly threads are cut, but without cutting into the seam allowance.

Seam Finishes on Medium- to Heavy-weight Fabrics

On the Conventional Machine

Stitch: 3-step zigzag (Fig. 3.11A) ———
Stitch length: 1–1.5, or fine ———
Stitch width: 4–6 ———
Foot: transparent embroidery ———
Needle: #80/11–12 ———
Stitch: double overlock (Fig. 3.11B) ———
Stitch length: preset ———
Stitch width: 4–5 ———
Foot: transparent embroidery ———
Needle: #80/11–12 ———

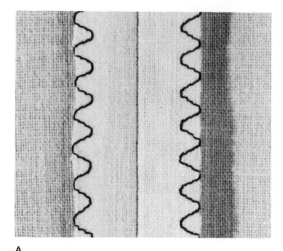

A

B

FIG. 3.11 Conventional 3-step zigzag (*A*) and double overlock (*B*) stitches used as seam finishes for medium to heavy fabrics.

1. Place fabric under foot so raw edge is even with the right side of the needle opening in the presser foot.
2. Overcast edge so the needle catches the fabric on the left and swings off the raw edge on the right.

HINT: If your machine has a fine-tune or elongation adjustment, you may have more success by elongating the stitch for heavier fabrics. Test on a scrap.

On the Serger
As with a conventional machine, use a longer stitch on medium to heavy fabrics.

2/3-thread serger
Stitch: 3-thread overlock (Fig. 3.12) _____
Stitch length: 3–5 _____
Stitch width: 4–5 _____
Needle tension: normal _____
Looper tension: normal _____
Needle plate: 5 mm _____

3/4-thread serger
Stitch: 3-thread overlock _____
Stitch length: 3–5 _____
Stitch width: 4–5 _____
Left needle tension: normal _____
Upper looper tension: normal _____
Lower looper tension: normal _____
Needle plate: 5 mm _____

FIG. 3.12 Serger 3-thread overlock stitch used as seam finish for medium and heavy fabrics.

3/4/5-thread serger

Stitch: 3-thread overlock —————
Stitch length: 3–5 —————
Stitch width: 4–5 —————
Left overlock needle tension:
    normal —————
Upper looper tension: normal —————
Lower looper tension: normal —————
Needle plate: 5 mm —————

Serge and overcast as described for fine fabrics.

JACKET CONSTRUCTION SEQUENCE

Fully Fused Front

In a lined, ready-to-wear jacket or blazer, a piece of interfacing is fused to the entire jacket front. This saves time and results in a crisp, tailored appearance in a fraction of the time it took to pad-stitch my college tailoring project. Because this is the largest area to fuse, it's important to use the appropriate interfacing and to fuse it properly. My favorite for summer-weight suiting is Pellon's Sof-Shape™. For loosely woven raw silk or linen, I like Stacy's Easy-Knit®. For heavier wools try Armo's fusible hair canvas or Stacy's Tailor's Touch. Use Chart 3.1 to help with your selection. For a more complete listing, see *Shaping Fashion: A Guide to Today's Interfacing* in the bibliography. Then test interfacing swatches on your fashion fabric to find what's best for you.

1. Cut jacket front interfacing using jacket front pattern piece as a guide. Trim away $\frac{1}{2}''$ (1.3 cm) all the way around. Fuse interfacing to wrong side of fashion fabric as described earlier in this chapter (How to Fuse).

2. Mark lapel roll line on interfacing.

3. To establish roll line on the lapel, use a piece of lighter weight interfacing than was fused on jacket front. Cut a triangular-shaped piece from the roll line to lapel point, using the jacket front pattern as a guide. Trim $\frac{1}{8}''$

(3 mm) inside roll line and $\frac{1}{2}''$ from seam allowances.

4. Fuse triangle to front lapels as shown in Fig. 3.13.

For a princess-line jacket, fuse interfacing on jacket front only. The side front piece is needed for shaping and fitting and therefore needs a softer hand. However, for fabrics that are very loosely woven and need more body, fully fuse side front pieces with a lighter weight interfacing than was used for jacket front. Good choices are Pellon's Sof-Shape or Stacy's Soft-Fuse™. For an unlined, loosely woven cardigan, you may want to underline both jacket front and back, and/or just the sleeves. To do this, use Stacy's Easy-Knit or Pellon's KnitShape™ to retain shape and durability and

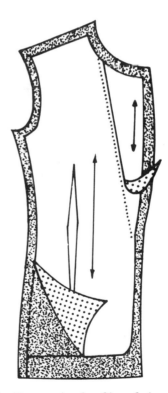

FIG. 3.13 Fuse a triangle of interfacing $\frac{1}{8}''$ (3mm) inside roll line to $\frac{1}{2}''$ (1.3cm) from raw edge.

to improve crease resistance. Even though Easy-Knit is supposed to be preshrunk, take a few minutes and preshrink it. It comes in white, black, beige, and grey. KnitShape comes in white and needs to be preshrunk. Either product should be cut following the lengthwise grain and can be used to underline a knit or woven garment. If you are using it as an underlining, don't trim seam allowances, as with other interfacing. Fuse the knit interfacing to the appropriate garment pieces, then repeat the fusing process press on the right side to give a strong, even bond.

Under Collar

The interfacing used in the under collar helps shape the roll line. Therefore, cut it on the bias per pattern markings and use slightly heavier fusible interfacing on the under collar than on the upper collar and front facing. Try fusible hair canvas, Pellon Pel-Aire, or Stacy Tailor's Touch.

1. Cut interfacing following pattern grain lines, using under collar pattern piece. Trim $\frac{1}{2}''$ (1.3 cm) from seam allowance.

2. Heat-baste and fuse interfacing on under collar pieces.

3. Seam under collar at center back and press seam open.

4. Using under collar pattern as a guide, trace the under collar stand on a piece of waxed paper, from roll line to seam line. Using waxed paper as a pattern piece, cut collar stand interfacing on the lengthwise grain and fuse $\frac{1}{8}''$ (3 mm) inside the roll line (Fig. 3.14).

5. Pin under collar on tailor's ham, and steam in the shape as shown in Fig. 3.15. Keep collar pinned to ham until the moisture has evaporated.

Upper Collar and Front Facing

In most cases, the upper collar and front facing should have a softer hand than the under collar. Therefore, use a lighter weight fu-

Clotilde

Clotilde

Fort Lauderdale, Florida

48

"With a name like Clotilde, who needs a last name?" At the age of six, Clotilde picked up a needle and hasn't stopped sewing since. After graduation from Miami University in Ohio, she worked in the wardrobe department of 20th Century Fox, where she learned manufacturers' techniques of garment construction. She continued to learn designers' tricks and techniques while sewing commercially for exclusive Beverly Hills boutiques.

After writing the book *Sew Smart,* Clotilde began a hectic touring schedule giving sewing seminars in all fifty states to thousands of home sewers. She continues to bring her "Sew Smart" message to university students and professors, cooperative extension agents, consumers, and professional sewing groups across the United States every year. She is president of her own notions company, Clotilde, Inc., which carries more than 1,000 items in its mail-order catalog and does business worldwide.

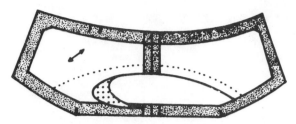

FIG. 3.14 After interfacing has been fused to under collar, another piece of interfacing is fused from roll line to neck edge.

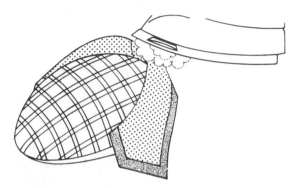

FIG. 3.15 Steam and shape under collar on tailor's ham.

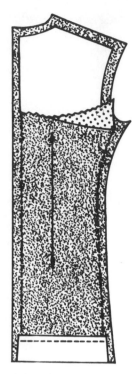

FIG. 3.16 Back interfacing. Pink lower edge to prevent a ridge from pressing through.

sible. I like Pellon Sof-Shape or Stacy Easy-Knit.

1. Cut interfacing using the upper collar and front facing pattern pieces. Trim $\frac{1}{2}''$ (1.3 cm) from seam allowance.

2. Heat-baste and fuse interfacing on upper collar and front facing.

Jacket Back

Because the upper back of a lined jacket gets a lot of stress, it should be interfaced. Use the pattern piece provided to cut the interfacing. If you don't have a pattern piece, cut back interfacing piece as shown in Fig. 3.16, starting $2\frac{1}{2}''$ (6.4 cm) below armhole. To prevent a ridge from pressing through, pink the edge as shown.

In Chapter 5 we will attach the collar to the jacket.

Hems

A jacket will hang and wear better if interfacing is used at the hems. This works well when you want a little more weight to a hemline in a knit cardigan or unlined jacket. Cut strips of interfacing for this purpose, or use Fold-a-Band or Fuse-n-Fold. One side is slotted $\frac{5}{8}''$ (1.5 cm) from one edge and the finished width is $1\frac{1}{2}''$ (3.8 cm), the recommended depth of most hems. Don't confuse it with similar products for waistbands. Fold-a-Band and Fuse-n-Fold are nonwoven, lightweight interfacings that add strength to hemlines without adding stiffness.

1. For bulky fabrics where seam allowances have been pressed open, trim seam allowance to about $\frac{1}{2}''$ (1.3 cm) within the depth of the hem (Fig. 3.17). **Note:** Be sure jacket fits before trimming away any seam allowance.

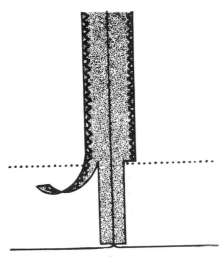

FIG. 3.17 Trim seam allowance to $\frac{1}{2}''$ (1.3cm) within the depth of the hem.

2. If hemming a garment with $\frac{1}{4}''$ (6 mm) seam allowances pressed to one side, twist seam allowance at the break of the hem so side seams are pressed toward the front and the hem allowance is pressed toward the back (Fig. 3.18).

3. Fuse Fold-a-Band or Fuse-n-Fold with the proper heat, moisture, and pressure so that

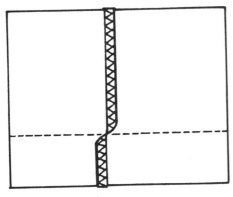

FIG. 3.18 For a $\frac{1}{4}''$ (6mm) seam allowance pressed to one side, twist seam allowance at the break of the hem so side seams are pressed toward the front and hem allowance is pressed toward the back.

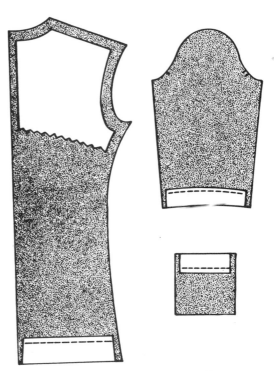

FIG. 3.19 Fuse interfacing to hem edges.

the wide part is fused to the hem allowance, and the slotted line is at the hemline (Fig. 3.19).

Speedy Sleeve Vent and Hem Finish

I like to push up my sleeves on summer weight jackets. I made a jacket and found the sleeves were too baggy at the wrist and used this technique to tighten them up.

1. Rather than turning up the hem, face the sleeve at the bottom edge. To do so, cut sleeve to desired finished length plus a $\frac{5}{8}''$ (1.5 cm) seam allowance.

2. To make a facing pattern, measure 4" (10 cm) up from bottom of sleeve and trace a facing including all pattern markings for the bottom of the sleeve. Remember to add seam allowance.

51

3. Fold sleeve pattern tissue in half the long way. With the back of the sleeve pattern right side up, find the halfway point between center fold and seamline. Draw a rectangular box, $3\frac{1}{2}''$ (9 cm) long and $\frac{1}{2}''$ (1.3 cm) wide (Fig. 3.20A). Place new facing pattern over sleeve pattern, and transfer rectangle to facing as shown (Fig. 3.20B). This rectangle is the new stitching line.

4. Cut and interface facings. Finish top edge of facing with the 3-step zigzag or super overlock stitch on the conventional machine or the 3-thread overlock on the serger. Before stitching underarm seam, place facing and sleeve pieces right sides together and stitch at $\frac{5}{8}''$ (1.5 cm), stitching around the rectangle as shown.

5. Clip and turn facing to wrong side of sleeve. Understitch seam allowance toward facing using the 3-step zigzag stitch (stitch length 1–1.5, stitch width 4–5, transparent embroidery foot). Edgestitch around vent (Fig. 3.21).

6. Stitch underarm seam, turn facing up, and blind hem.

FIG. 3.21 Edgestitch around vent.

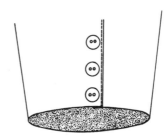

FIG. 3.22 Fold vent, and stitch buttons in place.

7. Fold vent as shown and stitch buttons to close it (Fig. 3.22).

TIPS ON TAILORING FOR MEN

There are a few differences in tailoring a jacket or blazer for a man—namely, the type of lining you elect to put into the garment (full or half) and the under collar treatment. Proportion of the jacket is also important.

A man's lined jacket, whether half or fully lined, has two inside pockets. In a full lining the back neck facing, normally used on a woman's blazer, is eliminated so the lining goes up to the collar. In a half lining, front pieces are lined and the back is lined to 3" (7.5 cm) below the armhole at the underarm seams. The traditional method of tailoring a man's collar is to pad by hand. In this book, you will see both the traditional approach and the speedy alternative (Chapter 5).

A well-fitting jacket should be long enough to cover the seat. Sleeves should touch the wrist bone, so the edge of the shirt cuffs show.

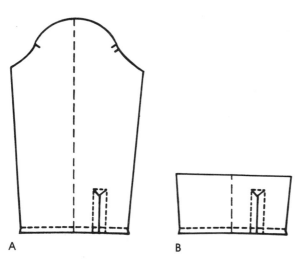

FIG. 3.20 *A*, On the back edge of the sleeve, draw a rectangular box halfway between underarm seam and center of sleeve. *B*, Transfer rectangle to new facing pattern.

52

Lapel length and pocket placement should be in proportion to the wearer's build. Lapel width and style are dictated by fashion; however, a conservative approach is always in good taste and enables the owner of the jacket to get a lot more wear out of it.

NEW PRODUCTS

I like any product or notion that makes my sewing go faster and easier. I urge you to try the following new products and come up with your own additional uses. You will find more new products by the time my book comes out. Keep a section in your notebook just for these, so you will keep up-to-date.

Knit Stabilizers in ¾" (2 cm) Tape

Easy-Knit and KnitShape™ are available in strip form, straight or bias cut, by the yard. They are used instead of twill tape to stabilize shoulder seams, to add body to narrow hems, to support buttonholes in knits, and to interface knit cardigans. Use the straight cut in areas that need stabilizing (shoulder seams, lengthwise seams). Use the bias cut for curved areas (circular hems, necklines).

Fusible Thermolam®

Thermolam is a lofty, crush-resistant, needle-punch fleece, available fusible or nonfusible, used in garment construction, quilting, and home decorating projects. The fusible is often easier to use, because it can be fused to a background fabric and won't shift. Use fusible fleece to make shoulder pads or to quilt small projects such as bibs, children's clothing, place mats, and handbags. Use two or three layers to create a mock-trapunto. Experiment. It's fun.

RolControl™

If you are sick of waistbands that roll or cut into your waistline after a nice dinner, try RolControl, a nonfusible waistline stabilizer. It is used in lieu of waistband interfacing, has stitching lines constructed into it for perfectly straight waistbands, and is easy to use (see Chapter 9). Do remember to preshrink it, and follow instructions on the package.

Wonder-Under™ or TransFuse™ in ¾" (2 cm) Strip

Wonder-Under and TransFuse are paper-backed fusible webs that are great for creating your own fusible fabric. I liked Wonder-Under by the yard for craft and decorative sewing, but I had to cut it into strips to fuse up a quick hem or to make a no-sew strap or belt. Now we have the best of both worlds, because it is also available in a 10-yard × ¾" (9 m × 2 cm) roll.

To use it, press the rough side of either product to the wrong side of your hem, let it cool, then peel off the paper and fuse hem up with a hot, dry press or iron. With the paper on the back, you can press it onto any fabric without using a Teflon pressing sheet, and it won't gum up your iron.

In Chapter 4 we'll learn the proper way to press as you sew. I've included some of my favorite sewing techniques to make the pressing go much faster. Whether you are making this jacket for yourself or a significant other, your hard work will pay off in compliments.

SUPPLY LIST FOR CHAPTER 4

- Jacket cut out, ready for construction
- Transparent tape
- Press or iron; travel iron
- Pressing cushions, tailor's ham, seam roll, mitt
- Adding machine tape
- Pins
- Waxed paper
- Seam gauge
- Sewing machine, serger, or both

Press As You Sew

In this chapter you'll learn the proper way to use a press or hand iron, and the accessories described in Chapter 2, to press your speed-tailored jacket as you sew. You'll also learn tips on how to stitch and press perfect collar points, pleats, and creases in pants, as well as other ideas to help with the rest of your sewing. If one or more of the techniques in this chapter are not part of your jacket project, make a sample of each to put in your notebook.

UNDER PRESSING AND TOP PRESSING

Under pressing is done on the inside of a garment during construction. Under pressing, with the custom pressing equipment discussed in previous chapters, is the way to shape a garment. Top pressing smooths a finished garment and is generally done with a press cloth to prevent marking and shine.

DARTS

All of us have figure flaws. The secret to a good-looking, well-fitting garment is to disguise the flaws—using a combination of properly placed darts, gathers, tucks, and seamlines and skill in stitching and pressing them.

Your jacket pattern has a dart at the waistline, bust, or shoulder. If your fabric is heavy, trim the dart away or slash to a $\frac{3}{8}''$ (1 cm) seam as far down as you can go to maintain the seam allowance. At the end of the slash, cut dart at an angle, halfway to the stitching line.

Straight Dart

1. For a straight dart, mark and pin, right sides together. Stitch from the widest part of the dart to the point, pulling pins out before stitching over them. If you're having trouble sewing straight, place a piece of transparent tape next to the stitching line to use as a guide. Sew *next* to the tape (Fig. 4.1). *Do not backstitch,* but leave about a 6″ (15 cm) thread tail.

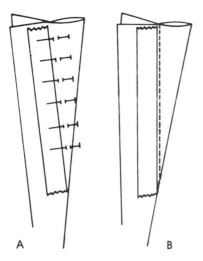

FIG. 4.1 Place a strip of transparent tape next to the stitching line (*A*), and sew next to the tape (*B*) for a straight dart.

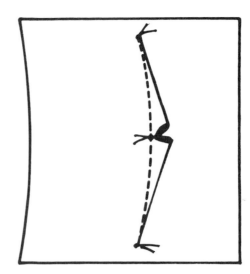

FIG. 4.3 Waistline contour dart.

2. Tie off thread ends. The best way to prevent threads from coming untied is to make a loop with both threads at the pointed end of the dart and pull the ends through (Fig. 4.2). Hold the loop at the fabric, pull thread ends through the loop, and snug it up to the fabric.

Waistline Contour Dart

Stitch a waistline contour dart in two steps.
1. Mark and pin dart as for straight dart. Baste if working on a particularly difficult fabric. Start at waistline, and stitch from the widest part to the point in one direction. Leave long thread tails.
2. Starting at the waistline again, stitch from the widest part to the point in the other direction. Leave long thread tails. Tie off dart at the middle and at the points as described above. Clip dart at waistline (Fig. 4.3).

Pressing Darts

Press stitching line from the row of stitches to the fold. This sets the thread and blends it into the fabric.

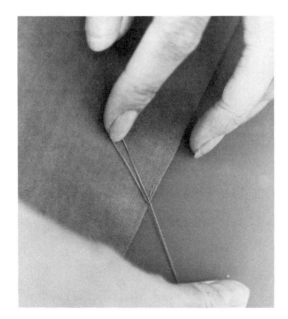

FIG. 4.2 Hold loop at the fabric, pull thread ends through the loop, and snug loop to fabric.

FIG. 4.4 Pressing dart with the press.

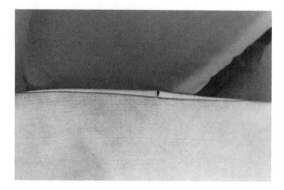

FIG. 4.5 Pressing waistline contour dart with the press.

With the Press

On the wrong side, place straight dart at an angle to the front of the press. Place wide end of dart toward you. Bring heating shoe down to the fabric and press dart so the heat presses to within $\frac{3}{8}''$ (1 cm) of the point (Fig. 4.4). For a waistline contour dart, press in two steps, using both ends of the press. Again, press to within $\frac{3}{8}''$ (1 cm) of the points. As with a straight dart, place dart at an angle with the wide end toward you (Fig. 4.5).

With the Hand Iron

Press either kind of dart flat by pressing in the direction it was stitched, from the stitching line to the fold and to within $\frac{3}{8}''$ (1 cm) of the point.

I like to shape darts over a ham with a hand iron. With right side down, press dart toward the center of the garment over the ham (Fig. 4.6). Turn fabric over and top press dart using a press cloth and shaping over the ham.

HINT: If you have a press, plug in your small travel iron and put ham on the press surface as if it were an ironing board.

For a slashed dart, press dart open as far as you can. Then slip a fine, metal knitting needle in the dart from the slash to the point, snugging the tip of the knitting needle up to the point of the dart. Press over knitting needle (Fig. 4.7).

HINT: For freshening up a dart, slip pressing mitt over your hand. With wrong side up, position dart over the mitt, and hold mitt up to the heating shoe of the press, *rolling,* not rubbing, the mitt against the heating shoe so dart is shaped over the curve of the mitt. Rubbing the fabric on the heating shoe might cause shine.

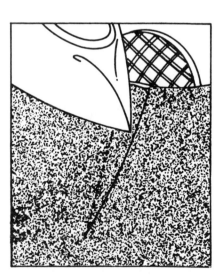

FIG. 4.6 With right side down, shape dart over a ham by pressing dart toward center of garment.

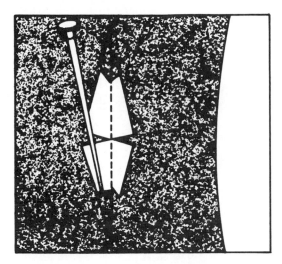

FIG. 4.7 Press dart open. Then slip a metal knitting needle in the dart snugging the tip up to the point, and press over it.

PRESSING SEAMS

Seams are under pressed open or to one side. For a crisp, flat edge, press against hard wood. For shaping, press against a padded surface.

⅝″ (1.5 cm) Seams Pressed Open

Set the stitches by pressing seam allowances flat and together with the press or hand iron.

With the Press
1. Open the seam allowances with the tip of your travel iron, pressing with the grain. Using steam or a dampened press cloth, touch the heating shoe to the surface of the fabric for a couple of seconds with half pressure.
2. To prevent seam allowances from pressing through to the right side, slip the padded sleeve cushion under seam allowance and press as described above. If you don't have a sleeve cushion, slip a strip of adding machine tape under each seam allowance and press (Fig. 4.8).
3. For a crisp result, slip a wooden yardstick under seam allowance and press as described above. As with the seam roll, the raw edges of the seam allowance fall away from the pressing surface. This method is great for long, straight side seams in sleeves and pants (Fig. 4.9).

With the Hand Iron
1. Place pattern piece wrong side up on a seam roll. Open the seam allowances with the

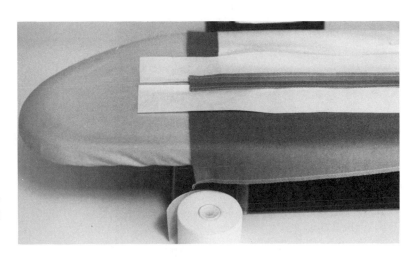

FIG. 4.8 Slip strips of adding machine tape under seam allowances to prevent them from pressing through.

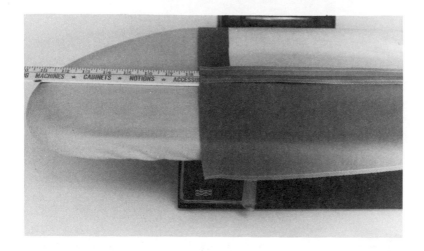

FIG. 4.9 Pressing seam open over a wooden yardstick.

tip of the iron, picking up the iron, pressing a couple of seconds, then picking it up again and moving down the seam allowance. Always press with the grain. The raw edges of the seam allowances fall away from the pressing surface when you use a seam roll, so they won't press through to the right side. If you are pressing a stiff or stubborn fabric, use steam and hold a tailor's clapper over seam allowance for a few seconds so the steam has a chance to penetrate and the seam can be pressed flat.

2. If you don't have a seam roll, place a strip of adding machine tape under seam allowances to prevent them from pressing through.

3. For crisp results, press seam open over the straight edge of a tailor board. Because the wood surface is narrow, the seam allowance won't press through on most fabrics.

4. For softer results, put the padded cover on the tailor board and press as described above.

$\frac{1}{4}''$ (6 mm) Seam Allowances Pressed to One Side

I use $\frac{1}{4}''$ (6 mm) seam allowances on knits, woven blouse weights, linings, sheers, swimwear, and lingerie. Generally, $\frac{1}{4}''$ (6 mm) seam allowances are pressed toward the center or

front of a garment, like darts. This way, the crack of the seamline is not seen when you are looking at the front of the garment. Shoulder seams and side seams are pressed toward the front.

With the Press

1. After stitching the seam, set thread by pressing seam with seam allowances flat and together.

2. With the right side of the pattern piece down, pin seam allowance toward garment front, pinning into the padded board.

3. Steam press seam to one side with travel iron, but not over pins.

4. Press seam again with press by bringing heating shoe to the surface of the fabric and using full pressure.

HINT: I often tug gently at either end of the seam while the heating shoe is down.

With the Hand Iron

1. Set thread in the seam by pressing seam allowances flat and together. Turn seam over, and press flat and together on the other side without sliding iron over the fabric.

2. Position seam on ironing board so it will be pressed toward the front. With iron in one hand, press seam, picking up the iron each time you move down the seam.

COLLARS

Collars frame our faces, so they should be stitched and pressed to perfection. This section tells how to stitch, clip, grade, and notch conventional collars for dress and blouse necklines. For tailored jacket collar and lapel instructions, skip to Chapter 5.

Use the proper interfacing on a collar. I use Pellon Shirt-Fuse™ for a crisp, dress shirt collar and on a man's dress shirt. For a softer, rolled collar, use an interfacing appropriate for the fabric (see Chart 3.1). Sheer fusible interfacings are available in a rainbow of colors for georgette, chiffon, batiste, handkerchief linen, etc.

The usual advice for fusible interfacing in collars is to use it on the top collar piece for a flat collar and on the under collar piece for a rolled collar. An exception, as I described in Chapter 3, is a tailored jacket. A jacket has a rolled collar, which means the back of the collar stands up from the neck edge, turns over, and breaks at the roll line. If you followed the usual rule, you would use no interfacing on the top collar piece. I want the upper collar and lapel of a jacket to have a crisp, tailored look and hand, so I interface both upper collar and front facing with a lighter weight interfacing than was used in the under collar.

Now let's take a closer look at making a good-looking collar on a dress or blouse.

Stitching Collar Points

The top collar should be larger than the under collar. If this provision is not made in the pattern, add $\frac{1}{8}''$ (3 mm) to the top edge of a lightweight fabric; $\frac{1}{4}''$ (6 mm) to the top edge of a medium-weight collar; $\frac{3}{8}''$ (1 cm) to the top edge of heavy fabric, tapering the line to the notched neck edge.

June Tailor, manufacturer of custom pressing equipment, says to increase the top collar pattern by retracing the top collar on a piece of waxed paper. Make the new cutting line using an adjustable hem gauge. Move the adjustable gauge the distance from the end of the rule that will be added to the top collar [$\frac{1}{8}''$ (3 mm), $\frac{1}{4}''$ (6 mm), or $\frac{3}{8}''$ (1 cm)]. Guide the adjusted gauge on the original cutting line, and use the point at the end of the rule to scratch in the new cutting line on the waxed paper (Fig. 4.10).

For perfect collar points, set your machine as follows:

Stitch: straight	_____
Stitch length: 2–3, or 10–15 stitches per inch	_____
Stitch width: 0	_____
Foot: standard zigzag (Teflon)	_____
Needle: #70/9 or #80/11–12 all-purpose	_____
Needle position: center; far left or far right if fabric puckers	_____

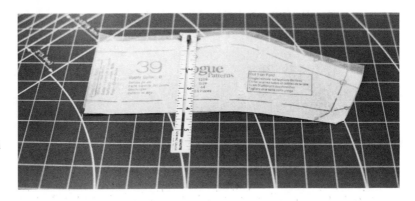

FIG. 4.10 Retrace a new increased top collar pattern using a piece of waxed paper and an adjustable hem gauge.

1. Interface top collar with appropriate fusible interfacing.

2. Place right sides together and pin collar together. With vanishing fabric marker, put a dot at each corner on top collar seam allowance.

HINT: To prevent collar points from curling up at the end, pinch and pin a tiny tuck in each corner of top collar, $1\frac{1}{2}$″ (3.8 cm) from the mark (Fig. 4.11). These tucks are called "tailor's blisters." The tuck allows more fabric at the points so the seamline falls toward the under collar.

3. With the top collar side up, stitch collar together on the $\frac{5}{8}$″ (1.5 cm) seamline. When you come to the corners, pivot collar slightly at the marks and take one stitch across the corner. Stop and pivot again.

HINT: For heavier fabrics, stitch collar points with a curved line of shortened, straight stitches. This is called "blunting" the point. Finish stitching collar. Tailor's blisters will be removed once the collar is turned.

Clip, Grade, Notch . . . or Not

A curved collar seam must be clipped, graded, and/or notched on the curve to eliminate bulk, so it lies down properly. I've always had a hard time remembering which layers of fabric to trim away so that the seam is graded properly. The following technique is unorthodox, but it's simple, requires no guesswork, and I like the results.

1. Press seam allowances flat and together with hand iron or press to set the stitches.

2. Cut away bulk from collar points. Clip into seam allowance $\frac{1}{8}$″ (3 mm) away from stitching line. Turn collar by holding the seam allowance at the corner toward the under collar. Remove tailor's blisters.

3. Using the tailor board, press seams open over wood, using the appropriate straight or curved edges of the board (Fig. 4.12).

4. For a lightweight shirt collar, top press collar with press or hand iron using a press cloth.

HINT: For a permanent press, moisten seamline with a mixture of half white vinegar, half water.

Margaret Dittman

Azle, Texas

"Sewing and quilt making have always been major elements in my life," says Margaret Dittman. "My grandmother, who raised me, made quilts from anything and everything. She was a true folk artist, using color lavishly and creatively, blending fabrics and techniques with wild abandon. From her, too, I adopted my artistic philosophy of free will and predestination: It's more fun to start with what you have on hand (the predestination part), then find a clever way to use it (free will). My grandmother, Delpha Anne Elizabeth Taylor, was what you'd call poor in worldly goods and money, but rich in talent and ideas. She accepted whatever anyone wanted to give her and in turn would give you anything she had. From her, no doubt, I got my love of scraps. From my mother, Golda Cooper, I learned precision—well, I'm in the process of learning it. Golda can make anything. She used to scout shop windows, then go home and make my sister and me the dresses and coats she'd liked in ready-to-wear.

"My favorite things to sew are quilts and wearables. My favorite techniques are spinning, weaving, Seminole and Afghani piecework, couching, and incorporating shisha mirrors. I like sewing with leather. I like using Folkwear patterns. I'd rather live in the

Margaret Dittman

country than in the city. My favorite places so far are my farm outside of Fort Worth, Texas, and the tiny village in the Sangre de Cristo mountains of northern New Mexico where my son was born in a hundred-year-old adobe house.

"My studio (oh lucky me) is a building separate from the house. Its former status was either servants' quarters or a rental apartment. The three rooms are tiny, and I lack a big open wall to pin designs onto, but the windows open onto my garden, the horses, and the rising moon. I have the freedom and privacy to make enormous messes and to play strange music at high volume.

"The résumé of an adventuress makes for interesting reading. I've done just about everything one can do to make a living—except waitressing. I tried it one night and left in tears. Now I always tip generously.

"I make my living by sewing quilts and wearables and by writing. In 1982 I took the job as editor of *Needle & Thread* magazine, the first job I'd ever had that I could sink my teeth into. Now that magazine has merged with *Needlecraft for Today,* and I'm co-editor of that. My first book was published by Chilton in the spring of 1988. *The Fabric Lover's Scrapbook* presents clever ways to sort, store, and use fabric scraps and remnants. One of my major ongoing projects is a charm quilt in shades of red. Four-inch squares of red and red print fabrics are welcome and can be sent to me at P.O. Drawer D, Azle, TX 76020."

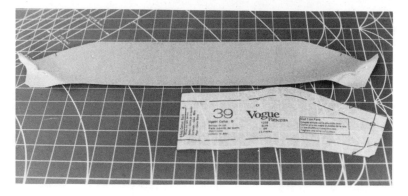

FIG. 4.11 Pin "tailor's blisters" 1½″ (3.8cm) from corner stitching line.

Your shirt collar is done. For heavier collars press seam allowances toward under collar and go on to the next steps.

5. From the right side, press seam allowance toward under collar and understitch using the following machine settings:

Stitch: 3-step zigzag ———————
Stitch length: 1–1.5 or 20 stitches
    per inch ————————
Stitch width: 4–5 ————————
Foot: transparent embroidery ————————
Needle: appropriate for fabric ————————

The 3-step zigzag stitch flattens the bulk and helps roll the seam to the underside without topstitching (Fig. 4.13).

6. Trim out excess seam allowance with appliqué or tailoring scissors. Top press collar flat using a press cloth.

7. If you haven't cut the top collar larger than under collar, hold finished collar in one hand to form a slight roll. The under collar will look larger. Pin collar together at neck edge and trim away excess seam allowance from under collar.

Collar Stand Application and Pressing

Most pattern instructions tell you to stitch the collar to the stand, machine stitch the back stand to the neck edge, and finish the stand

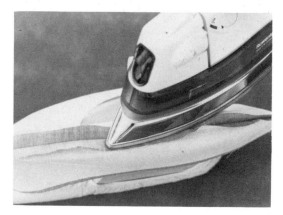

FIG. 4.12 Press seams open over wooden tailor board.

FIG. 4.13 Understitch seam allowance to under collar using the 3-step zigzag. Trim away excess seam allowance.

by slip-stitching it to the inside of the neck edge. With this method, the collar may be off center, and the slip-stitching gives the shirt a homemade look. To insure that the inside of the collar stand looks custom made and that the collar is properly centered in the stand, try this method adapted from David Coffin's *Custom Shirt Book:*

1. Interface inside stand and top collar with fusible interfacing appropriate for the fabric.

2. Make the shirt collar as described above. Fold collar in half, and mark the center back.

3. Stay-stitch shirt neck edge. Clip neck edge to within $\frac{1}{8}''$ (3 mm) of stay-stitching. Mark center back of neck edge.

4. Fold collar stand pieces in half to mark the center back. Also mark where the shirt and collar will fit into the stand. Sandwich shirt between inside and back collar stands, stretching stands to fit neck edge (Fig. 4.14).

5. Stitch stands to shirt, sewing from the center out, stopping $\frac{5}{8}''$ (1.5 cm) from each end. Trim neck edge seam to $\frac{1}{4}''$ (6 mm).

6. Hold collar on stands, matching center back and collar positioning marks. Double-check that collar is centered. Remove collar from stand.

7. Roll shirt fronts out of the way and pin back and inside stands together, matching collar positioning marks. Shorten your stitch length, and stitch from where you stopped at the neck edge around to collar positioning marks (Fig. 4.15). Do not backstitch. You may have to make minor adjustments later. Trim stand seam allowance to $\frac{1}{4}''$ (6 mm) around curve only. Clip top of both collar stands from raw edge where collar will be inserted, to collar positioning marks. Turn stand right side out and press so raw edges are out of the stand (Fig. 4.16). Try shirt on to be sure the pattern in the fabric matches and that the collar will be centered properly.

8. Pin finished collar to inside stand so top collar and inside stand are together. Back stand seam allowance is free. Stitch collar to inside stand.

9. Turn seam allowance toward the inside of stand. Tuck free seam allowance into stand,

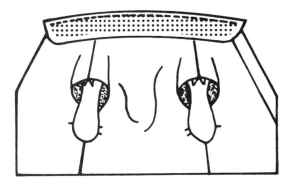

FIG. 4.14 Sandwich shirt between inside and back collar stands, stretching stands to fit neck edge.

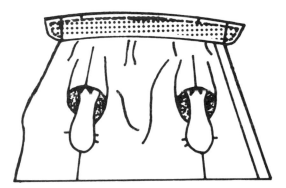

FIG. 4.15 Roll shirt fronts out of the way. Pin back and inside stands together. Stitch from where you stopped at neck edge around to marks.

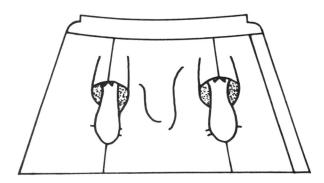

FIG. 4.16 Turn stand right side out so raw edges are out of stand.

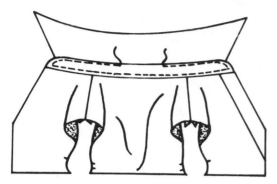

FIG. 4.17 Tuck free seam allowance into stand. Pin, press, and edgestitch around stand.

press, and edgestitch around collar stand, ⅛" (3 mm) from finished edge (Fig. 4.17). Set your machine as follows:

Stitch: straight   —————
Stitch length: 2.5, or 10–12 stitches
    per inch
Stitch width: 0   —————
Foot: buttonhole or blind hem   —————
Needle position: far left   —————
Needle: appropriate for fabric   —————

Position the inside of the right toe of buttonhole foot or blade of your blind hem foot against the finished edge and seamlines. As you sew, the toe or blade of the foot enables you to edgestitch evenly around the stand.

If your project does not include a collar stand, you will have to face the neck edge. To make the facing lie flat, and to make your garment look truly professional, try the following technique for understitching the facing.

UNDERSTITCHING FACINGS

1. Interface facing pieces with interfacing appropriate for the fabric (see Chart 3.1).
2. Finish raw edges where neckline facing will be stitched at the shoulder seams.
3. Seam facing at shoulder seams. Press seams open.

4. Finish outside raw edge so seam allowances are caught in the stitches. Stay-stitch neck edge of both facing and garment, so that you can clip the neck edge before collar and facing are attached.
5. Pin collar and neckline facing to garment, and stitch at the ⅝" (1.5 cm) seamline. Clip seam ⅛" (3 mm) from seamline.
6. Place neckline seam over tailor board; press neckline seam open.
7. Press entire seam allowance toward facing.
8. With the right side up, understitch facing, using the 3-step zigzag stitch (length 1–1.5, width 4–5). The stitch flattens bulk created by the five layers of fabric in the seam allowance (interfaced upper collar, under collar, and interfaced facings) so facings won't roll out of the neck edge. (Fig. 4.18).
9. Trim excess seam allowance, and press facing to inside of garment.
10. Anchor facing by stitching-in-the-ditch at shoulder seams from the right side.

SET-IN SLEEVES

When I first learned to sew, I wanted to make a dress with set-in sleeves. I couldn't figure out why the sleeve pattern was too big for the armhole. After struggling with what the pattern instructions called "ease," I was finally able to set in the sleeve by using every nasty word in my vocabulary, every pin in my pin cushion, and by hand-basting the sleeve in place before stitching.

After that experience, is it any wonder I avoided patterns with set-in sleeves? If that has happened to you, the following techniques will help clean up your language and open your closet to fashions with set-in sleeves.

Overcasting, Finishing, or Serging

If you plan to press the seams open, it's a lot easier to finish raw edges of the sleeve seams *before* the underarm seam is sewn. You

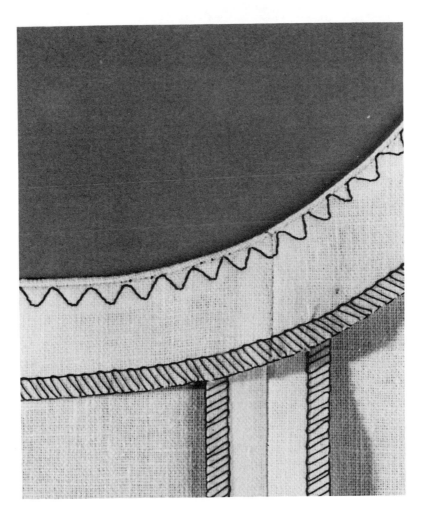

FIG. 4.18 Understitched facing.

are working with two sleeves, so the fastest way to finish each edge is to have both sleeve pieces in your lap, ready to stitch.

HINT: If you have difficulty telling the right from the wrong side of fabric, stick a piece of transparent tape on the right side of both sleeve pieces.

On the Serger
Stitch: 2- or 3-thread overlock ———
Stitch length: varies ———
Stitch width: 4–5 ———
Needle tension: normal ———
Upper looper tension: normal ———
Lower looper tension: normal ———
Needle plate: 5 mm ———

On the Conventional Machine
Stitch: 3-step zigzag ———
Stitch length: 1–1.5, or 20 stitches
   per inch ———
Stitch width: 4–5 ———
Foot: standard zigzag or
   transparent embroidery ———

Stitch: super overlock ———
Stitch length: preset ———
Stitch width: 4–5 ———
Foot: standard zigzag or
   transparent embroidery ———

1. With the right side up, place the raw edge of the first sleeve under the presser foot of your serger or sewing machine. Place fabric so overcasting stitches cover the raw edge of fabric.

2. When you finish serging or overcasting the first sleeve piece, place the second sleeve under presser foot as described above, *without* clipping threads between pattern pieces. Pattern pieces will resemble a kite tail with thread connecting the two.

3. Repeat to finish other raw edges of sleeve seam.

Sew and Press Underarm Seams

Machine settings for wovens
Stitch: straight _____
Stitch length: 2–2.5, or 12–15
    stitches per inch _____
Stitch width: 0 _____
Foot: standard zigzag _____

Machine settings for knits
Stitch: zigzag _____
Stitch length: 1–1.5, or 15 stitches
    per inch _____
Stitch width: 1–1.5 _____
Foot: standard zigzag _____

Pin right side of sleeve piece together and stitch at the $\frac{5}{8}''$ (1.5 cm) seamline.

HINT: If you put a piece of transparent tape on the right side of each sleeve as described in the preceding HINT, remove tape now.

Press the seam as follows.

With the Press
1. Press sleeve seam allowances flat and together to set the stitches.

2. Slip sleeve over sleeve cushion so seam allowance is up. Open seam allowance with tip of travel iron, pressing with the grain, without moving iron back and forth over the seam allowance (Fig. 4.19).

3. Dampen fabric with spritzer, or set press for steam setting. Bring heating shoe down to the fabric using *half* pressure. Press until all moisture has evaporated from fabric. Because sleeve is on the cushion, the seam allowance is absorbed into the cushion, so you rarely see ridges showing through to the right side.

HINT: If you dampen fabric too much and you can't press out the moisture, let sleeve air-dry with cushion still in place.

With the Hand Iron
1. Press seam flat and together to set the stitches.

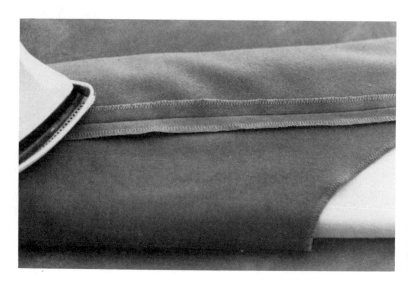

FIG. 4.19 With wrong side out, slip sleeve cushion into sleeve so seam is up. Open seam with tip of travel iron.

2. Press seam open by placing sleeve over seam roll. Place wool side against woolen or napped fabrics, synthetics, and blends requiring lower heat settings. Place cotton drill side of seam roll against cottons, cotton blends, linens, and linen blends.

3. If you don't have a seam roll, use a sleeve board and place a strip of wide adding machine tape under each seam allowance. Set iron on steam setting and gently open the seam with tip of iron, pressing with the grain. Press seam until fabric is dry.

Easing in Sleeve Cap

In preparation for easing in the sleeve cap, you will learn a new "finger posture" and manipulation of the fabric. This technique works on wovens, knits, Ultrasuede . . . anything. It just takes a little practice. Set your machine as follows:

Stitch: straight   _____
Stitch length: 2–3 or 10–12 stitches
    per inch   _____
Stitch width: 0   _____
Foot: standard zigzag or
    transparent embroidery   _____

To prepare the sleeve for the armhole, you will be sewing a row of ease stitches from notch to notch, ½" (1.3 cm) from the raw edge.

HINT: You need as much seam allowance as possible to hold onto at the right. Therefore, if you have a needle position on your machine, move the needle to the far right, and guide the raw edge of sleeve cap by the ⅝" (1.5 cm) seam guide on the needle plate.

Begin stitching at one of the notches, ½" (1.3 cm) from raw edge. Using index fingers on both hands simultaneously, pull fabric sideways, on the bias, exactly where the needle penetrates the fabric (Fig. 4.20). Some people call this "off-grain stitching." I call this the "pull and sweep method" because you pull the fabric sideways and sweep it back four or five stitches while sewing, then reposition your fingers for another pull and sweep.

HINT: For a better grip on the right, pull fabric with scissors points (Fig. 4.21).

Continue around sleeve cap until easing stitches have been sewn from notch to notch (Fig. 4.22). This pulls the fabric on the bias, thus closing up some space between the fibers. The stitches hold the fabric pulled on the bias creating ease, while the rest of the fabric returns to its original shape. If more ease is required, pull the fabric harder from side to side. If you have too much ease in the sleeve,

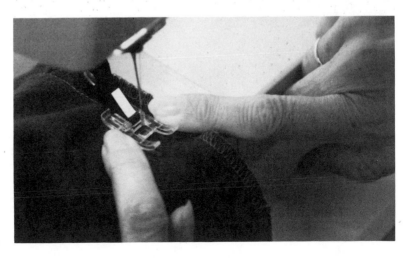

FIG. 4.20 Using both index fingers, pull fabric on the bias exactly where the needle penetrates the fabric.

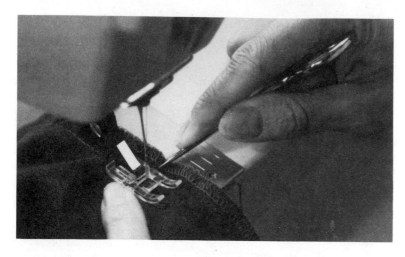

FIG. 4.21 For a better grip on the right, pull fabric with scissors points.

FIG. 4.22 Eased sleeve cap.

clip a thread or two to flatten out sleeve cap. The cap has an eased, rather than pleated or gathered, appearance.

Press and Shape Sleeve Cap

Most instructions recommend that you press the sleeve cap after the ease stitches have been sewn, thus "shrinking" the eased or gathered area with steam. Some suggest shrinking the fullness a couple of times so that the sleeve will fit the armhole. After successful preparation of the sleeve cap as described above,

this step is almost unnecessary. Your sleeve will look and fit better, however, if it is shaped on a tailor's ham or pressing mitt before final stitching.

With the Press

1. With wrong side out, place sleeve over curved end of pressing mitt.

2. Pin sleeve cap to mitt.

3. Set press on steam setting, or lightly dampen sleeve cap, then press mitt up on the heating shoe, pressing seam allowance only. Press until fabric is dry.

With the Hand Iron

1. With wrong side out, place sleeve over the larger end of tailor's ham so sleeve is positioned on the cotton drill side and the seam allowance is on the woolen side (Fig. 4.23).

HINT: The larger end of the ham is shaped like the top of your shoulder, so sleeve cap will be easier to shape. The smaller end can be used for children's sleeves.

2. There is about 1″ (2.5 cm) at the top of sleeve cap that is not eased, because it is cut across the grain. Starting at the uneased section of sleeve cap, center, and pin sleeve cap to the top of ham at the stitching line. Continue pinning sleeve to ham, just above the notch.

3. With steam, shape sleeve cap over ham, pressing the seam allowance only. Allow fabric to dry before removing sleeve from ham.

HINT: You can buy a stand for your ham that prevents it from rolling over while sleeve cap is drying.

FIG. 4.23   Shape sleeve cap over ham with steam, pressing seam allowance only. Place ham in stand to let fabric dry.

Final Stitching

Pin sleeve into armhole, matching notches, and permanently stitch in sleeve at the $\frac{5}{8}$″ (1.5 cm) seamline. Remember, the ease stitches were sewn $\frac{1}{2}$″ (1.3 cm) from raw edge, so they will not show after sleeve is permanently stitched.

HINT: If you sew with the eased side down, the action of the feed dogs helps ease in the fullness.

Trimming and Grading Sleeve Cap

Seam allowances always fall to the narrower seam allowance. Therefore, trim sleeve seam to $\frac{3}{8}$″ (1 cm) over top of sleeve from notch to notch. This causes the seam allowance to fall into the sleeve and maintains a well-rounded cap.

Trim jacket seam allowance to $\frac{1}{2}$″ (1.3 cm), and run a second row of stitching at the underarm from notch to notch, $\frac{3}{8}$″ (1 cm) outside seamline. Trim underarm seam allowance, close to second row of stitching.

Final Pressing

With the Press

With wrong side out, slide sleeve cushion or pressing mitt into sleeve, snugging it up to seamline. Place hand inside sleeve so cushion side is up. Gently touch and press seam allowance open against the heating shoe. This helps give sleeve cap a smooth, rounded shape at the seamline. To set stitches, turn sleeve allowances toward sleeve, and bring up to heating shoe to press (Fig. 4.24).

With the Hand Iron

With wrong side out, press sleeve seam allowance open over ham (Fig. 4.25). Then set the stitches by pressing it closed again with seam allowances toward sleeve. Avoid extending iron over seamline.

HINT: If you have a tailor board, use the padded accessories and use tip of iron to press seams and "soften" them into the garment.

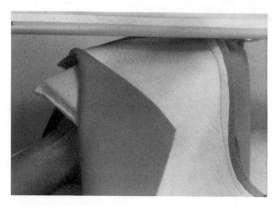

FIG. 4.24 With pressing mitt in sleeve, bring seam allowance up to heating shoe and touch it closed.

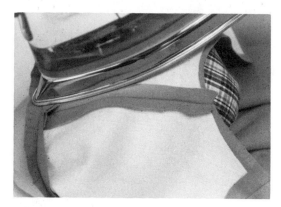

FIG. 4.25 With wrong side out, press seam allowance open over ham.

Inserting Sleeve Heads and Shoulder Pads

Sleeve heads and shoulder pads help shape out a shoulder and disguise figure flaws. Shoulder pads are sufficient shaping for most people, but sleeve heads can be purchased or made if they are needed, or if fashion dictates. To make a sleeve head cut a piece of polyester fleece 3″ × 5″ (7.5 cm × 12.5 cm). Fold it the long way so that one edge is 1″ (2.5 cm) wide.

Center and pin sleeve head in sleeve seam with fold against the seamline and wider half of head against the sleeve. Whipstitch head to sleeve seamline to support and round the sleeve cap.

You can make shoulder pads, too. I prefer using purchased ones, though; I figure the expense offsets the time it takes to make them. They are designed for all types of sleeves and come in many thicknesses. Some even have the sleeve heads built in.

Try the jacket on and insert pad so the top edge extends $\frac{3}{8}$″ (1 cm) into sleeve cap at seam. Pin pad in place along shoulder seam.

HINT: To help in placement, some shoulder pads are notched where pad is placed at the shoulder seam.

Remove jacket, turn wrong side out, and stitch pad to armhole seam allowance. Tack shoulder end to shoulder seam allowance to prevent shifting.

PLEATS AND PERMANENT CREASES

To press a permanent pleat or crease with the press or hand iron, dampen your press cloth with a mixture of half white vinegar, half water. To do this, put vinegar mixture in a bowl and sprinkle it on press cloth with a clean vegetable brush. If you're not sure of the fiber content, test vinegar mixture on a scrap first.

Pleats

Side pleats, box pleats, inverted pleats, soft pleats, sharp-fold pleats, topstitched pleats, edgestitched pleats—pleats of all kinds need pressing, whether during construction or after a lot of wear.

With the Press
1. Arrange pleats on the padded board.
2. Pin pleats in place, pinning fabric to both ends of the board.

Jackie Dodson

LaGrange, Illinois

"In school, I couldn't sew a straight line. We were making those awful quilted potholders, aprons, and boring stuff like that in home ec., so my mother did all my homework for me. I didn't do much sewing after that, until Chuck bought a machine for me after we were married.

"I taught myself to sew and really enjoyed it because I could always come up with something different that no one else was wearing. Then I joined the Embroiderers Guild in Chicago and learned how to stitch every kind of embroidery possible. I was introduced to machine embroidery and from that point, everything just clicked. My favorite medium is working with sheers and overlays."

If you have seen any of Jackie's work, you'll soon realize she is an artist. I asked her how she learned to think so creatively. She said, "I guess I've always had a pencil in my hand. My aunt taught my cousin and me block printing, beadwork, sketching . . . we even made our own looms as children. My dad was a good artist, too. As a result, I don't go anywhere without my sketch pad."

Besides her spectacular embroidery, Jackie has created the foundation of

Jackie Dodson

Chilton's *Know Your Sewing Machine* series. When she's finished, she will have authored and co-authored more than ten books. What an inspiration!

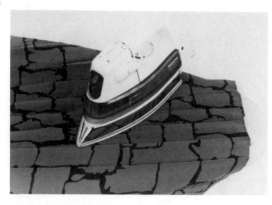

FIG. 4.26 Pin pleats at hem end. Hold waist taut with one hand and, with the iron in the other hand, press each pleat.

3. Spritz the fabric or press cloth, or set the press at steam setting. Bring heating shoe down and top press with full pressure for 3 to 5 seconds. Raise heating shoe, let steam escape, and press again. Press until moisture has evaporated from the press cloth. Repeat until all pleats are pressed. This way you can press many pleats at once and with 100 pounds (45 kg) of pressure, pleats are in to stay.

HINT: To press long pleats, start pressing the top of the garment, all the way around. Pull garment to the left, pin pleats as before, and press all the way around. Heating shoe should overlap previously pressed areas.

With the Hand Iron
1. Arrange pleats on ironing board.
2. Pin pleats in place at the hem end.
3. Spritz the press cloth or set iron at steam setting.
4. Hold waist end taut with one hand and hold the iron with the other (Fig. 4.26).
5. Press each pleat, picking up the iron and moving it down the pleat. Repeat as necessary until fabric is dry. The press cloth prevents shine.

Creases

To press correctly placed, permanent creases in a pair of pants, cut them on grain and make sure the pattern fits. Creases are pressed from the crotch down. The following preliminary step is used during garment construction. Final pressing is done after construction is complete.

With the Press
1. Construct pants, but do not yet attach legs at crotch.
2. With the right side out, hold pants leg upside down, so inseam and side seam are held together.
3. Place pants leg across padded board, from the knee down. The knee is to the left end of the board, the hem at the right; seams are at the front edge of the board (Fig. 4.27).
4. Dampen press cloth with white vinegar mixture, or set your press for steam.
5. Top press fabric, using full pressure, for 3 to 5 seconds. Raise heating shoe, let the steam escape, then press again until moisture has evaporated.
6. Lift pants leg and move it backward so seams are even with the back edge of board (Fig. 4.28). Press as before. Repeat for other pants leg.
7. Finish constructing pants. Press the rest of the crease (from knee to crotch) following the design lines. For final pressing, see Chapter 12.

With the Hand Iron
1. Follow steps 1–4 above.
2. Lower ironing board so you can exert more pressure on the iron. Place press cloth over pants leg and top press crease, pressing hard each time you move the iron down the crease.
3. Lift pants leg and move it backward so seams are even with back edge of board. Press as just described in step 2. Repeat for other leg.

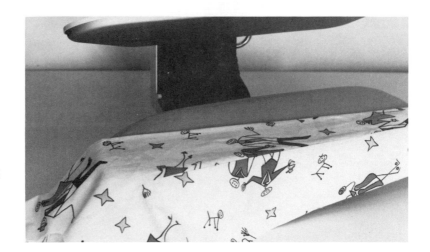

FIG. 4.27 Press pants leg from the knee down. The knee is to the left end of the board, the hem at the right; seams are at the front edge of the board.

FIG. 4.28 Lift pants leg and move it backward so seams are even with the back edge of board.

I hope you had enough practice to perfect some of the troublesome areas covered in this chapter. In Chapter 5 your jacket will begin to take shape. You'll learn how the upper collar, under collar, and lapels come together, a way to use the zigzag stitch to make a pocket welt with perfectly even lips, and a ready-to-wear technique of stitching a patch pocket on a jacket without topstitching it. I've also included some fast and professional ways to stitch in a zipper.

SUPPLY LIST FOR CHAPTER 5

- Patch pockets or welt pocket pieces cut for blazer
- 6″ (15.2 cm) fabric squares to practice techniques and put in notebook
- Under collar felt and hair canvas interfacing
- Braid
- 2 zippers
- ½″ (1.3 cm) transparent tape
- Pearl cotton

Tailoring Tips

Have you ever put a lot of time into a project and then never worn it because something just didn't look right? I have. In this chapter we will work on problem areas in tailoring which, if not done well, give a finished garment a homemade rather than hand-tailored look.

Try the suggestions for stitching the collar and lapels, and use one of the pocket applications on your jacket in progress. Stitch samples for your notebook to perfect the zipper insertions, braid application, and mitered corners.

INVISIBLE PATCH POCKET APPLICATION

I always wondered how to stitch patch pockets on a coat or jacket without topstitching them. I've seen it in ready-to-wear, knew it wasn't done by hand, and figured it was stitched with a special sewing machine that performed magic. Then a good friend, Karyl Garbow from Los Angeles, showed me this

technique, and I've used it ever since. The pockets must have round corners because they are stitched on from the *inside*. Here's how.

This technique is generally used for unlined pockets. I'm sure you want the pockets on your jacket lined, though, so I have modified the technique. Here's what to do:

1. Cut the pocket out and interface it with a lightweight fusible. Trim $\frac{1}{2}''$ (1.3 cm) from the interfacing seam allowance before fusing to the wrong side of pocket.

2. Cut pocket lining, and seam it to the top of the patch pocket as described in your pattern. Press pocket, right side out, and edgestitch lining and pocket together $\frac{1}{8}''$ (3 mm) from the raw edge.

3. Stay-stitch plus around the curved pocket corners, treating pocket and lining as one, as follows.

On the Conventional Machine
Stitch: straight stitch   _____
Stitch length: 2–3, or 10–12 stitches
    per inch   _____

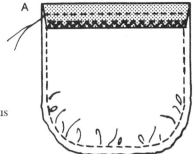 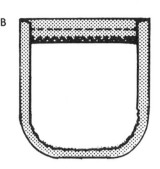

FIG. 5.1 *A*, Stay-stitch plus around pocket corners. *B*, Press seam allowance to inside.

Stitch width: 0 _____
Foot: transparent embroidery or standard zigzag foot _____

Starting at the inside top, stitch around pocket ¼″ (6 mm) from raw edge. When you get about 1″ (2.5 cm) above the first curve, stop and place your index finger behind the presser foot and hold the fabric very firmly. Begin stitching again holding the fabric firmly behind the foot so it bunches up. This is called "stay-stitching plus." Release the fabric across pocket bottom, then stay-stitch plus around the other curve. The stitches should ease the fabric into a curve at the corners (Fig. 5.1A). (Stay-stitching plus can also be used for hemming; see Chapter 11.)

On the Serger
Stitch: 3-thread overlock _____
Stitch length: 3 _____
Stitch width: 4–5 _____
Left needle tension: tight _____
Looper tensions: normal _____
Needle plate: 5 mm _____

Leave about a 5″ (12.5 cm) thread chain to start. Guiding the fabric so the knife will not cut it, start 1″ (2.5 cm) above the curve and serge around the corner. Continue around to the second corner stopping 1″ (2.5 cm) above the curve. Chain off another 4″–5″ (10 cm–12.5 cm). The tightened needle thread will cause the fabric to ease into a curve at the corners. If more ease is needed, tighten the

needle thread tension more and write the setting in the space provided above.

The needle thread is the shortest and straightest in the chain. With a pin, pull out the needle thread from one of the chains. This thread is used to adjust ease around pocket curves.

4. Press seam allowance to the inside, adjusting ease at the corners (Fig. 5.1B). If you serged around the corners, adjust ease with the needle thread you pulled out of the chain.

HINT: Press pocket corners around a pocket former so that both corners are pressed in exactly the same shape (Fig. 5.2).

5. Loosen upper tension and set your sewing machine as follows:

Stitch: zigzag stitch _____
Stitch length: 4–6 _____

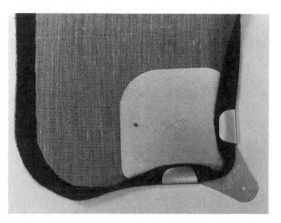

FIG. 5.2 Press pocket corners around pocket former (photo courtesy of Nancy's Notions).

Stitch width: 4–6 _____

Foot: transparent embroidery _____

Bobbin threaded with contrasting
    thread _____

6. Baste pocket, guiding the work so the needle takes one stitch into the pocket, one stitch into the jacket front (Fig. 5.3). Reset upper tension to normal, rethread bobbin with matching thread, and set your machine as follows:

Stitch: straight (wovens); zigzag
    (knits) _____

Stitch length: 1.5–2, or 15 stitches
    per inch _____

Stitch width: 0 (wovens); 1 (knits) _____

Foot: embroidery or transparent
    embroidery _____

7. Reach into the pocket and spread open the seam allowance. The zigzag basting stitches look like ladder rungs across the seamline.

8. Place foot over seamline, centering ladder rungs under the foot (Fig. 5.4). Stitch all the way around the inside of the pocket at the seamline.

9. Pull basting stitches out by pulling bobbin thread (Fig. 5.5).

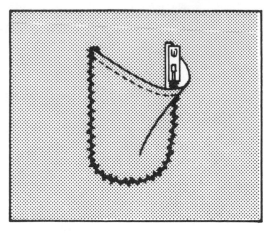

FIG. 5.4 Place foot over seamline, centering ladder rungs under foot.

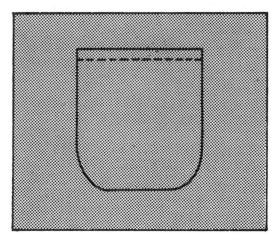

FIG. 5.5 Pull basting out, trim seam allowance inside pocket, and press.

10. Carefully trim seam allowance inside pocket to $\frac{1}{4}''$ (6 mm).

11. Press pocket.

12. (optional). Sometimes I like to reinforce pocket tops with a triangular-shaped line of topstitching at each corner. If you choose not to topstitch, the pocket is tough to fix if it comes unstitched at the corners when the jacket has a full lining.

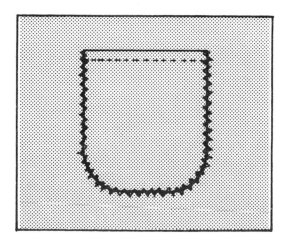

FIG. 5.3 Baste so needle takes one stitch into pocket, one stitch into jacket front.

With the Press

Place a press cloth over pocket, use steam or dampen the press cloth, and bring heating shoe down to pocket using *half* pressure for about 3 seconds. Release pressure, let steam escape, and press again using half pressure. Continue until moisture has evaporated from fabric.

With the Hand Iron

Place press cloth over pocket. With the steam setting, gently top press pocket area, picking up the iron, then putting it down over the pocket. Turn off the steam and continue pressing as before until the fabric is dry.

SPEEDY WELT POCKETS

I used to omit pocket welts from patterns that called for them because I found them difficult. But I love pockets and the look of pocket welts. When I discovered an easy way to make bound buttonholes, I applied the same technique for pocket welts, and now I always include them (Fig. 5.6). Set your sewing machine as follows:

Stitch: zigzag stitch _____
Stitch length: 0.8–1, or fine setting _____
Stitch width: 4–6 _____
Foot: transparent or metal
    embroidery _____

1. Carefully mark welt piece and pocket welt placement on jacket front or lining. I like to use tailor tacks.
2. Place welt piece on jacket front, right sides together, matching marks.
3. Starting on the left side at one end of the welt, zigzag to the other end, stopping with the needle in the right side of the stitch. Lift the presser foot and pivot the fabric 180 degrees.
4. Zigzag down the other side of the welt so the columns of zigzag stitches are parallel. Stop at the end of the welt (Fig. 5.7).

FIG. 5.6 Pocket welt.

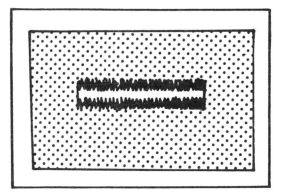

FIG. 5.7 Zigzag so columns of stitches are parallel, stopping at the end of welt.

5. Set your machine for a straight stitch, stitch length 2 (12 stitches per inch), and stitch a box around the outside of, but as close as possible to, the zigzag stitches (Fig. 5.8A).
6. Cut the welt open down the center. At each end, make angled clips to the straight-

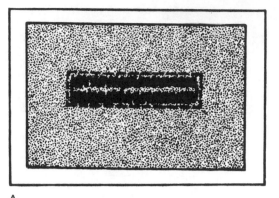

A

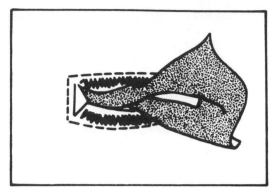

A

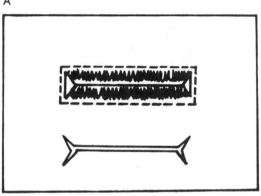

B

FIG. 5.8 *A* Stitch a box around the outside of zigzag stitches. *B*, Cut welt open down center, making angled clips to each corner.

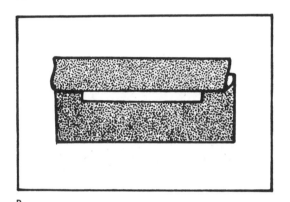

B

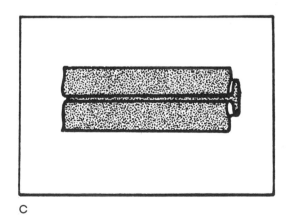

C

FIG. 5.9 *A*, Turn welt facing through opening. *B* and *C*, Fold fabric back over zigzagged sides to form lips.

stitched corners of the box, forming little triangles. Don't worry about cutting through some of the zigzag stitches at the ends (Fig. 5.8B).

7. Turn welt facing through the opening (Fig. 5.9A). To form the lips, fold the fabric back over the zigzagged sides. This insures both lips of the welt are the same width (Fig. 5.9B,C).

8. Top press lips toward the center of the welt using a see-through press cloth. Sew a few locking stitches at each end over the triangle to square up the welt (Fig. 5.10A).

Rebecca Dumlao

Corvallis, Oregon

Rebecca is a busy mother of two. She's written *The Expectant Mother's Wardrobe Planner* (Chilton, 1986) and *A Woman's Lifelong Wellness Planner* (anticipated 1989 release), has ghostwritten sewing articles for a prominent home economist, and has revised sixth grade nutrition workbooks for Glencoe Publishing (a division of Macmillan). As executive director of the Multiple Sclerosis Society, she has developed volunteer and public relations programs and has coordinated an eighteen-agency "Fashion Show for the Disabled," focusing on attractive, functional clothing for twelve disabled models.

"I have no sewing room. Instead, my current work space is a corner of my kitchen with a makeshift setup of two relic tables which support my sewing machine and serger. The best part is the view. I sit in front of the sliding glass door looking toward my herb garden and the backyard. Over the ridge is the local Honda dealership!

"This is far from The Ultimate Sewing Center . . . and less exquisite than sewing spaces I've had in the past, but it works for me."

Rebecca Dumlao

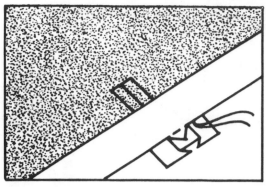

A

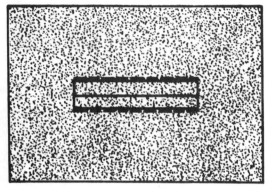

B

FIG. 5.10 *A,* Sew locking stitches at both ends to square up welt. *B,* Stitch-in-the-ditch along long sides of welt.

9. From the right side of jacket front, stitch-in-the-ditch along long sides of welt (Fig. 5.10B).

JACKET COLLAR AND LAPEL

Upper Collar and Front Facing Unit

On most necklines, the top and under collar are sewn together, turned and sandwiched between the neckline and neckline facing. In a tailored jacket, this method does not work.

The fabric is too heavy because the upper collar, under collar, front facing and neckline facing all are interfaced. Therefore the upper collar is stitched to the front facing, and the under collar to the body of the jacket. If you are using a felt under collar, see the special instructions later in this chapter.

1. Double check that both front facing and upper collar have been marked accurately. I use tailor tacks here. Stitch front and back facing pieces together. Press seams together, then open. If you are making an unlined jacket, finish the outside edge of facing unit with the 3-step zigzag [stitch length 1 (fine setting), stitch width 4–5], or serge with a 3-thread overlock.

2. Stay-stitch neckline seams on upper collar and front facings at the neck edge.

3. Pin upper collar to facing, right sides together. Clip neckline curves $\frac{1}{8}''$ (3 mm) above stay-stitching on both upper collar and facings, so collar fits smoothly.

4. With the facing side up, stitch collar and facing together, stopping precisely at the marks on either end of the collar (Fig. 5.11).

Under Collar and Jacket Back

In Chapter 3, you fused each under collar piece with a medium-weight interfacing, stitched the under collar together at the center back, then fused another piece of lighter weight interfacing from the roll line to neck edge over the seam. You shaped the under collar by pressing it and letting it dry on the ham. Now you are ready to attach it to the neckline of the jacket. Shoulder seams are stitched and pressed open, and the under collar placement is marked on the neck edge.

1. Stay-stitch neck edge of under collar and jacket.

2. Pin under collar to jacket at the seamline, right sides together, matching marks and notches. If necessary, clip into jacket neck edge $\frac{1}{8}''$ (3 mm) above stay-stitching so under collar fits. Stitch, jacket side up, and press seam flat, then open (Fig. 5.12).

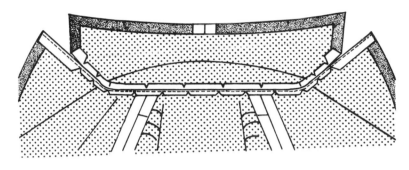

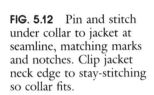

FIG. 5.11 Pin and stitch upper collar and facing together. Clip curves so collar fits smoothly.

FIG. 5.12 Pin and stitch under collar to jacket at seamline, matching marks and notches. Clip jacket neck edge to stay-stitching so collar fits.

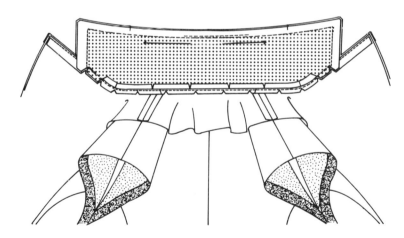

FIG. 5.13 Starting from center back, stitch collar together, stopping at the collar and lapel junction.

Putting Under Collar and Upper Collar Together

The easiest way to put the upper and under collars together is:

1. Pin collar pieces, right sides together, matching marks at collar points and where upper collar joins the facing and under collar joins jacket back. Fold down and pin neckline seam allowances of upper and under collars so they aren't caught in the stitching.

2. Starting from the center back, stitch collar together, stopping at the collar and lapel junction (Fig. 5.13). At junction do not back-

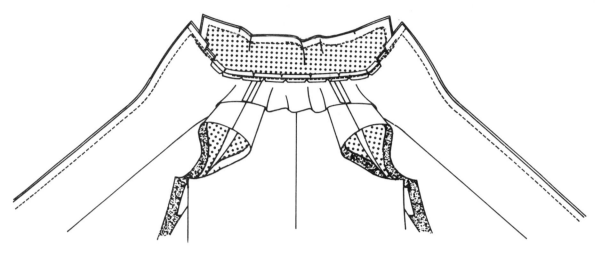

FIG. 5.14 Stitch front facing to jacket front, starting at the four-point closure. Blunt the corner of lapel.

stitch. Remove fabric, leaving long thread tails (you may need the extra thread length to remove a stitch or two and to tie off seam later).

HINT: Remember to take one or two stitches across the corner at the collar to blunt the point for sharp collar points (see Collars, Chapter 4).

3. Repeat for other side of collar, reinforcing seam at center back.

4. Press seam flat.

THE FOUR-POINT CLOSURE: JOINING COLLAR AND LAPEL

1. With right sides together, match marks and pin front facing and jacket front together. At the junction of the four points (upper collar, under collar, front facing and jacket front), pin neckline seam up, out of the way, so it does not get caught in the stitching.

2. Stitch front facing to jacket front, starting at the four-point closure to the bottom, stopping where pattern indicates (Fig. 5.14). Remember to take a couple of stitches across the tip of lapel to blunt the point. Press seams together.

3. Cut away excess fabric from four-point junction. Press upper collar and under collar

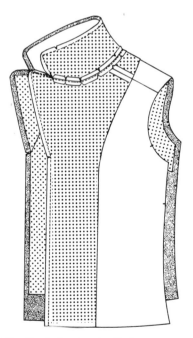

FIG. 5.15 On jacket lapel, clip into seam allowance at bottom of roll line.

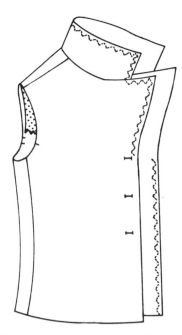

FIG. 5.16 Understitch lapel to roll line. Understitch facing from roll line to jacket bottom. Understitch seam allowance toward under collar.

neck edge seam allowances open over an un-padded tailor board.

4. Turn jacket right side out. Hand stitch both neckline seams together, stitching through the seam allowance so upper collar and under collar are joined. This prevents collar pieces from shifting.

5. On jacket lapel, clip into seam allowance $\frac{1}{8}''$ (3 mm) from stitching line at the bottom of roll line (Fig. 5.15). Trim lapel corners diagonally and turn front facing right side out.

6. Press lapel seam allowance toward jacket

front. With the right side up, understitch seam allowance down to the clip at the bottom of roll line (see Understitching Facings, Chapter 4).

7. If your jacket is curved at the bottom, clip seam allowance around the curve. Press remainder of the seam allowance toward front facing and understitch (Fig. 5.16). Carefully trim away excess seam allowance from front facing and lapel. Understitching enables jacket front and lapel to lie properly without top-stitching.

8. Press the seam allowance at the top of the collar toward under collar. From the right side, understitch seam allowance toward under collar as close to the points as you can get your presser foot (Fig. 5.16). Again, under-stitching helps the collar lie well, so topstitch-ing is not necessary.

9. On under collar, trim excess seam allow-ance to understitching.

FELT UNDER COLLAR
Preparation

In a traditionally man-tailored jacket, the collar is worked almost entirely by hand. The under collar is generally made of French mel-ton, but it's difficult to find, so ask your fa-vorite fabric store if they carry wool under collar felt. It doesn't have to match the fabric, just blend.

1. Cut under collar from felt as shown on the pattern piece. Cut hair canvas interfacing, using under collar pattern.

2. Pin interfacing to under collar, wrong sides together, and baste along the roll line. Shaping collar over your hand, pad-stitch with

FIG. 5.17 Pad-stitch with short chevron stitches from roll line to neckline seam. Pad-stitch remainder of under collar from roll line to seamline.

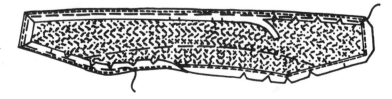

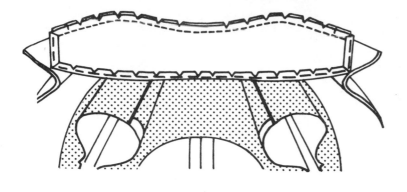

FIG. 5.18 Miter corners of upper collar.

FIG. 5.19 Pin and stitch upper collar to facing/lining unit.

short chevron stitches, perpendicular to neck edge, from roll line to neckline seam.

3. Lightly pad-stitch the remainder of under collar from roll line to seamline so stitches are parallel to the top (Fig. 5.17). Trim seam allowances away from under collar and interfacing.

4. Stay-stitch jacket neck edge.

Application

1. The lining and facing sections must be stitched together and, where appropriate, inside pockets completed. On a man's jacket, there is no back neck facing, so the upper collar is stitched to the facing/lining unit.

2. Stay-stitch neck edge of upper collar.

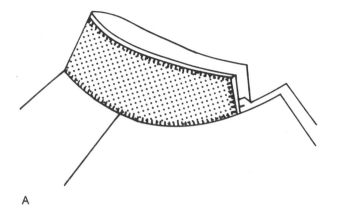

A

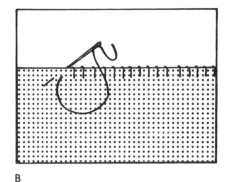

B

FIG. 5.20 *A* and *B* Fell-stitch under collar to upper collar.

3. Miter corners of upper collar. Trim corners $\frac{1}{8}''$ (3 mm) from miter. Press miter and seam allowance to the wrong side (Fig. 5.18). Turn collar right side out.

4. Pin and stitch upper collar to facing/lining unit, to marks where the collar and lapel come together. Clip neck edge to staystitching so upper collar fits (Fig. 5.19).

5. Stitch front facing and lining unit to jacket as described in The Four-Point Closure, above. The upper and under collars will be joined by hand later.

6. Place wrong sides of upper collar and felt under collar together so all seam allowances are enclosed. Baste. Top press and shape collar with a little steam over the seam roll using a press cloth. Try jacket on dress form or the person you're making it for to check that the under collar does not show at the neckline when the collar is turned down. If under collar does show, remove basting, trim away a little more seam allowance, then baste again.

7. By hand, fell-stitch under collar to upper collar (Fig. 5.20).

CHANEL TRIM

Coco Chanel simplified tailoring in the 1920s and 1930s with the creation of the Chanel suit. This style is popular today and is

FIG. 5.21 Chanel suit.

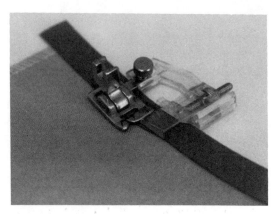

FIG. 5.22 Slip fabric in the guide between folded edges of the braid.

marked by the use of fold-over braid around the neck, down the front, and around the bottom of the jacket. The Chanel styling eliminates time-consuming collar and lapel construction, the traditional pleat at the sleeve, and hems and vents at the bottom and back of the jacket (Fig. 5.21).

I recently made a Chanel suit that went together so fast once it was cut out, I was wearing it the same day. The toughest part was stitching the fold-over braid. But I found a wonderful presser foot that is adjustable for up to $1\frac{1}{2}''$ (3.8 cm) braid [$\frac{3}{4}''$ (2 cm) when it's folded over]—perfect for a Chanel jacket, boiled wool jackets, or any time you want to use wide fold-over braid.

1. Thread braid through foot, adjusting for the width of the braid.

2. Leaving a length of braid behind the foot, slip fabric in the guide between the folded sides of the braid and begin sewing (Fig. 5.22). I used a straight stitch, stitch length 2.5–3. For a decorative treatment, use one of the closed or open embroidery stitches available on your sewing machine. Sew straight edges or curves. The foot holds everything in place so you don't miss stitching the trim to the fabric.

HINT: My Chanel jacket is made of a silk and linen blend. I did a fully fused front using Pellon's

Sof-Shape, then made the jacket and a separate lining, including the sleeves. I put the lining in the jacket and machine basted around the neck, down the front, around the bottom, and at the bottom of the sleeves to be sure the lining wasn't pulling on the jacket. The last step was attaching the braid with the special foot. It all went unbelievably fast.

3. The only drawback to the foot is stitching corners. So, about $2''$ (5 cm) from the corner, lift the foot and move it around the corner, still threaded with braid, being sure there is enough braid to fold a miter at the corner. Begin stitching braid on jacket again $2''$ (5 cm) from the corner as before. To finish the corner, go back and pin loose braid to jacket, folding a miter at the corner. Stitch braid down with your transparent embroidery foot.

MITERING CORNERS

Mitered corners are usually done at the pleat or vent at the bottom of a tailored sleeve, on place mats, table runners, and at the corners to bind a blanket or quilt. I've seen all kinds of tools to help miter corners, but this is the easiest way I've found:

1. Fold and press hem up the desired width.

2. Fold a triangle at the corner, the depth of the hem (Fig. 5.23).

3. Fold the edge perpendicular to the hem, over the triangle made in step 2. Crease and press (Fig. 5.24).

4. With a water-erasable marker, mark the angle of the miter on the fold with a line in the corner, and on the first hem folded in step 1 (Fig. 5.25).

5. Unfold the corner. When connected, your lines will make a large triangle in the corner. This is your stitching line.

6. Place right sides together, stitching on the lines marked in step 5. Trim seam allowance to $\frac{1}{4}''$ (6 mm) and press seam open. Turn mitered corner to the right side and press again.

Lois
Ericson

Tahoe City, California

When I caught up with Lois, she was between teaching a week-long artist-in-residence program in upstate New York called "Quilting by the Lake" and starting her eleventh book.

Lois's interest was originally in weaving, which undoubtedly led her to pursue the Studies in Fine Arts and Design program at San Diego State. Then the sewing bug bit her, and sewing has been her passion ever since.

When asked how long she's been sewing and what keeps her motivated to write about her craft, she says, "I've been sewing for 35 years but rather than having one year of experience 35 times, I am always looking for a new approach to an old idea." True to her word, her current book project, called *Pleats,* is about using pleated fabric in contemporary, nontraditional ways.

When she isn't writing, she's creating artwear for local and national galleries and art exhibits.

For more information about her books, write Lois Ericson, P.O. Box 1680, Tahoe City, CA 95730.

Lois Ericson

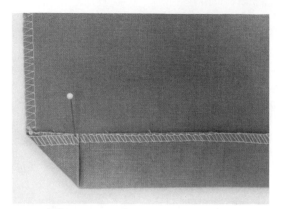

FIG. 5.23 Fold a triangle at the corner, the depth of the hem.

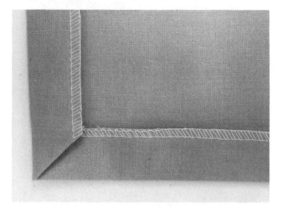

FIG. 5.24 Fold edge over triangle to make miter.

SERGER BRAID

You can create the look of braid by using pearl cotton, ribbon, or yarn in the loopers of your serger. If you are using something heavy such as yarn, ribbon, or size #3 or #5 pearl cotton, use it in upper looper only. Size #8 pearl cotton or fine knitting-machine yarn can be used in both upper and lower loopers.

I prefer the widest look I can get so I use the 5 mm needle plate. On some sergers, the

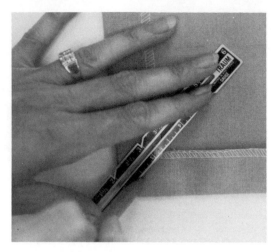

FIG. 5.25 Mark angle of miter to indicate stitching line.

lower stationary cutter can be moved over to the far right another 1–3 mm, giving a 7 mm width. However, don't try moving the blade over yourself unless you know what you're doing. I used this technique to bind off the raw edges of the coat in Fig. 5.26.

Set your serger as follows:

Stitch: 3-thread overlock _____
Stitch length: 3–4, depending on
  weight of cord or ribbon _____
Stitch width: widest _____
Needle tension: normal to tight
  (normal sewing thread) _____
Upper looper tension: loose or
  bypass _____
Lower looper tension: normal for
  thread, loose or bypass for pearl
  cotton _____
Needle plate: 5 mm _____

1. Test setting on a scrap. The decorative thread should be smooth on top, and the stitches should lock at the edge of the fabric. Guide the raw edge so the blades do not cut the fabric. The stitches should be solid and

FIG. 5.26 Edges of coat are bound with the serger using ribbon through the upper looper.

close together, like a satin stitch, so the raw edges are bound off without a lot of the fabric peeking through.

2. Once you have tested for proper tension settings, be sure you have enough decorative cord and that it will not catch on anything while you are serging.

Drop the ball of pearl cotton on the floor behind the serger. If you are using two balls, put each in a Ziplock bag and seal most of the top closed so that the balls do not get tangled. When I use ribbon, I put floral wire through the center of the spool and wire it over a nail attached to the wall behind the serger. This way the ribbon pulls off smoothly without twisting, just as toilet paper pulls off the holder on the wall.

3. Serge around fabric edge. For an outside corner, stitch to the corner, leaving the needle in the highest position.

HINT: If you are trimming off a seam allowance, clip 2″ (5 cm) at each corner and serge to the corner (Fig. 5.27).

Gently pull some slack in the needle thread and lift the presser foot. Pull the stitches off stitch fingers and turn fabric so the first stitch will form at the corner. Put presser foot down and pull needle slack back above the tension dial. Serge (Fig. 5.27).

For an inside corner, clip $\frac{1}{4}″$ (6 mm) into corner. Fold fabric into a straight edge and serge (Fig. 5.28).

FIG. 5.27 Turning an outside corner with a serger.

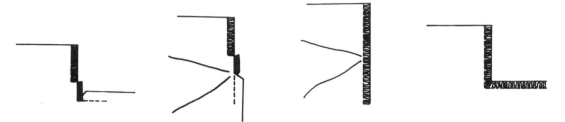

FIG. 5.28 Turning an inside corner with a serger.

ZIPPERS

Have you avoided a pattern with a zipper? I have, because, unfortunately, most instructions tell us to buy a 7″ zipper for a 7″ opening. Try as I might, the zipper pull gets in the way, and I sew an unwanted bulge at the top of the zipper opening. Also, most instructions say to stitch the zipper in from the wrong side. In a centered application I usually end up with one skinny side and one fat side on either side of the zipper teeth because I can't see where I'm going. For a lapped application, I end up with an uneven row of stitching for the same reason.

The following techniques are designed to eliminate both problems, so you'll never avoid a pattern with a zipper again. Make stitch samples for your notebook; then perfect these techniques on your next dressmaking project.

The 4-minute Zipper

1. Mark zipper placement. Place fabric right sides together. Loosen upper tension, set your machine for a long straight stitch, and baste zipper opening at the $\frac{5}{8}$″ (1.5 cm) seamline. Remove fabric from the machine, clip threads and return upper tension to normal. Complete stitching the seam on the $\frac{5}{8}$″ (1.5 cm) seamline so regular stitching and basting stitches meet. It's tough to repair a hole in the seamline just below a zipper; by stitching the seam in two steps you almost eliminate this problem.

2. Buy a zipper at least 1″ (2.5 cm) longer than needed and place it face down in the seam allowance, in the zipped position, on the inside of the seam. The zipper pull must be on the extra length of zipper tape (Fig. 5.29). For a lapped zipper application, stitch right side of zipper as instructed on zipper package, again with zipper pull on the extra length of zipper tape. Press.

3. Instead of hand or machine basting zipper in place, tape across the back of it with $\frac{1}{2}$″ (1.3 cm) transparent tape every 1″ to $1\frac{1}{2}$″ (2.5 cm–3.8 cm) (Fig. 5.29).

4. On the right side of fabric, place a strip of $\frac{1}{2}$″ (1.3 cm) tape the length of the zipper, with the seamline centered for a centered application (Fig. 5.30). For a lapped application, place the straight edge of the tape along the basted seamline.

HINT: If you are using a napped fabric, test tape to be sure it won't pull off the nap or leave a mark. I prefer using the cloudy rather than the shiny type, because it shows up well on dark fabrics and isn't as sticky.

5. Using the tape as a guide for your zipper foot, stitch in the zipper from the right side of garment, sewing next to, not through, the tape. This way the stitching lines are parallel (Fig. 5.31).

HINT: Stitch both sides of zipper in the same direction so that the fabric won't shift (i.e., stripes and plaids will remain matched after basting is removed).

6. Remove tape from right and wrong side of garment; remove basting stitches by pulling the bobbin thread. Pull zipper pull to the bottom of the zipper.

FIG. 5.29 With zipper pull up on extra length of zipper tape, tape zipper into position, every 1–1½″ (2.5–3.8cm).

FIG. 5.30 Position tape on right side of fabric, centering the seamline.

FIG. 5.31 Stitch zipper from right side, using tape as a stitching guide.

7. If the zipper is at a waistline or neckline, stitch on the facing or waistband, backstitching over the teeth at the top of the zipper. Don't worry; it won't hurt the needle (Fig. 5.32).

8. Cut top of zipper off and finish waistband or facing as described in the pattern instructions.

The waistband or facing prevents the zipper from coming off track. You've used a zipper longer than needed, so there isn't a bulge from sewing around the zipper pull at the top, and the stitching is even, because you've stitched from the right side of the fabric.

Handpicked Zipper by Machine

The detail that separates handmade from couture is a handpicked zipper. Even, hand-sewn stitches on either side of the zipper identify the garment as well-made.

Have you ever struggled with a handpicked zipper? One time you pick up too little fabric; the next, too much. Because the sewing machine is more precise than the unpracticed hand, use this method instead. All you need is a sewing machine with a blind hem stitch.

1. Follow step 1, above to baste seam allowance where zipper is to be inserted. Buy a zipper 1″ (2.5 cm) longer than the pattern calls for. I've found zippers with the tricot-like tape are lightweight, pliable, and easiest to work with.

2. Place zipper face down in the zipped position, centering the teeth over seamline. The zipper pull must be up on the extra length of tape, out of the way.

3. Using extra-long straight pins (quilting pins work well), pin zipper from the wrong

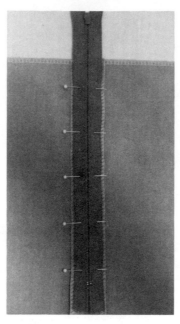

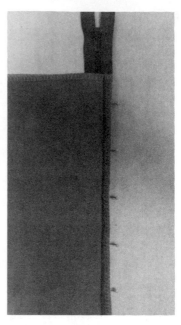

FIG. 5.32 Pull zipper pull to bottom of zipper. Pin and stitch waistband or facing.

FIG. 5.33 Pin zipper from wrong side, using long pins.

FIG. 5.34 Fold seam allowance back to where pins enter fabric. Zipper is under work.

side so pin enters zipper tape and fabric $\frac{1}{4}''$ (6 mm) from the teeth. Then pin, under teeth, up to the other side (Fig. 5.33). Place pins 1″ (2.5 cm) apart.

4. Set your sewing machine as follows:

Stitch: blind hem   ————
Stitch length: 2, or 10 stitches per
   inch   ————
Stitch width: 2–2.5   ————
Foot: blind hem or zipper*   ————

*If your blind hem foot has a narrow toe on the left, use it for this technique. Otherwise, use the zipper foot. You may want to experiment.

5. Fold seam allowance back to where the pins enter fabric (Fig. 5.34). Zipper will be under your work. Blind-stitch so straight stitches sew into seam allowance and zipper tape, and the zigzag stitches bite into the fold of fabric. Remove pins as you go so you do not stitch over them. When machine-picking a zipper, the stitches must show on the right side of fabric. Therefore, be sure needle bites into fold enough to create the proper effect.

6. Repeat for other side of zipper. The machine-picked stitches should be spaced evenly across from each other. Set your machine so the pick stitch on the second side is across from the pick stitch on the first side. Stitch and press.

7. Remove basting stitches. Anchor bottom of zipper tape to the seam allowance by hand. Move zipper pull to bottom of zipper.

8. Stitch waistband or facing, catching the top of the zipper in the seam.

9. Cut top of zipper off. Zipper teeth will not dull your scissors. Finish waistband or facing. The fabric stops the zipper from coming off track.

HINT: If pull should come off track, don't rip and start all over. Remove the metal stop at

92

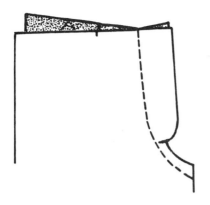

FIG. 5.35 Baste zipper opening. Clip into seam allowance.

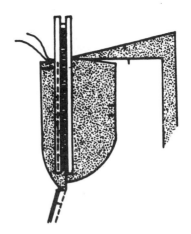

FIG. 5.37 Stitch left side of zipper to left extension.

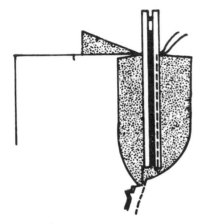

FIG. 5.36 Stitch right side of zipper to right zipper extension.

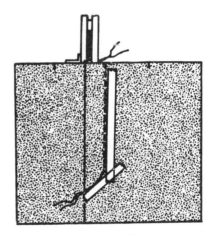

FIG. 5.38 Topstitch zipper from right side, stitching next to tape.

bottom of zipper and slide pull on track from the *bottom.* Remember to put metal stop back, or bar tack across teeth at bottom of zipper.

This technique takes a little practice, but once perfected, zippers can be stitched in quickly, securely, and in places that, in the past, have been difficult to reach using traditional techniques.

Speedy Fly-Front Zipper

1. Buy a zipper at least 1″ (2.5 cm) longer than zipper opening. Baste front crotch seam

from bottom of crotch to waist. Use a $\frac{5}{8}''$ (1.5 cm) seam allowance, continuing as if the fly front extension is not there. Clip into seam allowance as shown in Fig. 5.35.

2. Working from the wrong side, place closed zipper on the right zipper extension so the left edge of zipper tape is next to the seam. Stitch right side of zipper to zipper extension *only,* close to the edge of zipper tape (Fig. 5.36).

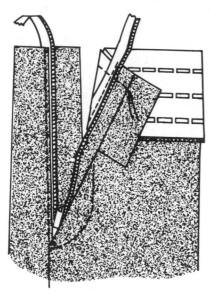

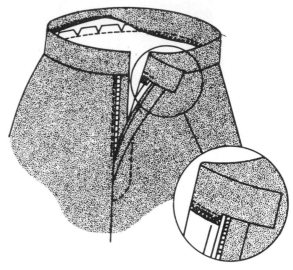

FIG. 5.39 Stitch waistband.

FIG. 5.40 Finish waistband by stitching-in-the-ditch, in the crack of the seam.

3. Pull zipper to left side so extension is taut. Be sure there are no puckers. Stitch left side of zipper to left extension (Fig. 5.37).

4. Topstitch zipper from right side, using strips of transparent tape as a guide and stitching next to the tape so topstitching is straight and even. Curve stitching at the corner if desired (Fig. 5.38). Move zipper pull to bottom of zipper.

5. Interface waistband. Trim long un-notched edge $\frac{1}{2}''$ (1.3 cm) and overcast with the 3-step zigzag or overlock on the conventional machine or the 3-thread overlock on the serger. Sew the notched edge of waistband to waistline as instructed in pattern instructions (Fig. 5.39). Backstitch a couple of times over zipper coil. Cut zipper tape off even with the $\frac{5}{8}''$ (1.5 cm) seam allowance.

6. Finish ends of waistband as shown in pattern instructions. Pin finished waistband edge over waistband and press. With the right side up, stitch-in-the-ditch guiding the needle in the crack of the seamline (Fig. 5.40).

HINT: Use the blade of the blind hem foot or inside of the right toe of the buttonhole foot to open the crack in the seam. Adjust the needle position so the stitch is hidden in the ditch.

Your jacket should be taking shape by now. The sleeves are in, and the collar and lapels are stitched. I hope the zipper applications will be helpful for a pair of slacks or a skirt you are making to go with your jacket.

In the next chapter I'll share my favorite tailored buttonhole techniques with you.

SUPPLY LIST FOR CHAPTER 6

- Pearl cotton
- 6″ (15.2 cm) fabric swatches for notebook samples
- Interfacing fused on swatches

Tailored Buttonholes

My first tailoring project was a light pink, basket-weave wool suit. The jacket had 16 bound buttonholes, ¾″ (2 cm) long. My professor recommended that I use a metal tool designed to make perfect bound-buttonhole lips. The fabric raveled so badly that none of the buttonholes turned out the same size. If I had only learned one of the tailored buttonhole techniques in this chapter, I might have worn the suit more than once.

In this chapter I'll share three techniques I use to make buttonholes on tailored jackets.

1. For lighter weight fabrics, plaids or tweeds, I like to make a corded stretch buttonhole. The cording gives extra support under the stitches so the buttonhole is sturdy without looking heavy.
2. The "handworked" buttonhole by machine is a stretch buttonhole, using topstitching or silk twist thread through the needle. It simulates a handworked buttonhole, but it's much easier.
3. Finally, I found a way to make a bound buttonhole that would have worked on my pink wool suit.

As with any buttonhole, make samples on a scrap. Use the same thicknesses of fashion fabric and interfacing as the finished garment will have to insure the buttonhole is the proper length for the button. Once perfected, put your buttonhole samples in your notebook.

CORDED STRETCH BUTTONHOLE

This buttonhole can be used on knits or wovens. For an almost invisible buttonhole on a knit, cord this buttonhole with yarn from the knit fabric. The buttonhole can also be used on a lightweight wool crepe or flannel (Fig. 6.1).

Set your sewing machine as follows:

Stitch: overlock   ———
Stitch length: preset, 0   ———
Stitch width: 2 and 4 (see instructions)   — ——

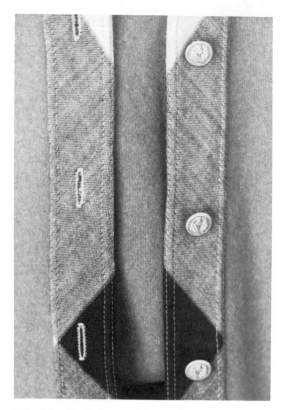

FIG. 6.1 Corded stretch buttonholes.

Foot: buttonhole or transparent
    embroidery   ———
Needle: #80/11–12 all-purpose   ———
Thread: to match fabric   ———
Needle position: left   ———
Pearl cotton, embroidery floss or yarn to
    match fabric for cord under buttonhole.

1. Generally, buttonholes are placed $\frac{1}{2}''$ (1.3 cm) from the finished facing edge. To mark buttonhole placement, place a $\frac{1}{2}''$ (1.3 cm) strip of transparent tape even with finished facing edge. Place another strip of tape parallel to the first to mark the length of buttonhole. Your buttonhole will be sewn between the strips of tape (Fig. 6.2).

2. Place a piece of matching cord or yarn under the left side of the buttonhole foot. The

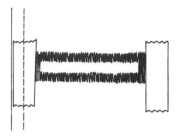

FIG. 6.2 Mark buttonhole placement using $\frac{1}{2}''$ (1.3cm) tape.

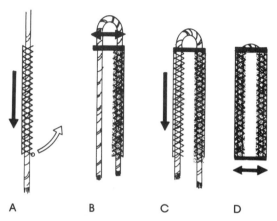

A   B   C   D

FIG. 6.3 A, Stitch left side of buttonhole, stopping with needle in right side of the stitch. B, Pivot and pull cord around under left side of foot; sew bar tack. C, Reset width, then stitch second side of buttonhole. D, Bar tack again. Pull threads between facing and jacket front and tie them off.

buttonhole foot has a groove on the underside behind the needle, so the cord guides easily. Starting at the edge of tape closest to the finished facing, stitch down the left side of the buttonhole, stopping with the needle in the right side of the stitch (Fig. 6.3A).

3. Lift the presser foot and pivot the fabric 180 degrees. Pull cord or yarn around and place it under the left side of buttonhole foot.

HINT: Do not snug the loop up to the needle; it will be pulled up to the bar tack after the

Robbie Fanning

Menlo Park, California

Robbie Fanning

"I'd like to show you a picture of me in my sewing room, but even a fish-angle lens wouldn't help—you'd back up to get far enough away and fall into our bed.

"We have a tiny house and I sew along one wall of the bedroom. My husband rescued a two-drawer table from the dump, which has been my sewing table for years. I have my serger next to it on a rolling computer table, so I can pull it out to make an L when I sew. This means nobody can walk through the bedroom when I'm sewing. I can't open the door to my office, either, because I have the ironing board set up in front of it.

"When we were first married, I used to complain about our lack of space. Then one day I saw a picture of a Greek woman sitting outside her tiny room on a tiny chair, embroidering exquisite garments. That shut me up. You can do a lot with whatever you have.

"I truly love to sew. Sometimes I don't even care whether I finish what I'm working on; the process itself is relaxing and satisfying to me. My favorite activity is to come home from work and listen to Books on Tape (address in Sources of Supply) while I sew—oh joy!"

Robbie Fanning has a degree in writing and publishing from the State University of New York. She learned sewing from her mother and writing from her father, both by osmosis. To date she has written ten books with her husband, Tony, including *The Complete Book of Machine Embroidery*, which is the keystone book of Chilton's Creative Machine Arts series, for which she is editor. She writes a column for *Needlecraft for Today* magazine, is a contributing editor for *Threads* magazine, writes articles for many other publications, and is series editor for the CMA series. She also has her own publishing company, Open Chain Publishing.

buttonhole is made. Put presser foot down and take the needle out of the work.

4. Set stitch length to 0, stitch width to 4, and bar tack the end of the buttonhole with a few stitches, being sure bar tack is wide enough to cover both sides of the cord (Fig. 6.3B).

5. With the needle out of the work, reset stitch length to the preset position, stitch width to 2. Sew the second side of the buttonhole (Fig. 6.3C).

6. With the needle out of the work, again set the stitch length to 0, stitch width to 4. Make bar tack as before. Pull on one side of cord or yarn loop so it snugs up to the bar tack. Pull threads and cord/yarn ends to the back of the buttonhole or between facing and jacket front. Tie threads off (Fig. 6.3D).

"HANDWORKED" BUTTONHOLE BY MACHINE

I love the look of a handworked buttonhole but have never acquired the skill. The following buttonhole is a stretch buttonhole variation. If made with silk twist or heavy topstitching thread, it looks like a handworked buttonhole and can be used on either knit or woven fabric (Fig. 6.4).

To make a "handworked" buttonhole by machine, thread a size #90/14 all-purpose or topstitching needle with heavy topstitching thread or silk twist to match the fabric. Make the stretch buttonhole as described above, without cording it. Because you are using the overlock stitch (a stretch stitch) to make the buttonhole, you don't need interfacing or stabilizer under the buttonhole. When used on a knit the buttonhole stretches and recovers without stretching out of shape. On a woven it looks handmade.

EASY BOUND BUTTONHOLE

This is a smaller version of the Speedy Welt Pocket in Chapter 5. Because each buttonhole

FIG. 6.4 "Hand-worked" buttonholes by machine.

is made by your machine, the length and width of the lips should be consistent on each buttonhole.

Set your sewing machine as follows:

Stitch: buttonhole	_____
Stitch length: 0.5–0.8 or fine or buttonhole setting	_____
Stitch width: buttonhole setting	_____
Foot: buttonhole	_____

1. Carefully mark buttonhole placement on jacket front.

2. Place buttonhole facing on jacket front,

FIG. 6.5 *A*, Place buttonhole facing on jacket front. *B*, Make a machine buttonhole desired length, omitting bar tacks.

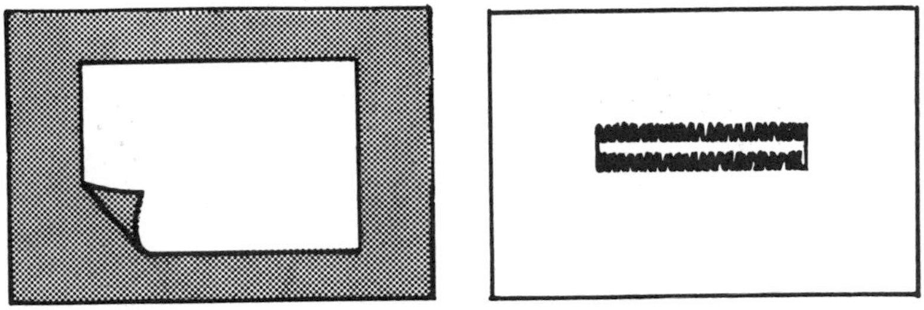

A

B

FIG. 6.6 *A*, Stitch a box around the perimeter of buttonhole. *B*, Cut buttonhole open down the center and clip into corners as shown.

A

B

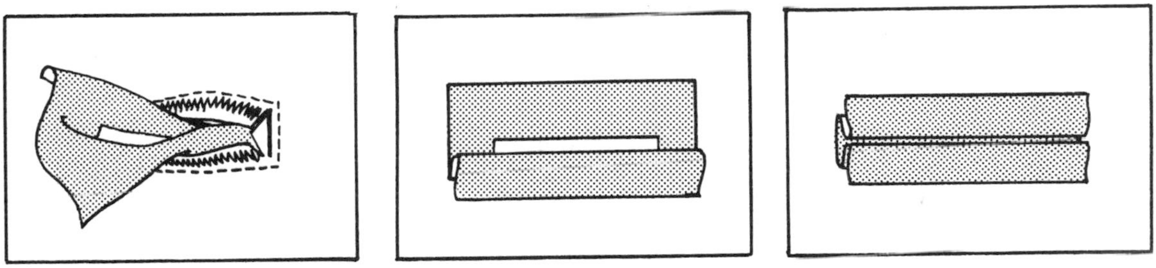

A

B

C

FIG. 6.7 *A*, Turn facing through buttonhole. *B* and *C*, Fold fabric back over zigzag stitches to form lips.

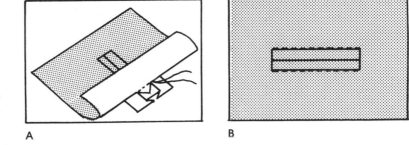

FIG. 6.8 *A*, Sew a few locking stitches to square up ends. *B*, Stitch-in-the-ditch on long sides of buttonhole.

A

B

right sides together, matching marks (Fig. 6.5A).

3. Starting on the end closest to the finished facing edge, make a buttonhole the desired length. If possible, omit bar tacks (Fig. 6.5B).

4. Set your machine for a straight stitch, stitch length 2 (12 stitches per inch), and stitch a box around the outside of, and as close as possible to, the zigzag stitches (Fig. 6.6A).

5. Cut buttonhole open down the center. Before cutting to the ends, make angled clips to the straight-stitched corners of the box, forming little triangles. Don't worry about cutting through some of the zigzag stitches or bar tacks at the ends (Fig. 6.6B).

6. Turn buttonhole facing through the opening (Fig. 6.7A). To form the lips, fold the fabric back over the zigzagged sides. This insures that the lips of the welt are the same width (Fig. 6.7B,C).

7. Top press lips toward the center of the buttonhole using a see-through press cloth. Sew a few locking stitches at each end over the triangle to square up the ends (Fig. 6.8A).

8. From the right side of jacket front, stitch-in-the-ditch on long sides of buttonhole (Fig. 6.7B). Trim excess fabric from wrong side of buttonhole, leaving enough fabric so lips will not ravel.

9. To finish front facing under bound buttonhole, baste buttonhole closed over the lips, and push pins through both ends of buttonhole and facing to mark the back (Fig. 6.9A). Cut a slit the length of the buttonhole (Fig. 6.9B). In the center of the slit, clip fabric about $\frac{1}{8}''$ (3 mm). This makes it easier to fold facing under. Fold facing fabric under and slip-stitch front facing to back of bound buttonhole (Fig. 6.9C).

HINT: On lighter weight fabrics, make another easy bound buttonhole on the facing as described in steps 3–5 above, with this exception: Turn buttonhole facing through buttonhole creating a box shape. Press box so the lips are pressed to the *outside* of the box. It will look like a rectangle and will frame the back of the buttonhole. Whipstitch facing to back of bound buttonhole by hand.

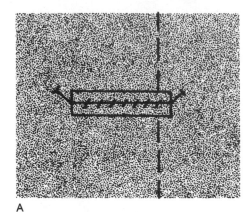

A

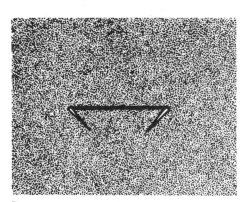

B

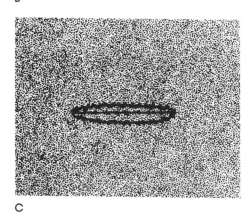

C

FIG. 6.9 *A,* Baste buttonhole closed, and push pins through. *B,* Cut a slit the length of the buttonhole. *C,* Clip, fold facing under, and slip-stitch.

Aren't these techniques more professional and easier than taking your finished jacket to a tailor to make the buttonholes for you? In the next chapter, I'll share some topstitching ideas you may want to try on your jacket in progress or save for other sewing projects.

SUPPLY LIST FOR CHAPTER 7

- Pearl cotton, floss, yarn, ribbon
- Narrow braiding foot
- Long-nosed tweezers
- Nylon mono-filament thread
- Beads
- Easy-Knit tape
- Pearl trim
- Tear-away stabilizer
- Freezer paper
- Dressmakers carbon
- Burnishing tool or empty ballpoint pen
- Water-soluble or vanishing marker

Topstitching

Topstitching defines design lines and makes a garment more tailored or sporty. In this chapter we'll look at topstitching needles, accessories, and decorative topstitching possibilities on both the conventional sewing machine and the serger.

NEEDLES FOR TOPSTITCHING

I've used a number of different needles for topstitching. If topstitching with thread used for dressmaking, use the same needle as for construction. For a bolder look, use two threads through the same needle—a size #80/11–12 is usually big enough. If using a heavy polyester or silk-twist topstitching thread, use a size #90/14 or topstitching needle. A topstitching needle has an elongated eye that accommodates heavier thread and is designed to prevent the thread from shredding and skipping stitches. I've also used size #8 pearl cotton through a size #100/16 needle for topstitching.

Specialty needles for topstitching are also available. The double-eye needle is designed to be threaded through the bottom eye for normal sewing. The top eye is used for topstitching when a long (7–8mm) saddle stitch is desired. Some machines saddle stitch using a short needle. Both the double-eye and short needles work on the same principle. Set your machine for a zigzag stitch and the needle skips every other zigzag, making a long straight stitch.

Built-in topstitching features and accessories are available for most machines and work similarly to the short or double-eye needle. Consult your manual or local sewing machine dealer to find out what is available for your machine. But topstitching with special threads through the needle is only one method. Special threads can also be used on the bobbin.

I never overlook an opportunity to find interesting threads to use in the bobbin of my sewing machine. I've topstitched with floss used to tie fishing flies; fiber, yarns, metallic cords, and ribbons found in knitting and weaving stores; and unusual cords, yarns, and cordonnet found in antique stores, flea markets, or grandma's trunk. If I can get it on the bobbin, I try it. You'll see how in the Reverse Embroidery section of this chapter.

TIPS FOR PERFECT TOPSTITCHING

1. Use a new needle.
2. If you want to pivot at the corner without skipping a stitch, pivot fabric around the needle while the needle is in the fabric and on its way up. Because the stitch cycle is complete at this point, the possibility of a skipped stitch is eliminated.
3. For straight topstitching, sew next to a piece of transparent tape.
4. If your machine is skipping stitches and you are using a new needle, try:

- Preshrinking the fabric
- Using a topstitching needle
- Using a size #90/14 stretch needle
- Far left needle position
- Far right needle position
- Skipping the last thread guide before thread enters the needle
- Tightening upper tension
- Oiling if your machine requires it—see your operator's manual
- Cleaning out the lint from under the feed dogs
- Using a straight-stitch foot or flat-bottomed presser foot that supports the fabric around the needle

COUCHING

Couching is a process of laying down cord, yarn, or fiber and stitching it to the right side of the fabric. This can be done to simulate long saddle stitching or crewel embroidery, or to create a texture or design on a solid fabric.

Saddle Stitching

Saddle stitching is a long, heavy topstitch, often seen on leather saddles and belts. It's sporty and is often used on khaki, wool flannel, and coating. To simulate saddle stitching, set your sewing machine as follows:

Stitch: blind hem   ———
Stitch length: 1–1.5, or fine setting   ———
Stitch width: 2, or wide enough to clear cord   ———
Foot: narrow braiding   ———
Needle: #70/9 or #80/11–12   ———
Thread: nylon monofilament or to match fabric and/or floss   ———
Accessories: embroidery, rayon, or silk floss; soft, supple fabric such as wool flannel, coating, or fleece   ———

1. Thread one or two strands of floss through needle hole or clip in the narrow braiding foot.
2. Test the stitch width on a scrap. The stitch should be just wide enough to stitch next to the floss on the right and swing over it when the blind hem zigzags to the left. The straight stitches bury themselves into the fabric next to the floss, while the zigzag stitch creates an indentation in the floss simulating a stitch (Fig. 7.1).
3. For a crisp corner, let the needle zig over the floss and zag back to the right side of the stitch. Pivot when needle is in the work but on its way up.

SIMULATED CREWEL EMBROIDERY

Did you know you could simulate crewel embroidery by machine, and do it so much faster? Use different types of yarns to create different effects. With the exception of two techniques, yarn, cord, or pearl cotton is couched to the fabric freehand, without a presser foot. Practice each technique by making a sample for your notebook. Figure 7.2

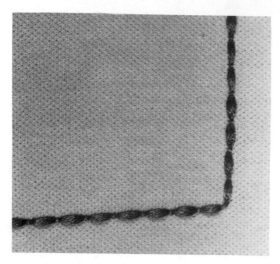

FIG. 7.1 Couching over floss with blind hem stitch and narrow braiding foot.

shows examples of these techniques stitched on the front and back yokes of western shirts.

Nylon monofilament thread will be used top and bobbin for the following techniques. Be careful not to overwind the bobbin and thread bobbin as for normal sewing thread. To prevent the top thread from spilling off the spool and tangling around the spool pin, place a fat plastic drinking straw (the type you get in fast-food restaurants), over the spool pin, then the spool of monofilament thread over the straw.

To prepare the fabric for freehand crewel embroidery, stretch fabric in a hoop or iron plastic freezer paper on the wrong side before embroidering. The freezer paper keeps fabric from puckering and is removed after embroidery is complete.

OUTLINING

An effective way to topstitch a pocket, yoke, or front tab is by outlining the area with yarn or braid. Set your machine as follows:

Stitch: straight _____
Stitch length: 2, or 12 stitches per inch _____

Stitch width: 0 _____
Foot: narrow braiding _____
Needle: #80/11–12 _____
Thread: nylon monofilament top and bobbin _____
Accessories: yarn or soutache braid _____

1. Thread or clip yarn or soutache in narrow braiding foot.
2. Stitch through yarn, attaching it to the area to be topstitched (Fig. 7.3).

NARROW CHAIN

You may prefer topstitching this way. I've also used this to create stems and vines.

Set your sewing machine as follows:

Stitch: straight _____
Stitch length: 4–6 _____
Stitch width: 0 _____
Foot: transparent embroidery _____
Thread: nylon monofilament top and bobbin _____
Accessories: pearl cotton, yarn, or narrow ribbon _____

1. Cut yarn double or four times the length needed for outlining or topstitching a particular area.
2. Pierce fabric with needle, leaving the foot up.
3. Double yarn or pearl cotton and place loop end around the needle. Cross yarn, left over right, and snug loop up to the needle. Put foot down.
4. Take one stitch leaving the needle in the fabric. Lift the presser foot and cross yarn again, left over right. Put foot down and take another stitch. Continue to stitch and cross the yarns without pulling yarn tight. The stems in Fig. 7.4 were done this way using pearl cotton rather than yarn.

HINT: Be consistent. If the left yarn is over the right, cross yarns the same way for the length of the topstitch.

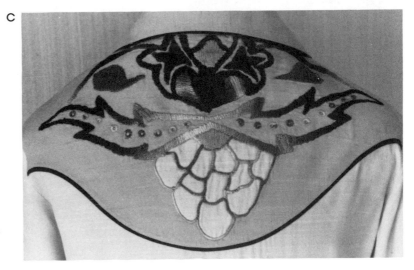

FIG. 7.2 *A*, *B*, and *C* Crewel embroidered yokes (by machine) on western shirts.

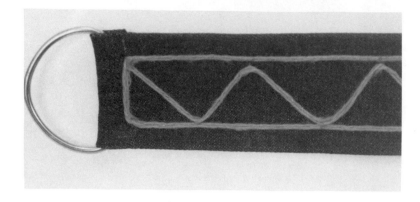

FIG. 7.3 Yarn was attached with the narrow braiding foot for topstitched effect.

5. When you're finished, pull threads and yarns to the back of the fabric and tie them off.

LOOPS

This is an easy way to create three-dimensional texture in the center of a flower or fur on an appliqué. You can emulate the hand yarn embroidery found on Austrian boiled wool jackets with freehand loops, satin stitches, and chain stitches.

1. Place the fabric in a hoop or iron freezer paper to the wrong side of the fabric. Set your sewing machine as follows:

FIG. 7.4 The stems were done with narrow chain using pearl cotton.

Stitch: straight	_____
Stitch length: 0	_____
Stitch width: 0	_____
Foot: none or darning foot	_____
Feed dogs: drop or cover	_____
Release pressure (optional)	_____
Thread: nylon monofilament top and bobbin	_____
Needle: #80/11–12 or #90/14	_____
Accessories: long tweezers (those that come with your serger work well)	_____

2. Place fabric under the needle. Lower the presser bar and turn the flywheel by hand, bringing the bobbin thread up through the fabric. Sew a couple of locking stitches to an-

chor thread and clip thread ends off at the fabric.

3. Place yarn end at the inside of the design and take a couple of locking stitches to anchor yarn to the fabric. Clip short yarn end off at the fabric.

4. With your work in one hand and long tweezers in the other, pull a loop the desired length and free machine stitch at the base of the loop between the tweezers and your fingers to anchor the loop (Fig. 7.5). Pull another loop and anchor it next to the first. Continue until the design is filled in. You can leave yarn loopy or cut it for a rougher texture.

SATIN STITCH

I fill in leaves, flower petals, and large areas of color this way. Again, use the nylon monofilament thread on top and bobbin, and set your machine as described above for this freehand technique.

1. Transfer your design to background fabric. Iron freezer paper to the back, or place the fabric in a hoop.

2. Bring bobbin thread up through the fabric, take a couple of locking stitches, then clip off thread at the fabric. Place yarn end at the edge of the outline. Sew a couple of locking stitches to anchor yarn to the fabric. Cut short yarn end off close to the fabric so it will not interfere with the design.

3. Hold the work with your right hand and the long length of yarn with your left. Starting on the right side of the design, move the work so that the machine needle walks across the design with a few straight stitches to the other side. Do not stitch through the yarn. *Note:* Each satin stitch yarn will be pulled across the design to cover the stitches that walk from one side to the other across the design.

4. With your left hand, draw the yarn taut across the design and anchor it with a few straight stitches at the design outline (Fig. 7.6).

5. Walk the needle to the right side of the design without stitching through the yarn, draw the yarn taut, and anchor it as before. Continue laying satin stitches across the de-

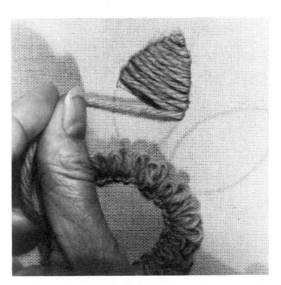

FIG. 7.5 Pull loop and free machine stitch at the base of loop.

FIG. 7.6 Draw yarn taut across the design, and anchor with straight stitches at outline.

sign, one next to the other. To anchor the ends, take a few locking stitches, cut threads off at the fabric, and pull yarn end through to the back and tie it off.

I have used yarn, pearl cotton, embroidery floss, and silk ribbon for this technique, and each gives a different look. Try a variety and make a sample of each for your notebook.

CHAIN STITCH

This is a great way to outline stems and branches or to create your own Chanel trim. Use one color yarn or blend them. It's fast, easy, and effective.

1. Press freezer paper to wrong side of fabric. If the chain stitch will be used to trim a jacket, be sure the fabric is interfaced or has a firm texture. For more stability, baste tear-away to the wrong side of the jacket. Transfer design line to background fabric. One thin line showing the direction to lay the yarn is sufficient.

2. Cut two or more strands of yarn the same length.

3. Set your machine as described above for loops. Bring bobbin thread up, lock the stitches, and clip threads at the fabric. Pierce fabric with needle, and loop the yarn around it. Stitch a couple of locking stitches.

4. With the needle in the work, twist the yarn as tight as desired, creating a twisted hank.

5. Following the yarn channels created by the twists, couch the yarn to the fabric. Continue this the length of the yarn. Anchor yarn ends by straight stitching through them.

6. Clip yarn at the fabric, pull yarn ends through to the back, or leave ends free to thread beads or to create fringe (Fig. 7.7).

CREATE TEXTURE ON A SOLID FABRIC

I recently gave a talk to the Kansas City chapter of the American Sewing Guild. Sue Green, a renowned serger expert, spoke at the program, too. She wore a cocoon jacket made

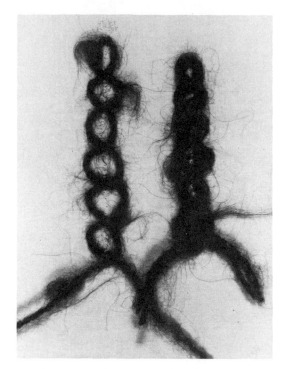

FIG. 7.7 Yarn chain stitch attached freely.

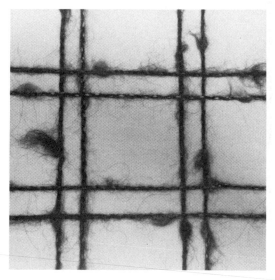

FIG. 7.8 Mohair yarn couched on background fabric.

out of a fabric with a large, abstract plaid on a black background. It appeared hand woven, but actually she had couched over gray and fuchsia strands of mohair yarn after the jacket was made. She explained that the jacket has one seam in the front, and she was afraid she couldn't match the design if it were couched on the fabric first (Fig. 7.8). The result was simple, effective, and striking.

REVERSE EMBROIDERY

As the name implies, reverse embroidery is done from the wrong side of the fabric. It emulates hand embroidery but is much faster. Pearl cotton, embroidery floss, ribbon, or cord is wrapped on the bobbin. The design is transferred to the wrong side of the fabric and you work upside down. I've used this technique in conjunction with a basting accessory or topstitching needle to topstitch a simple jacket (Fig. 7.9). The argyle design on the sweater vest in Fig. 7.10 was appliquéd, then the white and black rows of stitching were reverse embroidered.

Reverse embroidery works on sewing machines with removable bobbin cases or built-in bobbin cases, providing there is a tension

FIG. 7.9 Reverse embroidered topstitch using silk floss in the bobbin.

FIG. 7.10 Reverse embroidered sweater vest.

bypass hole or adjustable bobbin tension in the built-in bobbin case. If you have a removable bobbin case, buy another bobbin case from your dealer for reverse embroidery and any time you plan to change your bobbin tension. This way, one bobbin case is for normal sewing and the other for experimentation. Mark the experimental bobbin case with nail polish or marker so you keep them straight. If your machine has a built-in bobbin case, the bypass hole should be located at one o'clock or seven o'clock. Check your operator's manual, or check with your local sewing machine dealer if you can't find it.

Wind the bobbin by placing it on the bobbin winder and holding the cord or floss in your lap. Slowly wind the bobbin, guiding the floss on by hand as the bobbin turns. Do not overfill the bobbin.

For a removable bobbin case, thread heavy floss or cord through the hole located in the top or on the side of the bobbin case. If using a size #8 pearl cotton, cordonnet, or finer, then thread cord through normal bobbin tension of your experimental bobbin case and loosen the tension screw until the cord pulls as smoothly as standard sewing thread.

For a built-in bobbin case, thread cord through the tension bypass hole as described in your operator's manual. A number of stitches work well for reverse embroidery. Make a permanent record of the following decorative stitches plus all open or tracery decorative stitches available for your machine on a piece of striped pillow ticking (Fig. 7.11), and keep this sample for your notebook.

Set your sewing machine as follows:

Stitch suggestions: straight, zigzag, feather, smocking scallop, 3-step zigzag, smocking (honeycomb), cross stitch, etc. _____
Stitch length: varies _____
Stitch width: varies _____
Foot: embroidery _____
Needle: #80/11–12 all-purpose _____

Barb Griffin

Barb Griffin

Fort Collins, Colorado

This designer and author of *Pizzazz for Pennies* (Chilton, 1986) writes, "Just a brief note about how I work; I love the gridwork over my drafting table. I keep items up for at least two days before sending them off, to be sure they are okay. One brainstorm in the middle of the night might be great, while another is more like a trickle! So, I keep the

work up, along with a calendar filled with deadlines to nudge me on.

"My serger is kept on the edge of the table. I use it frequently now. The suction cups are great, as my table is on a slight angle. Off to the right of the table are vinyl-covered wire baskets that hold plastic boxes of buttons, bags of organized-by-color ribbons, thread, a stack of various weights of interfacing, and bags of miscellaneous trims (rickrack, pom-poms, bells, etc.). Off to the left—out of view—I have an old secretary/bookcase that is filled with fabrics separated into stacks by color. The top shelf is filled with current sewing books.

"Files and computer are in the dining room. I separate work into two areas: the designing and sewing of projects is done in my sewing work area. The actual writing about it is done at the computer. This setup causes a mental switching of gears from stitching to writing. I love both aspects of the work—so it's super!"

Not only has Barb written a book, but her original designs have been featured in *Child Magazine, Country Handcrafts Magazine, Crafts Magazine, Crafts with Simplicity Magazine* and *Needlecraft for Today,* to name just a few.

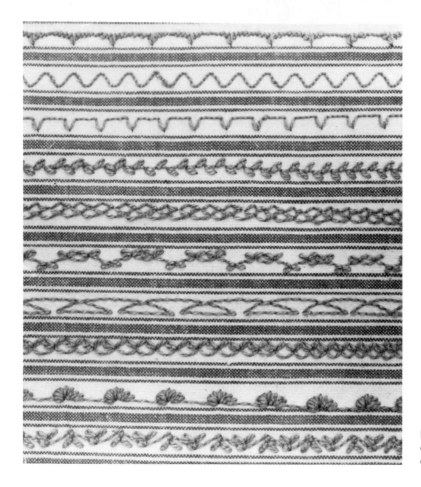

FIG. 7.11 Reverse embroidered stitch sampler on pillow ticking.

Thread: top threaded with thread to match the cord and fabric, or nylon monofilament; bobbin threaded with pearl cotton, embroidery floss, metallic yarn, etc. _____

Stabilizer: iron-on freezer paper or tear-away _____

Accessories: dressmaker's carbon and empty ballpoint pen or burnishing tool _____

HINT: If you are going to be changing bobbin colors a lot for one project, use nylon mono-filament on the top, so you don't need to re-thread for each color.

1. Place a piece of tear-away stabilizer on the wrong side of background fabric.

HINT: If you have access to a copy machine, cut tear-away the size of an 8½″ × 11″ (21.5 cm × 28 cm) piece of paper and put it in the paper tray. Then copy the design on the tear-away by running it through the copy machine.

2. If you don't have access to a copy machine, iron a piece of freezer paper to the wrong side of the fabric. Transfer the design by tracing it on the freezer paper with an empty ballpoint pen or burnishing tool and dress-

maker's carbon. I've found a dressmaker's carbon that washes out with water and comes in colors for light and dark fabrics (see Sources of Supply).

3. Place the right side of your work against the feed dogs and follow the design lines, using one or more of the stitches mentioned above (Fig. 7.12).

RUSSIAN EMBROIDERY

Russian embroidery is a method of reverse embroidery resembling hand needle punch. All you need is the smocking stitch and the ability to bypass the bobbin tension. I've used this technique to fill in the leaves (Fig. 7.13)

or to layer color on color for a three-dimensional look.

Set your machine as follows:

Stitch: smocking (looks like a
   honeycomb)   ————
Stitch length: preset   ————
Stitch width: 2–3   ————
Foot: transparent embroidery ————
Needle: #80/11–12 all-purpose ————
Thread: top threaded to match
   cord in bobbin, or with nylon
   monofilament; bobbin threaded
   with pearl cotton, embroidery
   floss, or other decorative cord ————
Stabilizer: iron-on freezer paper or
   tear-away   ————

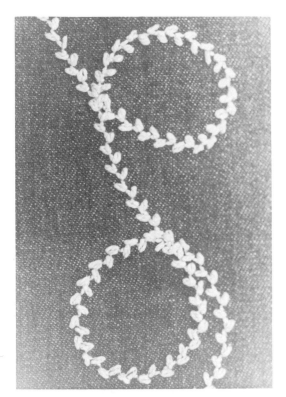

FIG. 7.12 Place fabric upside down and follow design lines, using open decorative stitches.

FIG. 7.13 Russian embroidery fills in the leaves of this design.

1. Stabilize the wrong side of fabric with freezer paper or tear-away. Transfer design to the wrong side of the fabric.

2. Starting on the outside of the design, sew a row of smocking stitches. Stitch around and around, working from the outside toward the center, so the rows of stitching are right next to each other. If stitches cross over one another occasionally, don't worry about it.

3. I have also used this technique as a single row of topstitching (Fig. 7.14). The inspiration came from a motif I saw stitched on a pair of cowboy boots.

TOPSTITCHING TECHNIQUES WITH YOUR SERGER

Besides using decorative threads, yarns, or ribbons through the upper and lower looper to create a Chanel trim with your serger (see Chapter 5), you can create interesting effects by flatlocking seams and tucks, couching over decorative threads, and attaching a string of pearls along an edge with your serger.

FIG. 7.14 Single row of Russian embroidery stitched in a motif inspired by a design seen on cowboy boots.

Flatlock Seams and Tucks

Flatlocking, often seen in ready-to-wear, is a method of stitching a seam together with a loosened tension, then pulling it apart so the decorative topstitch lies flat. To make a seam or tuck, set your serger as follows:

2/3-thread serger

Stitch: 2-thread flatlock	_____
Stitch length: 2–3	_____
Stitch width: 5 mm	_____
Needle tension: very loose	_____
Lower looper: very tight	_____
Needle plate: 5 mm (for a narrower flatlock, use 2 mm needle plate)	_____

3/4-thread serger or 3/4/5-thread serger

Stitch: 3-thread flatlock	_____
Stitch length: 2–3	_____
Stitch width: 5 mm	_____
Needle tension: very loose	_____
Upper looper: loose	_____
Lower looper: very tight	_____
Needle plate: 5 mm (for a narrower flatlock, use 2 mm needle plate)	_____

FLATLOCK SEAMS

1. Test seam on a scrap first.

2. Trim seam allowance to ¼″ (6 mm).

3. Place wrong sides together, making sure raw edges are even with each other.

4. Place raw edge under foot so most of the stitch forms on the fabric and the rest loops off the edge, over the stitch fingers. This is called "filling half the stitch" because fabric fills half of the stitch.

5. Serge and remove the fabric from the machine. Gently pull fabric at the seam so that the stitch pulls flat. If there is a ridge in the seam, loosen the needle tension. The loop side and ladder side of the flatlock stitch should be the same width (Fig. 7.15).

For fabrics that ravel, finish and press seam allowances to the wrong side of the fabric. Decide if you want the ladder or loop side out. For the loop side out, place wrong sides together. For the ladder side out, place right

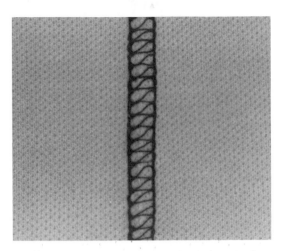

FIG. 7.15 Flatlock seam.

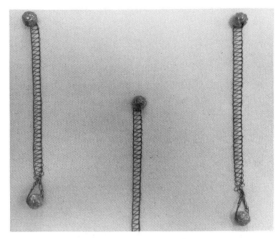

FIG. 7.17 Flatlock tucks with beads strung on free thread tails.

sides together. Place seam allowances together so folded edges are even. Flatlock along seamline and pull seam flat. With your conventional machine, straight stitch on either side of the flatlock seam.

To reinforce a flatlock seam, stitch, pull, and press seam flat. Fuse a piece of Easy-Knit tape on the wrong side of the flatlock seam.

Then straight stitch with a short stitch length on either side of flatlock (Fig. 7.16).

FLATLOCK TUCKS

1. Fold the fabric *wrong* sides together and press.
2. Place fold to the right, under the foot, so that it fills half of the stitch.
3. Serge and pull tuck flat, as described above.
4. For an added decorative effect, stitch flatlock tucks randomly on a piece of fabric. Thread beads on the free tails and tie the ends off by pulling them to the wrong side so beads stay in place (Fig. 7.17).

Couching

As with the conventional sewing machine, couching is a way to lay a strand or two of yarn, cord, ribbon, or floss on top of the fabric and stitch over it. To do this with your serger, set your machine for a 2-thread or 3-thread flatlock stitch, using thread that matches the yarn or cord you are couching over. For a bolder outline to the seam or tuck, use nylon monofilament thread through needle and loopers so that the color of the cord shows through the thread.

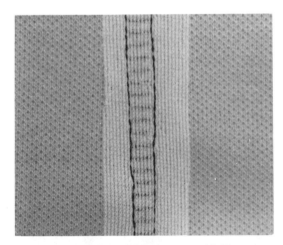

FIG. 7.16 Reinforce flatlock seam with Easy-Knit tape. Straight stitch on either side of flatlock to hold tape in place.

FIG. 7.18 Couching yarn or ribbon with flatlock tuck.

1. If your serger has a hole in the presser foot, thread yarn or cord over the toe of the foot and through the hole. If your serger does not have a hole in it, place yarn or cord under the presser foot. Rest the skein or ball on your lap, or let it drop to the floor.

2. With wrong sides together, place fabric under the foot, so the fabric fills half of the stitch and the cord guides along the cut edge of a seam or folded edge of a tuck.

3. Serge and remove fabric from the machine.

4. Gently pull seam or tuck flat. The yarn, cord, or ribbon lies under the stitch (Fig. 7.18).

Attaching a String of Seed Pearls or Sequin Trim

This technique is fast and makes attaching seed pearls to the edge of a hem or ruffle edge a snap.

Set your serger as follows:

2/3, 3/4, or 3/4/5-thread serger
Stitch: 2- or 3-thread overlock   ———
Stitch length: 5   ———
Stitch width: 5   ———
Left needle tension: normal   ———

Upper looper: normal   ———
Lower looper: normal   ———
Needle plate: 5 mm   ———
Thread: regular, woolly nylon, or
    nylon monofilament   ———

1. Remove presser foot.

2. If you can put the removable cutter in a nonworking position, do so. If you can't, be careful to guide the fabric and pearls so the blade will not cut the work.

3. Chain off 2"–3" (5 cm–7.5 cm), and place pearls or sequin trim to the right side of needle. Slowly stitch, catching the string of pearls in the thread chain. *Note:* No fabric is under needle at this point.

4. Fold and press a narrow hem or tuck in the fabric. Place fabric edge along right side of the needle plate, under pearls or sequins. If your blade is in working position, be sure fabric edge and trim are to the left of the blade. Slowly attach fabric to thread chain (Fig. 7.19). Pull the fabric through the serger so it runs slowly enough to prevent stitches from piling up over the pearls or sequins.

5. Finish each end by cutting off the pearl/sequin trim the desired length. Unravel the thread chains, pull threads to the wrong side, and tie them off.

FIG. 7.19 Pearl trim attached to edge of fabric with the serger.

Next time you topstitch, be different. Refer to your notebook full of topstitching samples from this chapter, or experiment with your own ideas. It makes the difference between ordinary and couture.

Next, we'll put the finishing touches on your jacket by lining it. Only about 6″–7″ (15 cm–18 cm) of hand stitching is necessary to stitch a full lining into your jacket. The rest is done by machine. Read on, and see how easy it is.

SUPPLY LIST FOR CHAPTER 8

- Jacket lining cut and marked
- #70/9 sewing machine needle
- Hand needle and thread
- Lining scraps cut into 6″ (15 cm) squares

Linings

I always wondered how manufacturers stitched a lining in a jacket without hand-work. After a lot of trial and error, I figured out how it's done and will share the technique with you in this chapter for your jacket-in-progress. I'll also show you how to ease a skirt lining into the waistline of a skirt before attaching a waistband and how to finish the hem in your skirt lining in a fast, decorative way.

FINISHING LINING IN A PARTIALLY LINED JACKET

If you are making a partially lined man's jacket, the lining has been stitched in with the collar application (see Chapter 5). To finish the back lining section, fold a narrow hem at the lower edge and machine stitch $\frac{1}{4}''$ (6 mm) from hem edge.

Finish the exposed back of the jacket by cutting hem and vent interfacing $\frac{1}{4}''$ (6 mm) less than the finished width, so interfacing will not show. The exposed seams should have

been finished before the jacket was constructed by overcasting the edges with the 3-step zigzag or double overlock on your conventional machine or by using a 2/3-thread overlock on your serger.

The front lining side seams are turned to the wrong side, pressed, and slip-stitched to the jacket side seam allowances (Fig. 8.1).

To finish the sleeve lining, turn lining hem up as described on the pattern and slip-stitch it to the hem of the jacket sleeve.

MACHINE STITCHED AND TURNED LININGS

Some experts recommend stitching a lining in a tailored jacket by hand. My attempts have been unsuccessful because I'm impatient, do not have a practiced hand at slip-stitching, and feel machine stitches are much sturdier than hand stitches. Therefore, all the linings I stitch into my own tailored jackets are done by machine. This is how I do it.

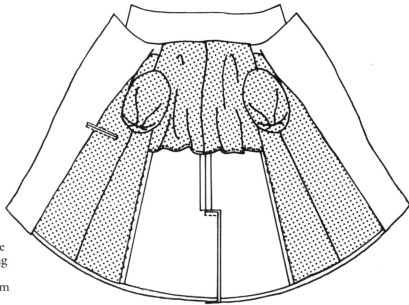

FIG. 8.1 Front lining side seams are turned to wrong side, pressed, and slip-stitched to jacket side seam allowances.

Attaching the Body of Lining

Before lining the jacket, pin or hand-baste jacket hem as described in pattern instructions. The raw edge of facing pieces should also be finished with the 3-step zigzag or overlock stitch on your conventional sewing machine or 2/3-thread overlock on your serger.

1. Mark and machine stitch the pleat or tuck down center back of lining piece. I make permanent stitches where indicated on the pattern piece, then baste the remainder of the pleat closed. Press pleat to one side.

2. Stitch all lining pieces together (front, side front, back, and sleeves) to form a complete lining unit. Clip and press seams open as you did for the jacket. Press hems in bottom of jacket lining and sleeve lining with width described in the pattern instructions.

3. Stay-stitch around neck edge.

4. Pin lining to jacket facing, right sides together, matching seams, raw edges, and center backs. Clip lining neck edge to stay-stitching, so lining and facing pieces match.

5. Stitch lining in at a $\frac{5}{8}''$ (1.5 cm) seam allowance, starting at the center back and sew-

ing to 3" (7.5 cm) above the lower edge of one front facing. Repeat for the other side (Fig. 8.2).

6. Clip seam allowance where necessary. Press lining seam allowance together. Turn

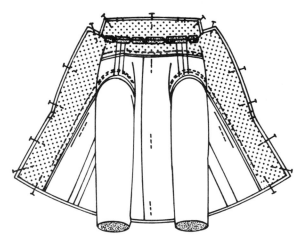

FIG. 8.2 Stitch lining starting at center back, to 3" (7.5cm) above lower edge of front facing.

lining and jacket right side out. Top press lining at facing edge.

Attaching Sleeve Lining

Most instructions tell you to slip-stitch the sleeve lining to the sleeve hem or sleeve cap of the jacket. I've done this, but was constantly catching the stitches in my jewelry, or the

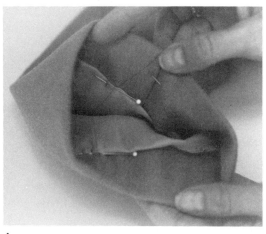

A

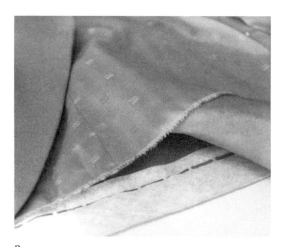

B

FIG. 8.3 *A,* Pin sleeve lining to sleeve hem. *B,* From bottom of jacket, reach between jacket and lining, up into sleeve.

stitches didn't hold around the armhole. I discovered this faster, more secure method for machine stitching the lining into a jacket sleeve at the hem.

1. Push sleeve linings through jacket sleeves. At the underarm seams, pin the turned up hem of sleeve lining to the hem of jacket, pinning through hem layers only (Fig. 8.3A).

2. Hold the sleeve hem where you have pinned the lining to the jacket sleeve with one hand. With the other hand and from the bottom, reach up between the lining and jacket, then down into the sleeve to the place where the hems are pinned together (Fig. 8.3B).

3. Grasp both hem allowances firmly, and pull sleeve through between the lining and body of jacket. Pin the sleeve hem of the lining to the sleeve hem of the jacket so raw edges match (Fig. 8.4). Smooth the fullness of the lining away from the hem, and stitch sleeve lining to the hem of jacket sleeve with a $\frac{5}{8}''$ (1.5 cm) seam allowance. *Note:* Before stitching, be sure sleeve lining is not twisted in the sleeve.

4. Turn sleeve right side out.

5. At hem end of the underarm seam, stitch-in-the-ditch the width of sleeve hem allowance from hem edge to where lining is stitched

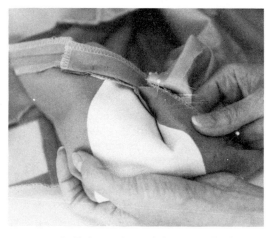

FIG. 8.4 Pull sleeve through between the lining and body of jacket. Stitch sleeve lining to hem of jacket sleeve.

in the sleeve (Fig. 8.5). This prevents the lining from pulling and the hem of the jacket from drooping. Let the excess fullness from lining drop into place and press. The fullness keeps the lining from pulling inside and makes the jacket more comfortable to wear.

6. Repeat for other sleeve.

7. Catch-stitch sleeve lining to jacket sleeve seam at the underarm and top of sleeve cap.

Finishing Jacket and Lining Hems

The hems on both jacket and lining should be pinned or hand-basted and pressed per pattern instructions. Press jacket and lining seam allowance at front facing toward the lining.

1. Hold jacket so lining hangs free. Reach into jacket between lining and body of the jacket. At one end of hem edge, grasp hem allowances of both lining and jacket, right sides together, and pull hem edge through the opening at the bottom or back vent of jacket.

2. Pin lining and jacket hem edges, right sides together, matching seams, raw edges, and center backs.

3. Starting at one end, stitch hem edges of lining and jacket together with a $\frac{5}{8}''$ (1.5 cm) seam allowance, stopping about 6"–7" (15 cm–18 cm) from the other end.

4. Turn jacket right side out. Pin remainder of jacket lining and hem together, smoothing

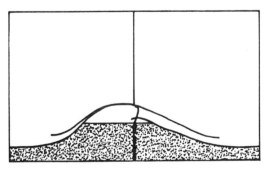

FIG. 8.5 Stitch-in-the-ditch the width of sleeve hem allowance.

lining fullness away from the hem. Slip-stitch the rest of the hem.

5. At side seams, stitch-in-the-ditch the width of the hem allowance so hems will not droop. Let the extra length of lining fall down over the hem and press.

6. Slip-stitch lining to facing, allowing for hem drop on both sides.

EASING SKIRT OR PANTS LINING INTO WAISTBAND

When it comes to lining a skirt, I like how it feels on my body, but I don't like to spend a lot of time on it. Sue Hausmann from Chicago showed me this quick trick. If you're in a hurry to line a skirt, this is the way to do it. Even if you're not in a hurry, this is the way to do it.

1. Construct the skirt of fashion fabric, except for putting on the waistband.

2. Cut skirt lining per pattern instructions. If your pattern does not have a skirt lining, make your own pattern.

For a pleated skirt, use two pattern pieces for the lining, both cut on the fold. The waistline measurement should be 2"–3" (5 cm–7.5 cm) bigger than the finished waistline measurement. Hip should also measure 2"–3" (5 cm–7.5 cm) bigger than actual hip measurement for ease. Stitch side seams using a $\frac{5}{8}''$ (1.5 cm) seam allowance, leaving a 7"–10" (18 cm–25.5 cm) slit on either side at the bottom and leaving a slit at zipper opening. Topstitch around slits so they lie flat.

For a skirt with a back pleat, use three pattern pieces for the lining. Cut front lining piece on the fold. Cut back lining pieces as shown in Fig. 8.6. Notice that rather than cutting the vent for the pleat, I've cut a gentle curve at the pleat. You'll see why in a moment.

For other styles, cut lining by using existing skirt pattern. Do not mark or stitch darts or gathers.

3. Stitch side seams together and press seam allowance open or to one side.

To quickly finish the curved and bottom edges of the lining for the skirt with the center back pleat, cut lining so it is 1″ (2.5 cm) shorter than hemmed length of skirt. Do not stitch seam together down center back. Open lining flat (Fig. 8.7), and overcast curved and bottom edges. Use the 3-step zigzag or double overlock stitch on the conventional machine or the 2/3-thread overlock on the serger. Stitch center back seam together at the $\frac{5}{8}''$ (1.5 cm) seamline, stopping 1″ (2.5 cm) above the curve. If there is a zipper in the center back, baste lining together the length of the zipper. Remove the fabric from the machine and clip threads. Shorten the stitch length; then finish stitching center back seam to 1″ (2.5 cm) above the curve. Press the seam allowance open; topstitch around the basted seam allowance on both sides of the seamline, the length of the zipper. Remove basting stitches to create a slit for the zipper opening.

4. Do not stitch darts, gathers, or tucks in the top of the lining, as may be described in the pattern. Pin lining into skirt matching top raw edges, side seams, and center front or center back. Lining will be fuller than waistline opening.

5. Set your machine for a straight stitch, stitch length 3 (9 stitches per inch). Use the embroidery foot.

6. Starting at the zipper opening, $\frac{1}{2}''$ (1.3 cm) from raw edge, place the top of the skirt and lining under the foot so the lining side is down against the feed dogs.

7. Begin stitching slowly, holding the skirt layer firmly in your right hand at the first pin, but preventing it from feeding normally through the machine. Let the lining feed normally through the machine. The feed dogs feed the lining into the waistline, automatically easing in the excess fullness. The more firmly you hold the top layer, the more excess is eased into the layer underneath. Ease the lining into the waistline from pin to pin. No darts, no gathers, no fuss, no muss (Fig. 8.8).

8. Now your skirt is ready for one of the waistband treatments discussed in Chapter 9.

Pati Palmer

Portland, Oregon

Pati Palmer is president of Palmer/Pletsch Associates, a 15-year-old sewing book publishing and promotion company. She has co-authored or edited eleven books, which have sold more than 2 million copies.

Pati is also co-designer, with Susan Pletsch, of a line of more than 200 Personalized Instruction™ patterns for McCall's Pattern Company. The pair are the only designers licensed by a pattern company who do not also design ready-to-wear clothes—and they are number one in sales for McCall's. But how did all this start for Pati?

"I started sewing when I was 10," says Pati. "Mom sewed, and I used her scraps to make doll clothes. The first thing I made for myself was a dirndl skirt. I didn't use a pattern. Mom helped me with the zipper, I gathered the fabric onto a waistband and had a skirt. It was easy to sew, didn't take a lot of time, and I was so pleased with myself.

"The first machine I owned was a Singer Featherweight, which I traded in for my grandmother's treadle machine. I had it

Pati Palmer

refinished—it's just beautiful and is part of my antique sewing machine collection.

"My first formal sewing lesson was as a sophomore in college." After graduating from Oregon State University with a degree in home economics, concentrating in clothing and textiles, Pati became an educational consultant for the Armo interfacing company of New York. She then became corporate home economist for Meier and Frank, an Oregon department store.

At Meier and Frank, she taught ten sewing classes per week and, at the time, admitted knowing little about fitting other people. "There was a woman who wanted to enroll in one of my classes who had a double D cup. I honestly didn't know how I was going to fit

her, so I told her all the classes were full. After that, we came up with the idea of five front-fit patterns designed to fit each bust size." This concept and the pants fitting pattern were the beginning of the successful line of Palmer/Pletsch patterns.

I asked Pati when she has time to sew now that she is a wife, mother, and president of her own company. "I occasionally take a week off and sew. The rest of the time I organize my projects so that when my daughter is down for a nap, I get a lot of sewing done in short periods of time." It also helps to have a well-organized sewing room. If you're interested in seeing more of Pati's "Ultimate Sewing Center" you can see it in her new sewing video.

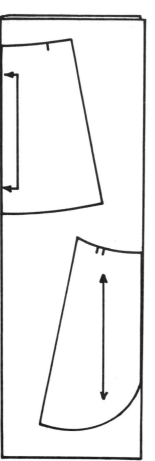

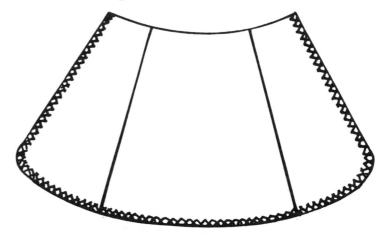

FIG. 8.6 Cut front lining piece on the fold. Cut two back lining pieces with a gentle curve at the pleat.

FIG. 8.7 Stitch lining together at side seams. Open lining flat. Overcast curved and bottom edges.

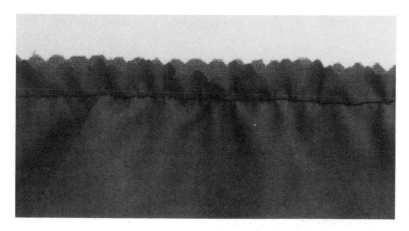

FIG. 8.8 Lining eased into waistline of skirt.

HEM FINISHES

As a young home economist, I went to the American Home Sewing Association conventions and was often impressed with other, more experienced home economists in the industry. One of them was Karen Holmquist. Her hallmarks were her sense of color and fashion, and her incredible sewing skills. I'll never forget a classic Vogue dress made of, and lined with, a fabric we called whipped cream. She made a fabric flower out of the scraps to wear on the belt, and she hemmed the lining as described below. I love this method of finishing lining hems and do it every chance I get. It gives me an opportunity to use my decorative stitches, is fun, and is almost as fast as machine blind hemming.

One-Step Method

PREPARATION

1. Let skirt hang overnight so hem can be measured accurately.
2. Hem skirt as described in Chapter 11.
3. If you have a dress form, put the skirt on the dress form inside out. If you don't have a dress form, call a friend over or get your husband to mark the lining for your skirt so it is 1″ (2.5 cm) shorter than the finished length of the skirt.
4. Pin and press lining hem without pressing over pins.

STITCHING

On a scrap, test a few decorative stitches on a doubled layer of lining fabric. Try one of the following stitches on different stitch widths and lengths. Tighten and loosen tensions for other effects and keep your test swatches in your notebook. Set your sewing machine as follows:

Stitch suggestions: scallop, arch, loops, brackets, or any tracery design	_____
Stitch length: varies	_____
Stitch width: 4	_____
Foot: standard zigzag (Teflon)	_____
Needle: #70/9 all-purpose	_____
Fabric: lining scraps	_____

When you have decided which stitch or stitches to use, run the first row of decorative stitching 1½″ (3.8 cm) from the folded hem edge. Be sure the presser foot is resting completely on a double layer of fabric. Run another row of decorative stitching a presser foot width away from the first, then a third row of decorative stitching a presser foot width away from the second (Fig. 8.9). Stitch as many or as few rows as desired. Stitch with matching or contrasting thread, using a single needle or double needle. The possibilities are endless.

Trim excess hem allowance up to the stitch.

Two-Step Method

Pin and press lining hem as described above. At the hem edge stitch a shell tuck. Set your sewing machine as follows:

Stitch: reverse blind hem	_____
Stitch length: 1.5, or 15 stitches per inch	_____
Stitch width: widest	_____
Foot: standard zigzag (Teflon)	_____
Needle: #70/9 all-purpose	_____

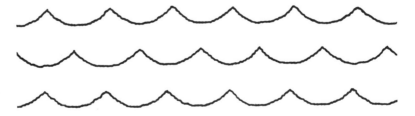

FIG. 8.9 Run three rows of decorative stitching a presser foot width away from each other to secure a lining hem.

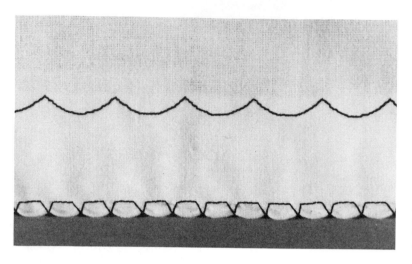

FIG. 8.10 Run one or more rows of decorative stitching above the shell tuck. Trim excess hem allowance up to the stitch.

Place the folded edge, right side up, two-thirds of the way under the presser foot. The needle takes a few stitches on the fabric at the left, then zigzags off the edge at the right. The needle must swing completely off the edge of the fabric, or you may end up with a skipped stitch. The zigzag stitches draw the fabric into a tuck or scallop.

Experiment with the stitch suggestions above (one-step method), and run one or more rows of decorative stitching 1" (2.5 cm) above the shell tuck. Trim excess hem allowance up to the stitch (Fig. 8.10).

Your jacket should be done, with the lining stitched in, pressed, and ready to wear. It's taken a little experimentation, some trial and error, but I hope you are pleased with the results. With this chapter, I also hope you are working on a pair of slacks or a skirt to go with your speed-tailored jacket. Next you will see three professional ways to install a waistband.

SUPPLY LIST FOR CHAPTER 9

- Waist-Shaper™, Fold-a-Band, or RolControl
- 1" (2.5 cm) waistband elastic
- 6" (15 cm) fabric squares for notebook

Waistbands

Waistbands should be an even width, and fit comfortably without rolling or binding. Before products were introduced to help make the perfect waistband, I cut my interfacing carefully, stitched the waistband precisely, and still ended up with an uneven waistband that rolled. In this chapter I'll show you three methods of applying a waistband. Two use helpful products such as Waist-Shaper and RolControl, and the third has elastic in it.

WAISTBAND USING WAIST-SHAPER OR FOLD-A-BAND

Waist-Shaper™ and Fold-a-Band™ are fusible, precut interfacings perforated for straight, even waistbands. Both are wrinkle-resistant, machine-washable, dry-cleanable, and work well on medium to heavy fabrics. For lighter weight fabrics, I cut it in half along the perforated slots and use only one side. Use either product as follows:

1. Cut waistband interfacing the length needed for the waistband, minus seam allowances on either end. One side is wider than the other and becomes the inside of the waistband.

2. With the rough, coated side down and the wider side on the unnotched side, place the center slots along the foldline. Place either the straight edges or narrow slotted lines along seamlines (Fig. 9.1).

3. Set iron or press on the wool setting. Set hand iron for steam. With the interfacing up, place a damp press cloth over the work.

With the Press
Press 10 seconds with full pressure, lift the heating shoe, and let the steam escape. Press again until fabric is dry.

With the Hand Iron
Press 15 seconds with steam and as much pressure as possible. Move iron and press cloth down the length of the waistband, fusing as you go. Do not slide the iron. Turn work over

127

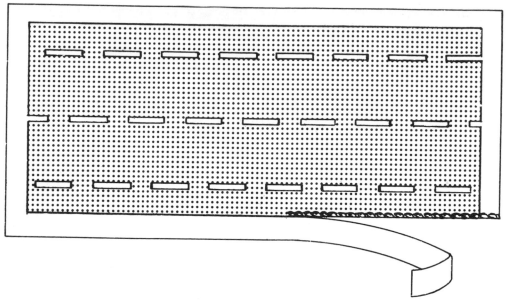

FIG. 9.1 Place straight edges or narrow slotted lines along seamlines.

and repeat fusing process another 15 seconds down the length of the band.

4. To eliminate bulk on medium to heavy fabrics, trim unnotched side of waistband to ¼″ (6 mm) seam allowance. To finish edge, overcast the raw edge with the 3-step zigzag or double overlock stitch on your conventional sewing machine, or with a 3-thread overlock on your serger.

5. With right sides together, pin and stitch waistband to waistline, matching notches. Try garment on to check the fit.

6. With right sides together, fold the waistband in half the long way along the slotted line. Fold the seam allowances up, toward center fold, and stitch each end of band without catching interfacing in the seamline.

7. Trim seam allowances and corners. Turn waistband right side out. Gently square the corners with a point turner and top press.

8. Press the waistline seam allowance up inside the band while pressing the inside of waistband down over the seamline.

HINT: At the ends, press the folded seam allowances under until the fold covers the zipper.

Then press the overcast, unnotched edge of waistband so it covers the seamline. Use this procedure for all the waistbands in this chapter.

9. Set your sewing machine as follows:

Stitch: straight   _____
Stitch length: 2–3, or 9–12 stitches
    per inch
Stitch width: 0   _____
Foot: blind hem or buttonhole   _____
Needle position: varies—move it so
    needle stitches-in-the-ditch   _____

From the right side of the waistband, place the blade of the blind hem foot or inside of the right toe of the buttonhole foot so that the needle stitches in the seamline. The blade and/or toe opens the seamline so stitches fall in the seamline or ditch. After the stitch is made, the fabric returns to its original position and almost covers the stitch. *Note:* Because the finished, unnotched edge covers the seamline, the waistband is stitched closed when you stitch-in-the-ditch (Fig. 9.2).

Donna
Salyers

Cincinnati, Ohio

Donna Salyers

"I've been sewing since age 9 or 10. I wanted pretty clothes and couldn't afford to buy them, so at first, it was out of necessity . . . but I found I just loved to sew. I'm only 5'2", so when I got older, it was difficult to find things that fit. And by the time I altered ready-to-wear, I could have made it, so I prefer to sew."

Donna is very busy with her weekly syndicated sewing column, starring in her own home sewing video series, hosting a half-hour cable TV program, and presenting sewing seminars around the country. Her series of 30-minute home sewing videos

("Sew a Wardrobe in a Weekend," "Re-Do a Wardrobe in a Weekend," "Super Time-Saving Sewing Tips," and "Craft and Gift Ideas") recently enjoyed some national attention when they were featured in *USA Today*. How does she do it all?

"My family is very supportive. I couldn't do all this without their support. My husband is my business adviser, and my son and daughter have even dressed up like clowns and passed out brochures at various events to promote my work."

For information on ordering Donna's videos, see the Source of Supply.

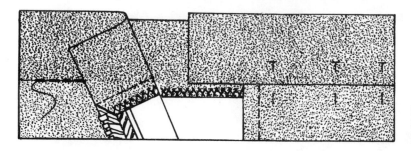

FIG. 9.2 Finish waistband by stitching-in-the-ditch on long side.

10. Top press waistband with the appropriate press cloth.

11. Stitch fasteners in place.

ROLCONTROL WAISTBAND APPLICATION

RolControl is a new waistband stabilizer. It is made by a continuous monofilament construction that prevents waistbands from rolling or creasing. It also has a $\frac{5}{8}''$ (1.5 cm) stitching guideline. To use it:

1. Preshrink RolControl the same way you intend to care for the finished garment. If garment is to be dry-cleaned, preshrink in hot water and hot dryer.

2. Do not interface waistband. Trim long unnotched edge of waistband to a $\frac{1}{4}''$ seam allowance and finish edge.

3. Cut RolControl the length of the waistband, including end seam allowance.

4. Pin and baste waistband to waistline, matching notches. Try garment on to check the fit.

5. Pin RolControl to the notched edge of waistband so the beige lines are over the seamline. Stitch between the two beige lines for a $\frac{5}{8}''$ (1.5 cm) seam.

6. With right sides together, fold band in half the long way. Fold the seam allowances up toward the center fold and stitch each end of band, catching the RolControl in the seamline. Stitch ends again $\frac{1}{8}''$ (3 mm) from first row of stitching.

7. Trim seam allowances and corners. Turn waistband right side out. Gently square the corners with a point turner and top press.

8. Press waistline and RolControl seam allowances up inside the band while pressing the inside of waistband down over the seamline.

9. Set your machine as described in step 9 of the preceding instructions, and stitch-in-the-ditch from the right side of waistband to secure it.

10. Stitch fasteners in place.

ELASTIC WAISTBAND APPLICATION

Have you ever sat down to a great meal and wished you could let out your waistband a bit before standing up? The following method of applying a waistband was devised by Sue Hausmann, from Chicago, for that very reason. You will need elastic the same width as your waistband.

1. Cut waistband per pattern instructions. Trim unnotched edge to a $\frac{1}{4}''$ (6 mm) seam allowance and finish edge.

2. Do not interface waistband. With right sides together, pin waistband to waistline edge, matching notches. Stitch, and try on for fit.

3. Use a piece of elastic the finished width of the waistband. Cut elastic $1''-1\frac{1}{2}''$ (2.5 cm–3.8 cm) smaller than waistband, including extensions, so it is comfortable.

4. Set your sewing machine as follows:

Stitch: zigzag
Stitch length: 3–4, or 6–9 stitches
    per inch ———
Stitch width: 3–4 ———
Foot: embroidery ———
Needle: #80/11–12 or #75/11 stretch ———

With the waistband side up, lay elastic along the seam allowance so the left edge of elastic is even with the seamline (Fig. 9.3). On the left edge, zigzag elastic to the seam allowance, stretching it slightly to fit the waistband.

5. With the right sides together, fold waistband in half the long way. Fold seam allowance up, toward center fold, and stitch each end of band, catching elastic in the seam.

6. Trim end seam allowance to $\frac{1}{8}"$–$\frac{1}{4}"$ (3 mm–6 mm). Turn band right side out. Gently square corners with the point turner and top press.

7. Press waistline seam allowance and elastic up inside the band while pressing the inside of the waistband down over the seamline.

8. Finish waistband by stitching-in-the-ditch on long side.

9. Stitch fasteners in place.

Try these techniques on your next three waistband applications, or make a sample for your notebook and see what works best for you. I use all three on different occasions, depending on the fabric and style of the skirt or pair of slacks.

Next I'll show you some decorative techniques I've used on my tailored suits. They're simple and fun and give each garment a look all its own.

FIG. 9.3 Lay elastic along the seam allowance, so left edge is even with seamline.

SUPPLY LIST FOR CHAPTER 10

- 9" (22.5 cm) woven (e.g., burlap, linen, kettlecloth) fabric squares for notebook samples
- Pearl cotton and thread to match fabric
- Sharp embroidery scissors
- Adding machine tape
- Tear-away stabilizer
- Embroidery hoop (5" or 7" spring type preferred)
- Water-soluble or vanishing marker
- Darning thread
- Wing needle
- Burlap
- Dressmaker's carbon and empty ballpoint pen

Chapter 10

Couture and Decorative Touches

Every time I make something, I try to give it character—give it my signature. It could be the way I match the plaid, use a border print, stitch the seams, create a pocket, or dress up the fabric by adding the texture of stitching to it. In this chapter, I will share four techniques I've used to create unique garments: cutwork, fagoting, hemstitching, and needleweaving. Perfect these techniques by making samples for your notebook, and use your new skills to give your handmade originals your signature.

THE INSPIRATION

The toughest part in creating an original design is finding the inspiration. Some of my inspiration comes from sketches, swatches, and stitch samples I keep in a stenographer's notebook. It fits easily in a purse or briefcase, and I use both sides of the paper. I take my notebook shopping, to sewing seminars and fashion shows, and anywhere else I think I might

find interesting ideas. When I do, I jot down stitch applications, make sketches, and record interesting garment details.

I also tear out ideas from magazines, mail-order catalogs, and the newspaper. My only problem is finding the time to stitch up all the ideas.

As you have probably deduced, my original designs stem from something I've seen or borrowed from someone else. By the time I translate it into stitchery, it looks so different from the original, I call it my own. Aren't I sneaky? Why don't you do the same? You'll be amazed how quickly you build an idea file to use as your springboard for creativity.

CUTWORK

I remember looking at my grandmother's table linens and, even at the tender age of seven, I had an appreciation of the artistry and hours of hand work necessary to create such beautiful pieces.

With today's technology, cutwork is much easier. I've tried a number of methods, and the following is my favorite. The satin stitches are raised, and the embroidery is sturdy enough to withstand years of wear and tear, such as in the suit in Fig. 10.1.

The best fabrics for cutwork are firmly woven linen or linen-like fabrics with a smooth hand or finish. The fabric used in my cutwork suit is a linen, silk, and rayon blend I found at a mill outlet store. When I cut out the pattern, I cut generous corners, leaving enough room for a hoop. Later I trimmed the excess

away after the embroidery was completed and hems turned up.

1. Trace and transfer the design onto the right side of the fabric, using dressmaker's carbon and an empty ballpoint pen.

HINT: Water-erasable or vanishing dressmaker's carbon is available in most markets. This way, the marks can be removed with clear water or will vanish in 24 to 72 hours. If you plan to stitch the cutwork in more than one sitting, you may find the water-erasable type better.

2. The area to be cut away must be reinforced so the stitching will not pull into the

A

B

FIG. 10.1 *A* and *B* Cutwork suit.

hole. Therefore, I like to cord around those areas with pearl cotton.

Set your machine as follows:

Stitch: zigzag _____
Stitch length: 1–2, or 12–20 stitches
   per inch _____
Stitch width: 2 _____
Foot: transparent embroidery or
   narrow braiding _____
Needle: #80/11–12 all-purpose _____
Thread: top and bobbin threaded
   with machine embroidery thread
   to match fabric _____
Accessories: size #5 pearl cotton to
   match fabric, 5"–7"
   (12.5 cm–18 cm) spring hoop,
   sharp embroidery scissors, tear-
   away stabilizer (optional) _____

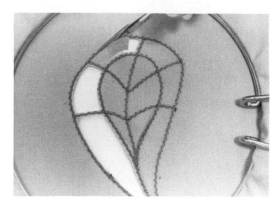

FIG. 10.2 Trim fabric away from the stitches with sharp embroidery scissors.

3. Place tear-away stabilizer under the fabric, or put fabric in a hoop, centering the design. Place a strand of pearl cotton under embroidery foot or in the clip of the narrow braiding foot. Couch over the pearl cotton with the zigzag stitch described above, following the design outline.

HINT: For more control, use the narrow braiding foot. Cord all areas before cutting away any of the fabric.

4. Using a sharp pair of embroidery scissors, trim fabric away from one side of the stitches (Fig. 10.2). Be careful that each shape is joined by fabric or bars of stitching to the base fabric. Otherwise, you may cord an area and cut a whole shape out of the fabric by mistake.

5. To clean up the edges and finish the cutwork, satin stitch over corded edges.

Set your machine as follows:

Stitch: zigzag (satin stitch) _____
Stitch length: 0.5, or fine setting _____
Stitch width: 3–4 _____
Foot: transparent embroidery _____
Needle: #80/11–12 all-purpose _____

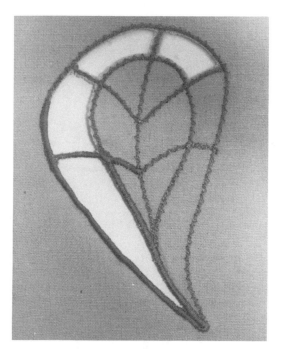

FIG. 10.3 Place corded edge under foot so needle catches the fabric on one side and swings over edge on the other; the finished stitch is shown.

Thread: top and bobbin threaded
with machine embroidery thread
to match or contrast with fabric _____
Tension: top slightly loosened _____

Place corded edge under the foot so the needle catches the fabric on one side and swings over the edge into open area on the other (Fig. 10.3).

FAGOTING

Fagoting is a method of attaching fabric to fabric, or fabric to trim, with a row of threads or cords. The beauty is in the open lacy look created by the fagoted stitches. Generally, fagoting is used on straight seams and edges. Because of its delicate nature, do not stitch fagoting in stress areas.

With the help of today's decorative machine stitches, I've discovered a number of fagoting techniques and use them to decorate pocket tops and table runners and to create interesting seamlines. One of my favorite projects was a dress that had gotten too short to be in style. Fortunately, I had kept the scraps. After fagoting the band to the hemline, it looked as if I had tried to disguise a too-short dress. But when I made bands and fagoted them to the bottom of the short sleeves, the dress looked great, better than it did new.

Simple Fagoting

This delicate treatment is often seen on blouses and christening gowns. Set your machine as follows:

Stitch: 3-step zigzag; feather _____
Stitch length: 0.8–1 or fine setting;
preset _____
Stitch width: 4–6 _____
Foot: fagoting or transparent
embroidery _____

Needle: #70/9 or #80/11–12 all-
purpose _____
Accessories: fagoting plate or
raised seam guide if available
for your machine _____
Thread: regular sewing or machine-
embroidery thread to match or
contrast with fabric _____
Fabric: medium-weight, firmly
woven cotton _____

1. Press seam allowance to the wrong side on both edges to be fagoted together. Place folded edges under the foot, right side up and next to each other, so there is a narrow space between them.

HINT: If you have a fagoting plate or raised seam guide to fit over your feed dogs, use this as the spacer and snug the folded edges against the guide in the plate to create the narrow space (Fig. 10.4). If you don't, draw two parallel lines on water-soluble stabilizer $\frac{1}{16}$" (1.5 mm) apart. Pin the folds along the lines. Later, remove the stabilizer.

2. Begin stitching. The needle catches a stitch in the fold on the left, travels across the space, then catches a stitch in the fold at the

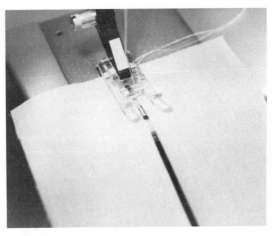

FIG. 10.4 Fagoting with plate or raised seam guide as a spacer.

right. Continue stitching until fagoting is complete (Fig. 10.5).

Rickrack Ladder Fagoting

I was looking for an interesting way to show off the seamlines of a six-gore linen skirt and jacket. I used thread to match the fabric and this closed fagoting technique (Fig. 10.6).

1. Finish raw edges with the 3-step zigzag or double overlock stitch on your conventional machine or the 3-thread overlock on your serger.

Set your sewing machine as follows:

Stitch: rickrack _____
Stitch length: 4–6 plus, or
    elongated _____
Stitch width: 4 _____
Foot: fringe, special marking or
    tacking _____
Needle: #80/11–12 all-purpose _____
Thread: regular sewing or machine
    embroidery top and bobbin _____
Tension: top loosened, bobbin
    normal _____
Fabric suggestion: suit-weight linen _____

2. Place fabric right sides together. Sew at the $\frac{5}{8}''$ (1.5 cm) seamline.

3. From the right side, pull seam open so ladder stitches are seen. For an open ladder, press the seam open. For a closed ladder, press the seam to one side. Decide what's best for the project and location of the fagoting.

Fagoting with Pearl Cotton in the Bobbin

For a heavier, crocheted look, you may prefer this technique. Experiment with the open or tracery decorative stitches on your machine, and make samples for your notebook. In this section you will learn one-step, two-step, and freehand methods of fagoting with pearl cotton in the bobbin. To do this, bypass the bobbin tension (see Reverse Embroidery in Chapter 7), or loosen the bobbin tension

Kathy Sandmann

Springfield, Minnesota

"I learned how to sew differently than most people I know in the industry, because no one in my family sewed. I taught myself and bought my first sewing machine at age eleven or twelve with my baby-sitting money.

"I never used the pattern guide sheet and didn't know anything about grainlines or other pattern markings, so when I ran into trouble, I had no one to ask what to do; I just worked it out."

Kathy went on to major in home economics at the University of Minnesota and has attended numerous sewing classes at various locations around the country. She married Dennis Sandmann in 1973 and didn't work outside the home for ten years so that she could be home with her four children.

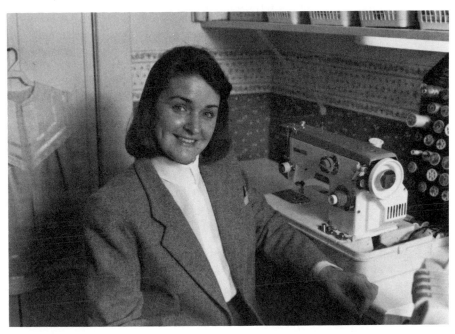

Kathy Sandmann

She was looking for a job she could do anywhere and one with flexible hours. One day she received a newsletter in the mail. It wasn't about sewing, but Kathy thought publishing a sewing newsletter was a good idea. With a lot of encouragement from her husband and a year's worth of market research, she began publishing *The Sewing Sampler,* a monthly newsletter devoted to fashion sewing. Since 1985, the newsletter has enjoyed great success. In January 1988 it was joined by *The Sewing Sampler—Children's Edition,* which is proving to be even more popular.

"The home sewing market has really changed. No longer do most sewers do it out of necessity; those who remain sew for a hobby and don't mind spending money on sewing publications, good fabrics, and supplies."

I asked her if her husband was as involved with the publications now as he was initially. She said he's "great at stuffing newsletters in envelopes, and when I get too far behind, he takes the kids away so I can get my work done. More than anything, he always encouraged me by saying 'Yes, you can do it. Yes. Yes. Yes.' So I did."

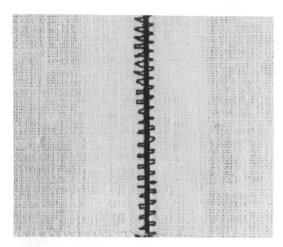

FIG. 10.5 Simple fagoting.

FIG. 10.6 Rickrack ladder fagoting on linen suit.

screw on your experimental bobbin case so the cord pulls through smoothly like regular sewing thread. You may have to increase your top tension slightly. Always stitch samples first to check tensions. Keep your successes for your notebook, noting stitch, width, length, and tension adjustments on each sample.

ONE-STEP METHOD

Follow instructions for Simple Fagoting, but thread your bobbin with embroidery floss, size #5 or #8 pearl cotton.

1. Finish raw edges of seam allowances with the 3-step zigzag or double overlock stitch on your conventional machine or the 3-thread overlock on your serger.

2. Fold seam allowances back and press them to the wrong side. With the wrong sides up and next to each other, guide the fabric so there is a slight space between the folded edges (use the fagoting plate or raised seam guide as a spacer if available for your machine).

3. Guide the fabric so that part of the stitch forms on the left fold, travels across the space, then catches into the right fold (Fig. 10.7). If the cord or floss is too dense, lengthen or elongate the stitch.

TWO-STEP METHOD

To get a wider space between the folded edges, one side of the fagoting is stitched, then the work is turned around and stitched again, so the stitches meet in the space between the fabric. Set your machine as follows:

Stitch suggestions: super stretch,
    loops, couching, scallops   _____
Stitch length: 4–6, elongated, or 4
    stitches per inch   _____
Stitch width: 4–6   _____
Foot: transparent embroidery   _____

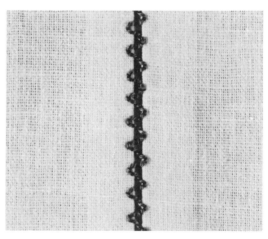

FIG. 10.7 Simple fagoting with pearl cotton in the bobbin.

Needle: #80/11–12 all-purpose ⎯⎯⎯⎯
Thread: top threaded with regular
 sewing or machine embroidery
 thread; bobbin threaded with
 pearl cotton or embroidery floss
 through tension bypass hole, or
 loosen bobbin tension ⎯⎯⎯⎯
Accessories: adding machine tape ⎯⎯⎯⎯

1. Before trying this on your fashion fabric, practice matching the stitch on a scrap. Use regular sewing thread top and bobbin. Some stitches, like the super stretch stitch, can be matched in either direction (Fig. 10.8). Once you have perfected matching, finish the raw edge with the 3-step zigzag or double overlock on the conventional machine or the 3-thread overlock on the serger. Fold the seam allowance to the wrong side and press.

2. Place a strip of adding machine tape under the folded edge. With the wrong side up and from the left, place the fold halfway under the foot so half of the stitch forms on the fabric and half of the stitch forms on the adding machine tape.

3. Turn your work around. With the wrong side up, place folded edge of the second piece of fabric under the foot as before. The needle will stitch on the fabric at the left and swing on the paper over the previous stitching at the right. The paper keeps the stitches uniform (Fig. 10.9).

4. Carefully rip the paper away from the stitching with tweezers. Depending on the stitch used, wet the paper for easy removal.

FREEHAND METHOD

Create your own fagoting by freely moving the fabric under the needle. In this method, I like to use size #8 pearl cotton in the bobbin. Set your machine as follows:

Stitch: straight ⎯⎯⎯⎯
Stitch length: 0 ⎯⎯⎯⎯
Stitch width: 0 ⎯⎯⎯⎯
Foot: none or darning ⎯⎯⎯⎯
Needle: #80/11–12 all-purpose ⎯⎯⎯⎯
Thread: top threaded with regular
 sewing or machine embroidery
 thread, bobbin threaded with
 #8 pearl cotton through tension
 bypass hole or loosened bobbin
 tension ⎯⎯⎯⎯
Pressure: released if possible ⎯⎯⎯⎯
Feed dogs: covered or lowered ⎯⎯⎯⎯
Accessories: tear-away or water-
 soluble stabilizer, water-soluble
 basting thread ⎯⎯⎯⎯

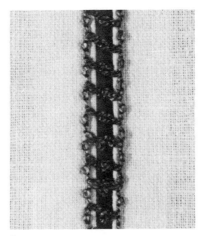
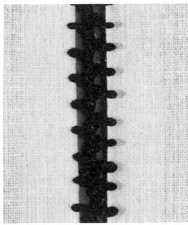

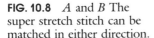

FIG. 10.8 *A* and *B* The super stretch stitch can be matched in either direction.   **A**

B

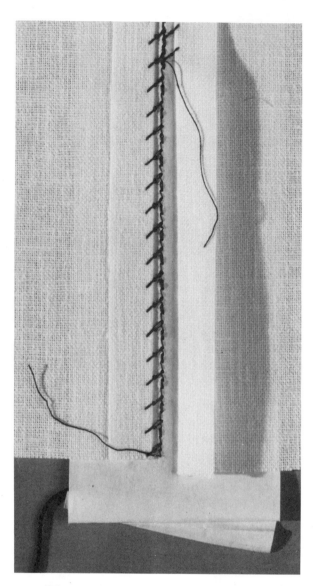

FIG. 10.9 Two-step method fagoting. Stitches are sewn off the fabric onto adding machine tape to keep them uniform.

1. Finish raw edges with the 3-step zigzag or double overlock stitch on your conventional sewing machine or the 3-thread overlock on your serger. Press seam allowances to the wrong side.

2. Cut a strip of stabilizer 1″–2″ (2.5 cm–5 cm) wide and the length of the fabric to be fagoted together. Using water-soluble basting thread, machine baste the stabilizer to the two edges to be fagoted so that the space between the folded edges is the desired distance apart (Fig. 10.10).

3. With the right side down, put the fabric under the needle and lower the presser bar. Take one stitch and bring the bobbin thread up through the fabric and hold it out of the way. Run the machine quickly and move your hands slowly, moving the work from side to side so the needle stitches on one fold, across the stabilizer then to the other fold. One of the easiest freehand designs to make is a series of script letter *L*s. To keep the size uniform, you may want to mark a dot every inch (2.5 cm) or so for a guide (Fig. 10.11).

HINT: Do not mark on the water-soluble stabilizer with a water-soluble marker or the marker may dissolve the stabilizer.

Remove stabilizer after stitching is complete.

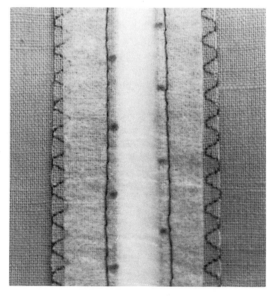

FIG. 10.10 Baste stabilizer to edges so space between folded edges is desired distance apart. Dots every 1″ (2.5cm) or so serve as guides for your design.

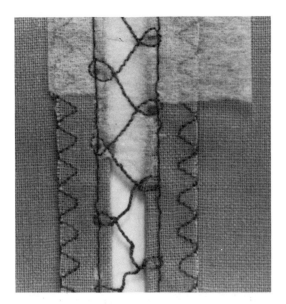

FIG. 10.11 Freehand fagoting.

Fagoting with Your Serger

In researching this technique I couldn't find a fagoting method I liked. I tried serging two pieces of fabric together with the flatlock stitch so part of the stitch formed off the fabric. I ended up with uneven stitches and very little space between the fabric strips. Then I tried the same method but put adding machine tape under the work. The stitches formed well over the paper to put space between the fabric strips, but the paper was difficult to tear away. The fagoting also had too many threads in it. So rather than paper, I incorporated a piece of contrasting ribbon or fabric into the seam, which fills the space between the fagoting and is stiff enough to keep the space between the fabric strips uniform. Make a sample of this for your notebook, and write the tension settings and stitch length on the sample for future use.

Set your serger as follows:

Stitch: 3-thread flatlock   ———
Stitch length: 2–3   ———
Stitch width: 4–5   ———

Left needle tension: very loose   ———
Upper looper tension: loose   ———
Lower looper tension: very tight   ———
Needle plate: 5 mm   ———
Accessories: $\frac{3}{8}$"–$\frac{1}{2}$" ((1 cm–1.3 cm)
  ribbon to contrast with fabric   ———

1. Finish raw edges, using the 3-step zigzag or double overlock stitch on your conventional sewing machine or the 3-thread overlock stitch on your serger. Press seam allowances to the wrong side.

2. Place right sides of fabric to be fagoted together, so folded edges are even. Place ribbon under both pieces of fabric so about $\frac{1}{4}$" (6 mm) of ribbon is exposed to the right of the folded edges.

3. Place fabric and ribbon under the foot so the needle stitches through the folded edges and the flatlock stitches form over the edge of the ribbon (Fig. 10.12). Serge slowly to guide evenly.

4. Pull fagoting open as for a flatlock seam and press. The ribbon becomes the back-

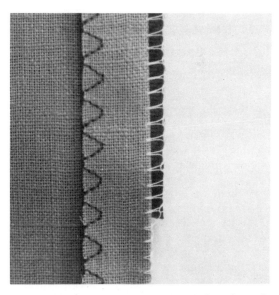

FIG. 10.12 Place work so needle stitches through folded edges, and stitches form over edge of ribbon.

FIG. 10.13 Fagoting by serger.

ground for the ladder stitches. Try this method on sleeve cuffs, pocket tops, or down a sleeve. It's fast, easy, and colorful (Fig. 10.13).

HEMSTITCHING

What Is Hemstitching?

Hemstitching has long been used to decorate borders and ends of fabric. From the turn of the century until recently, hemstitching has been used to stitch hems on fine linens by hand. Now we can simulate many of the techniques by machine with the use of a large needle, fine darning thread, and the hemstitches available on most sewing machines.

Fifteen years ago, I went to Europe and learned the fine points of hemstitching by machine. When I mentioned hemstitching in this country at the time, however, everyone thought I was referring to conventional hemming techniques. Because of the popularity of French hand sewing by machine (also called machine heirloom techniques), which incorporates hemstitching techniques on clothing, most people now understand the difference.

Jan
Saunders

Columbus, Ohio

"I started sewing as soon as I could hold a needle and thread. I've always loved it and mark significant events in my life around the craft. For instance, for my seventh Christmas I got my own sewing basket chock-full of embroidery floss, needles, a thimble (which my grandmother insisted I learn how to use, and I still do today), stenciled pillowcases, and fabric scraps. I finally had a place to stash all the doll clothes I was making.

"The next significant day was my tenth birthday, when part of my present was the privilege of using the sewing machine. I'll never forget Mom over one shoulder, Dad over the other, both trying to tell me how to sew straight.

"In college, three of my sorority sisters talked with me about how oblivious I was to everything around me when I was sewing. They felt for my own good I should be told so I could be aware of my obsession.

"For my twenty-first birthday Mom found me an old boat-shuttle treadle machine that

Jan Saunders

still worked. I can't tell you about the other gifts received on those occasions, but by then, I knew I wanted to make a living doing something in the home sewing field.

"I've worked for a major sewing machine company, a large fabric chain, and have traveled the country giving seminars to the loveliest people in the world, home sewers. After five years of writing, editing, and believing in the information I taught folks at my seminars, *Speed Sewing: 103 Sewing Machine Shortcuts* was published in 1980, became a book club selection, and launched me on a writing career.

"Since then, I have given more seminars to promote the book, written articles for numerous home sewing publications,

become a contributing author for Simplicity's *Simply the Best Sewing Book,* and met Robbie Fanning by proposing this book to her. That proposal led to two more co-authorships with Jackie Dodson for *Know Your Viking* and *Know Your White* (Chilton 1988, 1989).

"My husband, John Moser, is the man behind the camera, my best cheerleader and critic. We're expecting our first child this year, which is why you see me hiding behind the cutting table in the photo.

"I love to sew and will do almost anything to motivate others to love it as much as I do. I hope in reading this book you will get that shot in the arm we all need from time to time, so that you will continue sewing, experimenting, and growing with the craft."

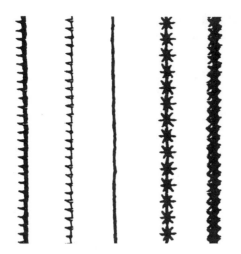

FIG. 10.14 Common hemstitches. *Left to right*: Point de Paris, picot, elastic straight stitch, daisy, Venetian hem stitch.

The most common hemstitches are identified in Fig. 10.14. What makes hemstitches unique is the number of times the needle stitches in and out of the same hole before the stitch pattern is complete. The needle acts like an awl, opening the fibers in the fabric, while the fine thread stitches and binds the hole open. The beauty is the texture created by the holes in the fabric.

If you don't have hemstitches available on your machine, you can create a hemstitch look using the straight stitch or zigzag. However, you must stitch through the holes again, or they will close around the stitch after cleaning or washing. The hole created by the wing needle is large enough for a small crochet hook to fit through. If you can crochet, keep the holes open by using them as a base, and crochet or tat off the edge.

Hemstitching Supplies

Fabrics I like best for hemstitching are firmly woven, all natural fabrics such as linen, handkerchief linen, organdy, and organza. Translucent sheers can be layered and stitched, then one or more layers trimmed away to create subtle color and shade changes.

The thread I like best is 100 percent cotton darning or hemstitching thread. It comes in white or black and two sizes, #70 and #100. Either works well. For colors, I like DMC size #50 machine-embroidery thread. It's a little heavier than darning thread, but works well for less intricate hemstitches.

I use either a wing needle (one size available) or a size #120/20 conventional sewing machine needle for hemstitching. Either needle pokes a hole by spreading the fibers apart in the fabric. For fragile fabrics such as batiste or silk organza, I prefer the size #120/20 needle because it won't tear the fibers as the wing needle sometimes will. For other interesting hemstitched effects and for creating my own entredeux, I like the double wing needle. It has a conventional needle on one side and a wing needle on the other.

To make your own entredeux, cut a strip of white organdy. Using the elastic stretch stitch, and with your double wing needle threaded with white darning thread, sew a row of stitching down the middle of the organdy strip. Turn the fabric around, and sew a second row of stitching so that the second row tracks in the holes created by the first row. For more information on this technique, see my book *Know Your Viking* (Chilton, 1988).

Here's How

I suggest making a hemstitch sampler of the stitches available on your sewing machine. Even though my machine automatically selects the stitch length and width, I prefer to hemstitch no wider than 3 mm. Otherwise, the stitches look too heavy for the delicate effect. You may prefer to change the width of your hemstitches, too. Record stitch settings on the fabric next to each stitch and put the sampler in your notebook. This will save you a lot of trouble next time you hemstitch a hankie, christening gown, or baby bonnet.

Set your machine as follows:

Stitch suggestions: Point de Paris,
  picot stitch, elastic straight stitch,
  daisy, Venetian hemstitch   _____
Stitch length: varies   _____
Stitch width: 2–3   _____
Foot: metal embroidery   _____
Needle: #120/20 or wing   _____
Thread: darning thread top and
  bobbin   _____
Tension: top slightly loose   _____
Fabric: firmly woven linen, organza,
  or organdy   _____
Accessories: spray starch or spray
  sizing   _____

1. Cut two 6" (15 cm) squares of fabric, and place one on top of the other.

2. Sew row after row of hemstitching, on the bias. Try the stitches suggested and other stitches on your machine. Remember to record special settings and tension adjustments for each stitch.

Hemstitching Applications

Rather than turning up and stitching a conventional hem in a linen top, I may hemstitch it as shown in Fig. 10.15. Combine rows of hemstitching with twin needle tucks and/or scallops to create your own hemstitched yardage for collars, cuffs, yokes, or bands.

Combine hemstitches and appliqués to create motifs on collars, dresser scarves, or table linens (Fig. 10.16).

Another way to use hemstitching is to pull weft or filling threads out of the fabric and finish each edge with a hemstitch (Fig. 10.17).

NEEDLEWEAVING

Needleweaving is a technique in which weft or filling threads are pulled from the fabric or canvas and the remaining threads are bound together in an abstract or uniform pattern. Examples of needleweaving have been seen on ancient Egyptian and Coptic embroideries of the sixth century, and elements of the art are incorporated into almost every other culture's embroidery. Ancient embroidery was done by hand, but modern technology has enabled us to simulate the technique by machine.

For your notebook sample, use a loosely woven fabric. Burlap works well. If you are making a linen or linen-blend suit, you may want to try this technique on a pocket or sleeve.

Abstract Needleweaving

1. On a 9" (23 cm) square of fabric, pull weft (crosswise) threads from the middle of the fabric so the open work is about 1" (2.5 cm) wide (Fig. 10.18).

2. Place fabric in a 7" (18 cm) spring hoop, stretching the drawn fiber area in the middle of the hoop. Remember, when you are embroidering on a machine, the right side of the fabric looks as if it is in the hoop upside down.

3. Remove the presser foot and set your machine for freehand embroidery:

FIG. 10.15 Hemstitched hem in linen top.

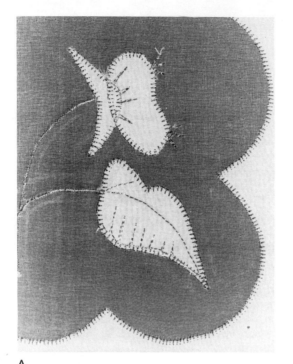

A

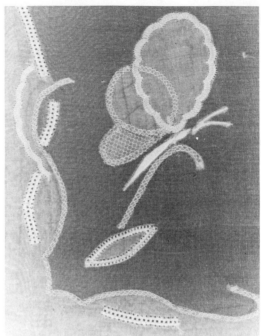

B

FIG. 10.16 *A*, and *B* Hemstitched motifs.

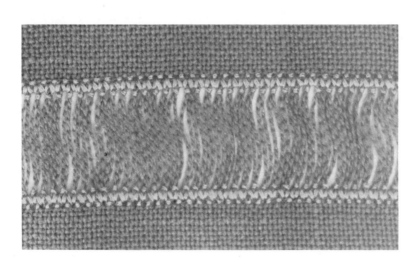

FIG. 10.17 Pull weft threads and hemstitch along both sides.

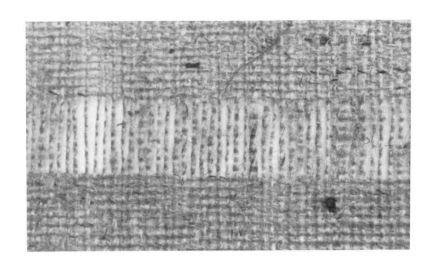

FIG. 10.18 Pull weft threads from middle of fabric.

Stitch: zigzag   ————
Stitch length: 0   ————
Stitch width: 4   ————
Foot: none or darning   ————
Needle: #80/11–12 all-purpose or
    #90/14 stretch   ————
Feed dogs: drop or cover   ————
Pressure: release to 0   ————
Thread: top and bobbin to match
    fabric   ————
Accessories: 7″ (18 cm) spring hoop   ————

4. Place work under the presser foot, and put the presser bar down. Even though you may not have a foot on the machine, the presser bar must be down to engage the upper thread tension. Take one stitch to bring the bobbin thread to the surface of the fabric. Take a couple of locking stitches, and clip thread ends at the fabric.

5. Starting at the top of the drawn fiber area and at one end, zigzag down two or three lengthwise fibers. Move the hoop slowly enough to create a satin stitch. When you get to the bottom of the drawn thread area, move the hoop over while sewing and stitch up, catching two or three lengthwise fibers, and satin stitch over them.

HINT: For more interest and texture, move up and down the lengthwise fibers, first catching one fiber, then two, then moving over to a bar that has already been stitched, in an abstract fashion (Fig. 10.19).

Move the hoop down the drawn fiber area as needed. I like the spring hoop for this technique because you leave the fabric anchored under the needle while releasing and moving the hoop.

6. Once all the lengthwise fibers have been satin stitched, turn the hoop 90 degrees. To finish the top and bottom of the needleweaving, set your machine on the widest zigzag stitch and satin stitch one edge at a time, freehand, guiding the fabric so that half of the stitch forms on the fabric and half of the stitch forms into the needleweaving. Run your machine quickly while moving the fabric slowly and smoothly under the needle. Repeat for the other edge. This cleans up the edge and creates an arch between the bars of needleweaving (Fig. 10.20).

Uniform Needleweaving

If you like more order to your life, you may want more order to your needleweaving, too. In this technique, all the bars are the same width and distance apart. All you do is separate the lengthwise fibers into even groups before satin stitching the bars.

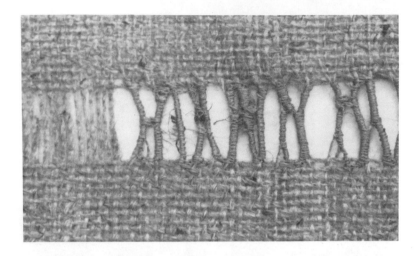

FIG. 10.19 Abstract needleweaving in progress.

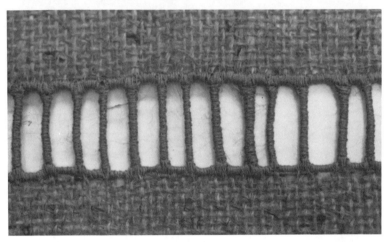

FIG. 10.20 Finish top and bottom with freehand satin stitch.

1. Pull weft (crosswise) fibers out of the middle of a 9″ (23 cm) square of loosely woven fabric as described in step 1 of the preceding instructions.

2. Find the rickrack stitch on your sewing machine. It looks like a zigzag stitch but has three or more stitches in each bar to give the appearance of rickrack trim. Set your machine as follows:

Stitch: rickrack _____
Stitch length: longest or elongated _____
Stitch width: 4–6 _____
Foot: transparent embroidery _____

Needle: #80/11–12 all-purpose or #90/14 stretch _____
Thread: top and bobbin to match fabric _____

3. Place the drawn fiber area under the presser foot so half of the stitch forms on the area where the crosswise fibers have been removed and half of the stitch forms on the fabric. The rickrack stitch organizes the lengthwise fibers into even groups (Fig. 10.21).

HINT: If you want the groupings to be closer together, shorten the stitch length. If you want them farther apart, lengthen the stitch.

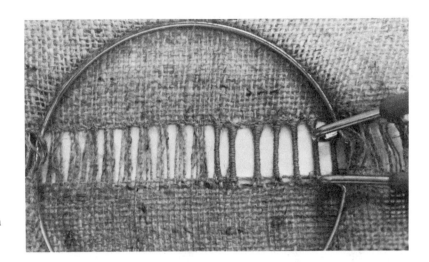

FIG. 10.21 Rickrack stitch divides fibers into even groups.

4. Remove fabric from the machine, and set your machine for freehand embroidery following steps 3 to 6 (Abstract Needleweaving), above.

My most successful needleweaving project was a linen suit. The cuffs, collar, and skirt were brown; the body of the jacket, off-white. The cuffs and collar were needlewoven so the off-white showed through the brown bars. If you choose to making a suit or jacket like this, the long edge of the collar must be cut on the straight of grain so the needleweaving is positioned evenly from the edge. In Fig. 10.22, the linen burlap pockets are needlewoven at the hem. The seam allowances would have shown if pressed to the inside of the pocket, so I finished the pocket edges with a corded satin stitch.

Corded Satin Stitch

This edge finish is commonly seen on embroidered European table linens. It has a smooth raised appearance, perfect for the pocket edges explained above. Finish around the 9″ (23 cm), needlewoven square and put it in your notebook.

1. Cut pocket, place mat, or table cloth, leaving the seam allowances around the edge intact.

2. Set your machine as follows:

Stitch: zigzag
Stitch length: 2–3, or 9–13 stitches per inch
Stitch width: 3
Foot: transparent embroidery
Needle: #80/11–12 all-purpose
Thread: top and bobbin to match fabric
Accessories: pearl cotton or embroidery floss to match fabric

Cut a strand of pearl cotton or embroidery floss four times the length needed to cover pocket edges. Starting $\frac{5}{8}$″ (1.5 cm) from raw edge, place needle in the fabric, leaving the foot up. Double the strand of pearl cotton or floss, then double it again, looping it around the needle so that you will sew over four strands. Put the foot down.

3. Couch over the four strands of pearl cotton or floss, sewing $\frac{5}{8}$″ (1.5 cm) from raw edge. Stitch a gentle curve at the corner (Fig. 10.23).

4. With a sharp pair of scissors, trim the seam allowance up to the stitches without cutting them. Using the same presser foot, set your machine for a wide satin stitch [stitch length 0.5 (fine setting), stitch width 4–5]. Place presser foot so the needle zigs on the fabric and over the cord on the left and zags slightly off the edge on the right. Satin stitch

149

FIG. 10.22 Linen burlap suit with needleweaving on pockets.

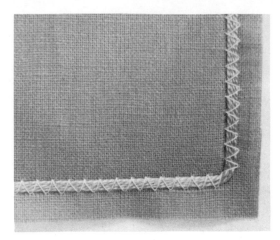

FIG. 10.23 Couch over four strands of pearl cotton.

stitching, so 2″ (5 cm) of cord is behind the foot. Put the foot down and couch over cord so the needle catches into the edge on the left and swings off the edge, over the cord, on the right. Work the extra length of cord to the wrong side of edge finish.

6. Repeat and cord the inside of the satin stitched edge.

7. To attach the pocket to the jacket, I stitched-in-the-ditch along the inside row of cording using thread matching the fabric (Fig. 10.25).

around the corded edge. When you get to the corner, use the inside of the corner as a pivot point and allow the satin stitches to flair out from the corner (Fig. 10.24).

5. Reset your machine for a longer, narrower zigzag [stitch length 2 (13 stitches per inch), stitch width 2]. Again, at the outside of satin-stitched edge, put the needle in the edge of the satin stitch, leaving the presser foot up. Cut a length of pearl cotton or floss the length of the pocket edge plus 4″–5″ (10 cm–12.5 cm). Place length of pearl cotton or floss along the outside edge of the satin

FIG. 10.24 Use inside corner as a pivot point so stitches flair out from the corner.

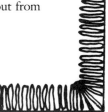

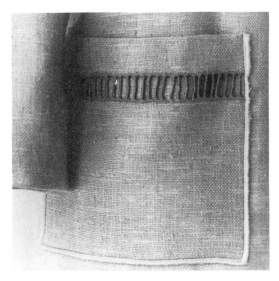

FIG. 10.25 Stitch pocket to jacket front along inside row of cording.

The techniques in this chapter are decorative but not time-consuming when used on a small part of a suit, such as a pocket, collar, or cuff. Take a little time planning something special for your next project. Then collect the compliments.

Next, we'll look at professional hemming techniques stitched on the conventional machine and serger.

SUPPLY LIST FOR CHAPTER 11

- Seams Great™
- Blind hem foot to fit your machine
- Pearl cotton
- 6″ (15 cm) knit, woven, and sheer fabric squares
- Elastic thread
- Easy-Knit tape

Chapter **11**

Hemming

Even though I'm usually hemming some-thing at the last minute, I don't take short-cuts in measuring, marking, or stitching. A poorly sewn hem reeks of "homemade." I just hem faster and more professionally, using the techniques in this chapter.

First we'll look at the traditional Hong Kong hem finish. It's more time-consuming than machine hemming techniques, but is beautiful on fine tailored clothing.

Next we'll look at a great way to ease in a full hemline without having to run a row of hand-basting, or worse yet, pleat or tuck in the fullness so the hem fits the shape of the skirt. Then we'll look at some practical and decorative hemming techniques for wovens and knits. Finally, we'll look at hemming al-ternatives on your serger, from serged blind hems to narrow rolled hems.

HONG KONG FINISH

This couture finish, recommended for heavy fabrics, is generally used on underlined gar-ments as a way to finish the seams by binding the raw edges of the underlining and fashion fabric together. The Hong Kong finish is also a popular hem finish. You can cut 1″ (2.5 cm) bias from the underlining or lining fabric for the binding, but it's easier to use a product called Seams Great.

Seams Great is a $\frac{5}{8}''$ (1.5 cm) strip of sheer tricot, cut on the bias. When stretched, the edges curl in, over the edge of the fabric. It doesn't fray, ravel, or run and is lightweight enough that it won't create unnecessary bulk. You can even use it around curves.

To use it, pull gently to determine which way it curls. Both edges will curl to the center of the strip. Center the raw edge of the fashion fabric in the curl of Seams Great. Straight stitch (stitch length appropriate for the fabric, transparent embroidery foot) $\frac{1}{8}''$ (3 mm) from raw edge. Because it automatically curls over the raw edge, both sides of the strip are stitched at once (Fig. 11.1).

To finish a hem where Seams Great has been attached, secure the hem with a hand blind hemming stitch (Fig. 11.2).

FIG. 11.1 Seams Great curls over raw edge so both sides are stitched at once.

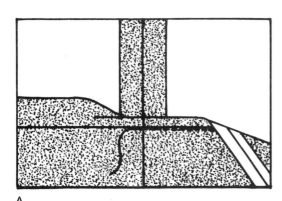

A

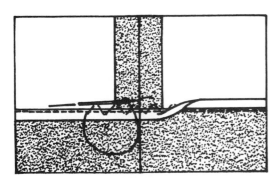

B

FIG. 11.2 *A* and *B* Secure Hong Kong hem finish with a hand blind hemming stitch.

STAY-STITCHING PLUS

Have you tried to stitch a 2″ (5 cm) hem on a circle or full A-line skirt? I used to pinch tucks in the hem allowance every so often, to take up the fullness. Often after the hem was pressed, the tucks pressed through to the right side of the fabric, and the hem appeared to have little points at the folded edge. Inevitably, someone would ask if I had made the skirt. I got tired of being humiliated, so I stopped making circle and full A-line skirts—until I learned a technique from the Bishop method, called "stay-stitching plus."

1. Let the garment hang overnight so an even hem can be marked. Have a friend or family member measure and mark the hem. Remember to wear the undergarments and shoes you plan to wear with the garment.

2. Measure hem allowance to desired depth. I don't like to use hem tape or lace because it creates unnecessary bulk. Therefore, I finish hem edges using the 3-step zigzag or double overlock stitch on the conventional machine or the 3-thread overlock on my serger. If you plan to finish your full hem edge with the serger, skip to Stay-Stitch Plus Instructions for Sergers, below.

Set your machine as follows:

Stitch: straight   _____
Stitch length: 2–3, or 10–12 stitches
    per inch   _____
Stitch width: 0   _____
Foot: transparent embroidery or
    standard zigzag   _____
Needle: #70/9 or #80/11–12 all-
    purpose   _____

Starting ¼″ (6 mm) from finished edge, place the index finger of your left hand behind the presser foot and hold the fabric very firmly. Begin stitching, holding the fabric so it bunches up behind the foot.

3. Hold the fabric as long as you can, release it, stop sewing, reposition your index finger behind the foot, and stitch again, holding the fabric firmly behind the foot.

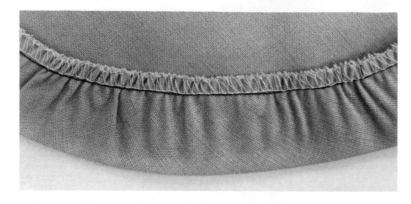

FIG. 11.3 Stay-stitch plus by holding fabric firmly behind the foot while sewing. The hem edge eases in and is shaped to fit skirt.

FIG. 11.4 Ease in hem edge with serger by tightening needle tension(s).

4. Repeat until you have stitched around the hem edge. Because you are holding the fabric behind the foot, the fabric eases in, so the hem allowance can be shaped into the skirt (Fig. 11.3).

Stay-Stitching Plus Instructions for Sergers

Set your serger as follows:

Stitch: 3-thread or 3/4-thread
   overlock   _____
Stitch length: 3   _____
Stitch width: 4–5   _____
Left needle tension: tight   _____
Right needle tension: tight _____
Upper looper tension: normal _____
Lower looper tension: normal _____
Needle plate: 5 mm   _____

1. Leave about a 5″ (12.5 cm) thread chain to start. Place fabric under foot so knives will not cut the fabric. Serge around hem edge. If more ease is needed, tighten needle tension(s). For less ease, loosen needle tension(s) (Fig. 11.4).

2. When you come around to where you started, hold the beginning end of the chain out of the way so it will not be cut off. End by chaining off another 5″ (12.5 cm) and without crossing stitches. This way, the ease can be adjusted by pulling the needle thread(s) on either end of the chain.

MACHINE BLIND HEMMING

There are two blind hem stitches—one for wovens, one for knits. They resemble each other; however, the stretch blind hem stitch

FIG. 11.5 *Left*, stretch blind hem stitch; *right*, blind hem stitch.

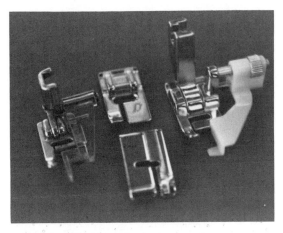

FIG. 11.6 Blind hem feet.

has one large zigzag followed by two or three smaller zigzag stitches (Fig. 11.5). The extra zigzags enable the stitch to stretch with the fabric.

Most conventional sewing machines made in the last 15 years have a built-in blind hem stitch. But if you're like a lot of people, you may not have used it because the stitch catches too much fabric and shows. A few tricks to an invisible blind hem work on both knit and woven fabrics.

First, use the blind hem foot designed for your machine (Fig. 11.6). The foot has a blade or groove under it, so when the hem is folded for stitching, the foot rides next to the fold to insure easy guiding.

Use a fine needle and fine thread for blind hemming. I use a #60/8 or #70/9 all-purpose needle and size #50 machine embroidery thread. A finer needle and thread will pick up less fabric for less visible results.

Use a blind hem stitch no wider than a 2 stitch width. The stitch should be just wide enough to catch a thread in the fold of the fabric.

Finally, loosen the upper tension slightly.

Depending on the weight and hand of the fabric I sometimes loosen or bypass the bobbin tension as well. The finer the fabric, the looser my tensions. To stitch a blind hem, set your sewing machine as follows:

Stitch: blind hem or stretch blind hem _____
Stitch length: 2, or 12 stitches per inch _____
Stitch width: 1–2 _____
Foot: blind hem _____
Needle: #60/8 or #70/9 all-purpose _____
Thread: #50 machine embroidery, one shade darker than fashion fabric _____
Tension: top loosened slightly, bobbin loosened or bypassed (optional) _____

1. Fold hem up desired amount. Pin hem so pins are perpendicular to hem edge and so the point of the pin enters the fabric $\frac{1}{4}''$ (6 mm) down from finished edge (Fig. 11.7). Press hem without pressing over pins.

HINT: On certain fabrics (e.g., wool or synthetic crepe or flannel) remove pins and put a strip of adding machine tape under hem edge before pressing to prevent a ridge from pressing through to the right side.

2. Fold hem to the outside of the garment, folding hem back to where the pins enter the fabric (Fig. 11.8). Place the fold under the foot so the body of the garment is to the left and the ¼″ (6 mm) extension is to the right of the needle.

3. Begin blind hemming. The needle takes a few straight or small zigzag stitches on the extension, then bites into the fold at the left of the needle, picking up a thread or two.

With a little practice, you will never stitch a hem by hand again.

4. Top press hem with steam, as follows.

With the Press
Place hem wrong side up so the finished edge is even with the front of the board and the body of the garment is in your lap. Using steam setting or a damp press cloth, press around hem until all moisture has evaporated from the fabric.

With the Hand Iron
Place garment right side up on the ironing board. Set iron for steam setting. Press entire skirt or garment, including the hem, following the lengthwise grain. Press until fabric is dry.

HINT: For a sharp crease, hold steam iron 2″ (5 cm) above hem edge so steam penetrates the fabric. Then press clapper over hem edge.

SHELL TUCKING

Shell tucking is commonly found on lingerie and children's clothing. It can also be used to decorate the hem of a skirt lining (see Hem Finishes in Chapter 8) or to trim a neck edge on a tank top or camisole. To shell tuck with the blind hem stitch, you must feed the fabric under the foot so the bulk is to the right. On smaller pieces, this is not a problem, but if you are shell tucking the bottom of a nightgown, it is cumbersome. Therefore, most conventional sewing machines have a reverse blind hem stitch available or a mirror image feature

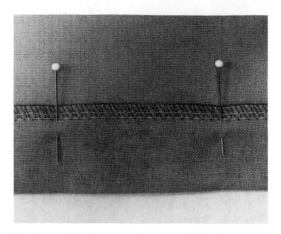

FIG. 11.7   Pin hem so pin enters fabric ¼″ (6mm) from finished edge.

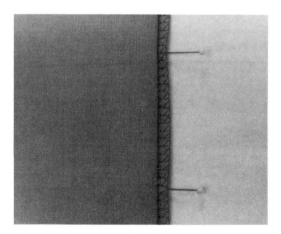

FIG. 11.8   Fold hem to outside and back to where pins enter fabric.

that turns the stitch over so the fabric can be fed with the bulk to the left.

Set your machine as follows:

Stitch: reverse blind hem   ———
Stitch length: 1.5–2, or 12–15 stitches
    per inch   ———
Stitch width: widest   ———
Foot: transparent embroidery or
    standard zigzag   ———

Claire Shaeffer

Palm Springs, California

"I've been sewing so long that I don't remember learning to sew. My mother and grandmother sewed for me out of necessity because I was a very skinny child; later I started sewing for myself.

"I wanted to be a professional dancer, but my parents didn't know this until it was time to go to college. My specialty was acrobatics, so I decided to go to Florida State and join the circus. Unfortunately, there wasn't a circus to join, so I majored in costume design until I quit school and got married."

From there, Claire helped put her husband through medical school, went back to school and got an associate degree in industrial sewing and fashion design and an undergraduate degree in art history. What does art history have to do with sewing? Claire says she enjoys studying the history of garments and how they were constructed.

Besides writing articles for *Woman's Day, Threads, Sew News,* and many other periodicals, Claire has written seven books, including *Sew a Beautiful Gift, The Complete Book of Sewing Shortcuts,* and *Claire Shaeffer's Sewing SOS.* Her latest book, *Claire Shaeffer's Fabric Sewing Guide,* was published by Chilton in the spring of 1989.

Claire teaches all levels of garment construction and fashion design at the College of the Desert. She also teaches

Claire Shaeffer

couture techniques in the summer program at Eastern Michigan University. Her philosophy in teaching sewing is to teach students how to think through a garment, rather than being a slave to the pattern instruction sheet.

The mother of two grown sons, this talented woman lives in Palm Springs, California, with her husband and two Labrador retrievers. She is also active in local philanthropic organizations.

Needle: #70/9 or #80/11–12 all-purpose   _____

Accessories: #5 or #8 pearl cotton to make a corded shell tuck (optional)   _____

Fabric suggestions: nylon tricot, T-shirt interlock knit, or lightweight silk or lining fabric   _____

1. Turn hem up desired amount, pin, and press. Do not press over pins.

2. Feed folded edge under the presser foot, so the needle stitches into the fabric at the left and swings completely off the edge at the right.

HINT: If the needle hits the folded edge, you may skip a stitch, so move the fabric over until the needle stitches completely off the edge.

3. For another decorative treatment, lay a strand of pearl cotton to the right, against the fold. Stitch so the needle couches over the cord (Fig. 11.9).

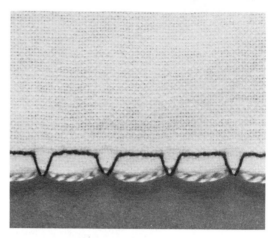

FIG. 11.9 Corded shell tuck.

STRAIGHT SINGLE-NEEDLE HEMS

This technique was discovered by Karyl Garbow from Los Angeles when she took a class from a clothing manufacturer. It's fast, easy, very durable, and looks as if the hem has been knitted into the fabric on extremely stretchy sweater knits.

The trick is using elastic thread in the bobbin. To do this, put the bobbin on your bobbin winder. Anchor the elastic thread to the bobbin; then as the bobbin turns, gently guide the elastic thread onto the bobbin by hand *without* stretching it. If your machine winds the bobbin in the machine, through the needle, wind the bobbin by hand without stretching the elastic thread. Thread elastic thread through the tension bypass hole, if you have one on your machine. Otherwise, use the experimental bobbin case and loosen the bobbin tension so the elastic thread has hardly any tension on it.

Set your machine as follows:

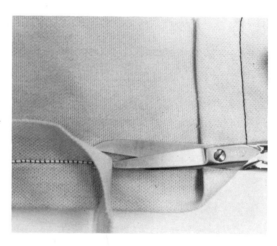

FIG. 11.10 Carefully trim excess hem allowance.

Stitch: straight   _____

Stitch length: 2.5–3.5, or 8–12 stitches per inch   _____

Stitch width: 0   _____

Tension: normal or tighten slightly   _____

Foot: transparent embroidery   _____

Needle: #80/11–12 all-purpose   _____

Thread: elastic thread in bobbin, cotton-wrapped polyester to match fabric in top   _____

Fabric suggestions: sweater knits, stretch terry cloth, velour, some jerseys

1. Turn hem up desired amount, pin, and press. Do not press over pins.

2. Place fabric under presser foot, right side up, so presser foot is resting on a double layer of fabric.

3. Stitch around hem desired amount from the hem edge. Pull threads to the back and tie them off. Carefully trim excess hem allowance up to the stitch (Fig. 11.10).

TWIN-NEEDLE HEMS

Straight Twin-needle Hems

When you bought your machine, did you get a twin or double needle in the box of accessories? Have you ever used it? One of my favorite sewing discoveries is what can be done with twin needles. Not only can you sew two parallel rows of straight or decorative stitching simultaneously; you can also hem, tuck, and smock with them. In this section, we will concentrate on hemming techniques.

Twin needles come in a range of sizes from 1.6/70(9) to 4.0/100(16). The first number indicates the distance between the needles (in millimeters); the second number indicates the size of the needle. The higher the first number, the farther apart the needles. I use the narrower needles for pin tucking and twin needle hems (Fig. 11.11). The 4.0/100(16) twin needle is great for stitching two parallel rows of topstitching approximately $\frac{1}{4}$" (6 mm) apart.

To insert the needles in your machine, the flat side of the twin needle shank is to the back. For this reason, twin needles are used in front- and top-loading bobbin machines only. In side-loading bobbin machines, the flat side of the needle is positioned to the right, so twin needles would be sitting in the machine sideways. Therefore, they cannot be used.

The easiest way to hem knits is with twin

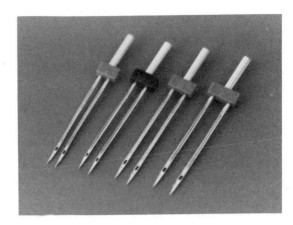

FIG. 11.11 Twin needles.

needles. There are two top threads and one bobbin thread, which causes the bobbin thread to zigzag. The resulting stitch provides the extra stretch necessary for knit hems. On lightweight fabrics, the zigzag stitch created by the bobbin thread pulls a tuck or ridge in the fabric. For a more pronounced tuck, tighten the upper tension; for a flat topstitch, loosen the upper tension.

Set your machine as follows:

Stitch: straight
Stitch length: 3, or 9 stitches per inch (or appropriate for the fabric)
Stitch width: 0
Foot: transparent embroidery (for medium and heavy fabrics) or standard zigzag (for lightweights and sheers)
Needle: 2.0/80(12) twin needle
Thread: to match fabric
Suggested fabrics: T-shirt knits, cotton or wool jersey, stretch terry cloth, velour

1. Fold hem up desired amount. Pin and press without pressing over pins.

2. Place fabric right side up, so the foot rests on a double layer of fabric. You'll find the stitches are more uniform this way.

159

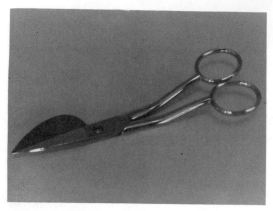

FIG. 11.12 Gingher's appliqué scissors.

FIG. 11.13 Shadow work done with twin needles on sheer fabric.

3. Begin sewing. If the fabric waves out of shape, lengthen the stitch. If the fabric puckers, shorten the stitch length.

4. Pull threads to the back and tie them off. Carefully trim away excess hem allowance up to the line of stitching.

HINT: The best tool for trimming away excess hem allowance is Gingher's appliqué scissors (Fig. 11.12). The pelican-shaped blade protects the body of the garment, while the sharp, pointed blade cuts away the excess fabric. This way you won't end up with a hole where it doesn't belong.

Decorative Twin-needle Hems

You can also use decorative stitches for a twin-needle hem. My favorite is the open scallop or scallop variation on sheer fabric like organdy or sheer tricot. The bobbin thread shows through the sheer fabric, creating a darker, shaded area between the two rows of stitching (Fig. 11.13). This is sometimes referred to as shadow work. Set your machine as described above; however, you will have to set a stitch width to create a scallop. Because twin needles are wider than a single needle, you won't be able to use the entire width of the stitch or you'll hit the needle plate. So remember to use a narrower width and test it

on a scrap first so that you won't break a needle. Some machines have a twin needle feature that automatically narrows the width of the stitch. Check your instruction manual to see if you have this feature on your machine.

Experiment with the decorative stitches available for your machine and make a stitch sampler for your notebook.

Set your machine as follows:

Stitch: open scallop or scallop
   variation   ———
Stitch length: varies   ———
Stitch width: 2–3   ———
Foot: embroidery or standard
   zigzag   ———
Needle: 2.0/80(12) twin needle   ———
Thread: one shade darker than
   fabric   ———
Fabric: sheer tricot or organdy   ———

1. Fold hem desired amount. Pin and press without pressing over pins.

HINT: If you do not want the twin needles to create a ridge or tuck, loosen the upper tension. If you want the bobbin thread to lie perfectly flat, loosen the bobbin tension or bypass it.

Starting at a side seam, place hem under foot so the foot is resting on a double layer of fabric.

2. Begin stitching. Unless your machine has a pattern-start setting, rarely does the scallop match perfectly at beginning and end. So you may have to "fudge" a little by holding the fabric back or pulling it slightly so the pattern matches.

3. Carefully trim excess hem allowance away up to the line of stitching. If the scallops are deep, I like to trim the fabric out from behind them.

SERGED HEM FINISHES

Blind Hem

Blind hem feet are available for many sergers. Check with your dealer to see if there is a foot available for yours. As with the conventional machine, blind hemming with your serger takes a little practice. But once perfected, it is very fast and professional. I suggest you perfect straight hems on draperies or interior design projects before attempting curved hems.

Set your serger as follows:

2/3-Thread Serger
Stitch: 3-thread overlock _____
Stitch length: 5 _____
Stitch width: 5 _____
Needle tension: very loose _____
Upper looper tension: n/a _____
Lower looper tension: normal _____
Needle plate: 5 mm _____
Foot: blind hem _____

3/4-Thread Serger
Stitch: 3-thread overlock _____
Stitch length: 5 _____
Stitch width: 5 _____
Left needle tension: normal _____
Right needle: remove _____
Upper looper tension: tight _____
Lower looper tension: very loose _____
Needle plate: 5 mm _____
Foot: blind hem _____

3/4/5-Thread Serger
Stitch: 3-thread overlock _____
Stitch length: 5 _____
Stitch width: 5 _____
Chain stitch needle: remove _____
Overlock needle tension: normal _____
Upper looper tension: tight _____
Lower looper tension: loose _____
Needle plate: 5 mm _____
Foot: blind hem _____

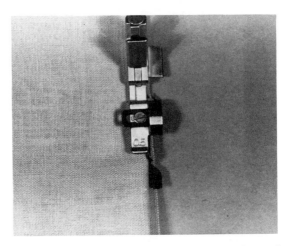

FIG. 11.14 Position hem under blind hem foot of serger leaving a $\frac{1}{4}''$–$\frac{3}{8}''$ (6mm–1cm) extension to the right of the needle.

1. Mark, pin, and press hem without pressing over pins.
2. Fold hem back as for blind hemming on the conventional machine, toward the right side of the garment. Leave a $\frac{1}{4}''$–$\frac{3}{8}''$ (6 mm–1 cm) hem allowance extension to the right of the needle.
3. Place hem under blind hem foot, wrong side up, so the fold is against the guide in the foot (Fig. 11.14).
4. Serge along raw edge so the needle just catches the fold of the fabric.

HINT: Most guides are adjustable. Adjust the guide so the needle catches one or two threads of the fold.

Flatlock Hem

This hemming treatment can be used on knits or wovens and can be used with the loop or ladder side out. If you are hemming wovens, stabilize the underside by pressing a strip of Easy-Knit tape to the wrong side of the seam and straight stitch on either side of the stitch with your conventional machine (Fig. 11.15).

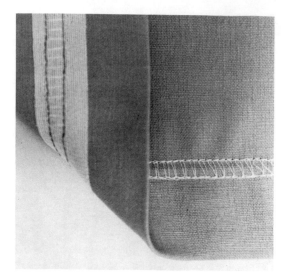

FIG. 11.15 For flatlock hems on wovens, stabilize underside with Easy-Knit tape, then straight stitch on either side.

Set your serger as follows:

2/3-Thread Serger
Stitch: 2-thread flatlock _____
Stitch length: 2–3 _____
Stitch width: 5 _____
Needle tension: very loose _____
Upper looper tension: n/a _____
Lower looper tension: very tight _____
Needle plate: 5 mm _____

3/4-Thread Serger
Stitch: 3-thread flatlock _____
Stitch length: 2–3 _____
Stitch width: 5 _____
Needle tension: very loose _____
Upper looper tension: loose _____
Lower looper tension: very tight _____
Needle plate: 5 mm _____

3/4/5-Thread Serger
Stitch: 3-thread flatlock _____
Stitch length: 2–3 _____
Stitch width: 5 _____

Chain stitch needle: remove _____
Overlock needle tension: very loose _____
Upper looper tension: loose _____
Lower looper tension: very tight _____
Needle plate: 5 mm _____

1. If possible, turn removable cutter or knife to nonworking position. For the loop side of the stitch out, fold a double hem up desired depth. For the ladder side out, fold hem as for a blind hemming, so the raw edge and fold are even.
2. Place hem under foot, garment side up, so the folded edge aligns with the edge of the needle plate or to the left of the removable cutter. Serge.
3. Pull fabric flat to create the flatlock hem. Top press.

Rolled Hem

This fine finish is seen on napkin edges and scarves. I've used it to hem edges of a georgette blouse (Fig. 11.16) and a tricot teddy. I have best results using 100 percent silk thread or woolly nylon on the looper for the 2-thread

FIG. 11.16 Rolled hem on georgette blouse.

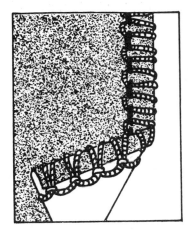

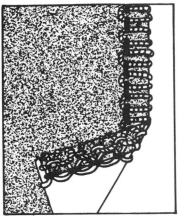

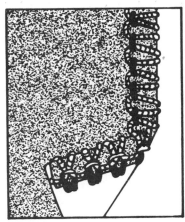

FIG. 11.17 Perfect rolled hem tensions.

FIG. 11.18 If lower looper loops on the underside, loosen upper looper tension and tighten lower looper tension.

FIG. 11.19 If needle thread is seen on the underside, tighten needle tension.

rolled hem and on the upper looper for the 3-thread rolled hem. I've found each serger is slightly different, even sergers of the same brand. Therefore, the settings below are a starting point. Test the settings on a swatch, and record them below and on the swatch for your notebook.

HINT: If you need more tension on the lower looper, loosen tension dial to 0, wrap the thread around the tension dial twice, and set tension for rolled hem. Then remember to unthread and reset lower looper tension for normal serging.

Set your serger as follows:

2/3- or 3/4/5-Thread Serger
Stitch: 2-thread rolled hem   _____
Stitch length: 1   _____
Stitch width: 1   _____
Overlock needle tension: very loose   _____
Lower looper: loose   _____
Needle plate: 2 mm   _____

2/3-, 3/4-, or 3/4/5-Thread Serger
Stitch: 3-thread rolled hem   _____
Stitch length: 1   _____

Stitch width: 1   _____
Overlock needle tension: loose   _____
Upper looper tension: tight   _____
Lower looper tension: very tight   _____
Needle plate: 2 mm   _____

1. Allow a ½" (1.3 cm) hem allowance.

2. Place fabric under foot, right side up, so excess hem allowance is to the right. Serge. Fine-tune tension settings for a perfect rolled hem (Fig. 11.17). If lower looper thread loops on the underside, loosen upper looper tension and tighten lower looper tension (Fig. 11.18). If needle thread is seen on the underside, tighten needle tension (Fig. 11.19).

Narrow Shell Hem

This finish is softer than a rolled hem and can be used on lingerie, skirt linings, silks, and crepe de chines. The fabric rolls and the stitches are farther apart than for a rolled hem, so the edge finish looks similar to a shell tuck made on the conventional machine.

FIG. 11.20 Narrow shell hem done on serger.

1. Allow a $\frac{1}{2}''$ (1.3 cm) hem allowance.

2. Place fabric under foot, right side up, so the hem allowance extends to the right of the needle. Serge (Fig. 11.20).

Your notebook should be bulging with techniques to use on your next project and in projects to come. Try one or all hemming techniques in the chapter to find your favorites.

Chapter 12 will help you with pressing techniques. You will learn how to press everything in your family's wardrobe as well as finished craft and needlework projects.

Set your serger as follows:

Stitch: 3-thread overlock _____

Stitch length: 3–4 _____

Stitch width: 2 _____

Needle tension: normal _____

Upper looper tension: tight _____

Lower looper: very tight _____

Needle plate: 2 mm _____

SUPPLY LIST FOR CHAPTER 12

- Press or hand iron
- Pressing ham
- Sleeve roll or sleeve board
- Press cloths
- Pressing cushions
- Pressing mitt
- Basket full of unpressed clothing

Chapter **12**

The Final Touch

Until recently, many of us have been spoiled by permanent-press clothing. I have friends who even got rid of their irons. But the trend has swung back to fabrics with a high natural fiber content. This means more pressing. So break out the iron and ironing board or your press, your basket of unpressed laundry, and press along with me.

We'll start with a shirt and pants, then press a skirt, dress, and blazer. I like my T-shirts and other knit items pressed, so we'll discover the best method for pressing knits. Finally, we'll press specialty items, from needlepoint to quilt blocks.

I've always been interested in what goes on behind the scenes at a dry cleaner, so I took a tour of two facilities—Colony Cleaners in a suburb of Detroit, Michigan, and Dublin Cleaners in a suburb of Columbus, Ohio. The following are the notes from my field trips.

A DAY AT THE CLEANERS

After cleaning, the dry cleaner first "blows out" the wrinkles with steam. Each garment is put on a specially designed former, the steam jets through the fabric, and the garment is ready for top pressing with a power steam press and finishing with a hand iron. Next to each power press is a hand iron and a sleeve board. Within close proximity is a puff iron to remove button marks and to freshen up ruffles. Commercial presses have steam generated from the bottom, top, or both, and most have a slightly curved board and heating shoe to conform to the curves in each garment. They also have a vacuum that pulls out the excess steam and moisture so clothing will not rewrinkle after pressing.

Because the presses are heated to the same temperature for all fabrics, the amount of pressure and the time the heating shoe is left down are determined by the fiber content. An experienced press operator knows the fiber content of each garment simply by touching it. With crepe or flannel, the press stays closed for about 5 seconds, so the fabric won't shine. For gabardine or an even-weave cotton, the press stays closed considerably longer. Silk, wool, acetate, rayon, and other synthetics are pressed from the wrong side with a steam press, then finished with a hand iron.

Press operators press and iron to finish a garment. As you recall, pressing is an up and down motion with an iron or press, in which steam does most of the work in shaping a garment. Ironing is a sliding motion used to smooth wrinkles.

Shirts are laundered and the starch is put into the shirt prior to pressing. Next, a shirt is dampened, then put on a shirt form. The hard-to-press wrinkles are then blown out with steam. Sleeves are pressed on a sleeve board or flat, and the rest of the shirt is pressed on a power press until it is dry.

Pressing a woman's synthetic, silk, cotton, or cotton-blend blouse is similar to pressing a shirt. However, once it is steam-pressed on a power press, it is turned inside out and finished with a hand iron. First the seams are ironed open or to one side, depending on how the blouse is constructed. Then shoulders, tabs, pocket flaps, collars and ruffles are smoothed with a hand iron, which explains why women's blouses are more expensive to have cleaned or laundered and pressed than men's shirts. After pressing and finishing, the blouse is hung on a hanger, and tissue paper is stuffed in the sleeves to keep the fabric in shape and to prevent crushing. *Note:* Silk or wool is never pressed until dry, but hung, shaped, and allowed to air-dry before the plastic bag is hung over it.

The top of a pair of pants is steamed on a pants form for 45 to 60 seconds to press the waistband and around pockets and the zipper. Pocket linings are ironed by hand. One whole leg at a time is pressed on the power press. The inseam is up and both sides of the leg are pressed to the crotch.

Corduroy pants are handled differently. The top is blown out, then each leg is done in four steps with lots of steam. The press is closed less time for corduroy than for gabardine.

The body of a skirt is top pressed on the power press. Lining is pressed from the wrong side. The waistband and seams are ironed open or to one side with a hand iron.

A blazer is put on a form with sleeve forms and blown out with steam before finishing. It is top pressed like a shirt, with extra care being taken in areas with multiple layers (pockets, pocket flaps, and lapels). Lapels are pressed first on the wrong side, then on the right side. Next, the shoulder is pressed with the lapel folded in place. The heating shoe is brought down lightly, and the area is steamed and brushed. The lapel is unfolded, and the blazer is put on the press like a shirt, right side up, and steam-pressed all the way around. Sleeves are ironed on a sleeve board and collar touched up with a hand iron. A wool blazer is hung on a hanger, sleeves are stuffed with tissue paper, and it is allowed to air-dry before a plastic bag is put over it.

Sweaters are steamed more than pressed. The sweater is laid flat on a power press. Steam shoots up through it; the heating shoe is not brought to the surface. It is patted and brushed with a horsehair drafting brush to prevent crushing. The ribbing is steamed and blocked into shape by hand. The sweater is folded with tissue paper and hung on a hanger like a pair of pants.

Wouldn't it be great to have all this equipment available at home? Unfortunately, most of us don't have this luxury, but we can achieve professional results through proper use of the pressing equipment we do have. Read on, practice with me, and admire your results.

GENERAL PRESSING INFORMATION

Iron with the lengthwise grain. If garment is cut on the bias, press seams open or to one side, and press/iron fabric following the lengthwise grain. *Exception:* If pressing a napped fabric, press with the nap.

If pressing a lot of clothing in one sitting, start with those items requiring lower temperatures, then increase heat as needed for the rest of your pressing.

Dry cleaners put each garment on a form and blow steam through it to eliminate the

Linda
McGehee
Williams

Shreveport, Louisiana

Linda McGehee Williams

Linda has been sewing since third grade. On her birthdays, a friend of the family would give her half-yard pieces of fabric to make doll clothes, "so I didn't have to use my mother's remnants all the time." In college Linda studied home economics, but switched to business because she knew she wanted to "work with sewing, but didn't want to teach in the school system."

She then taught classes and did some custom sewing, but she found she didn't enjoy either. Then she started sewing with suede. After seeing her creations, a friend suggested she teach a class at Shreveport-Bossier Vo-Tech Institute. When the response to her classes was excellent, Linda discovered, "I really enjoyed the teaching . . . I love to show people how to make things.

"One thing just led to another, like a chain reaction. When I taught classes, students started asking me for material and special scissors, so I started bringing some supplies with me to sell. Then I moved the classes to the shop, and we went from making suede outfits to making handbags, belts, cosmetics bags, and even eyeglass cases from scraps and remnants."

Linda's shop, named Ghee's, markets and mail-orders six handbag patterns, suede fabrics, and special notions that turn handmade bags into elegant replicas of expensive purses. You may have seen her ads in *Sew News* or attended one of her seminars at Bernina University, Viking Convention, Theta's School of Sewing, Palmer/Pletsch Creative Serger Workshop, or the American Sewing Guild Convention.

majority of wrinkles before final pressing. Follow the same idea by taking clothing out of the dryer and hanging it up before pressing.

HINT: When I travel, the first thing I do is take all my hanging clothes out of the garment bag. I hang them on the shower rod, turn the shower on the hottest setting and close the door so the bathroom fills with steam. The steam penetrates the fabric and, providing the clothes were well pressed before I packed them, the wrinkles hang out, so that only a light touch-up is necessary.

When using a press and pressing over uneven surfaces (e.g., pockets, pocket flaps, zippers, darts, gathers, etc.), place a pressing cushion under the uneven layers of fabric and press with half pressure. The seam allowances and uneven layers of fabric are absorbed into the cushion, so all wrinkles are pressed out and the fabric around uneven areas is pressed smooth.

Press or iron silk, acetate, rayon, and other synthetics on the wrong side. Cotton and linen are pressed or ironed on the right side. Dark colors are usually pressed or ironed from the wrong side to prevent discoloration and shine. Wool is usually steam-pressed so that some of the moisture is pressed out and the rest evaporates naturally.

Final press parts of a garment on a cushion, ham, or seam roll if these were used during construction, using the appropriate wool or drill side of the pressing tool.

After ironing or pressing a garment, put it on a dress form or hang it on a hanger so that all moisture can evaporate before you wear it.

To remove shine, dampen a sponge with warm water and run it over the shiny area. Lightly top press, using a press cloth.

To remove an overpressed look, hold steam iron $\frac{1}{2}''-1''$ (1.3 cm–2.5 cm) above surface of fabric, allowing steam to penetrate it. Brush up nap with a horsehair drafting brush while steam is still in the fabric.

In the information to follow, I will give you very detailed instructions on how to use a press and a hand iron. Please don't be intimidated by the number of steps it takes to press any given garment. The pressing techniques are designed for efficiency and are patterned after those used by the most experienced press operators. I hope through these words and photographs to help you press faster, better, and more professionally.

In each case, set the press or iron for the appropriate temperature setting. Depending on your equipment and the fiber content of the garment, use a dampened press cloth, the steam setting on your press or iron, or spritz the surface of the fabric or press cloth with warm water.

PRESSING A DRESS SHIRT

With the Press

1. With the body of the shirt to the left side of the press, place both sleeves on the board at the same time. Then remove the top sleeve to the left side.

HINT: The left end of the board is designed to fit the shape of an armhole seam, so place the sleeve on the board following this curve (Fig. 12.1).

Press one sleeve, then pull it toward you, off the board, placing it in front of the press. Put the other sleeve on the board and press.

2. Remove shirt from the press by pulling it off with your left hand at the collar. Let sleeves hang free. Put shirt into the press so collar is to the right, shirt tails are to the left, the body of the shirt is at the back of the press, and the sleeves are straight behind and to the right, so they won't wrinkle (Fig. 12.2).

3. Pull shirt over pressing board, snugging the shoulder up into the right end of the board. Press.

HINT: If there are difficult wrinkles, I pull the collar and shirttails taut on both ends while the press is closed.

4. Pull the shirt to the right and toward you to press the side from the bottom of the armhole to the shirttail, centering the side seam on the board. Press.

HINT: If pressing a tapered shirt, fold a dart at the shirttail to press the taper flat (Fig. 12.3).

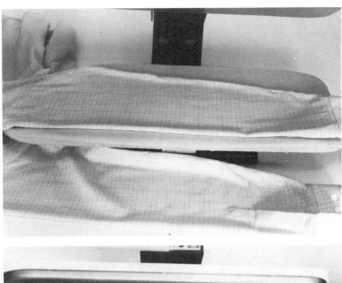

FIG. 12.1 The left end of the board is designed to fit the shape of an armhole seam.

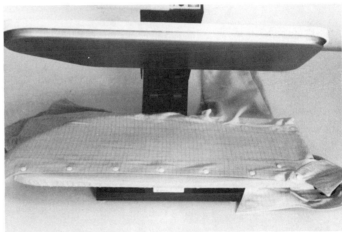

FIG. 12.2 Body of the shirt is at the back of the press, and sleeves are straight behind so they won't wrinkle.

FIG. 12.3 If pressing a tapered shirt, fold a dart at the shirttail to press taper flat.

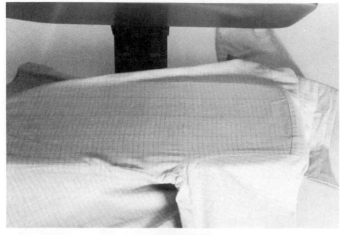

FIG. 12.4 Pull shirt toward you, snugging the back shoulder up to the right end of the board.

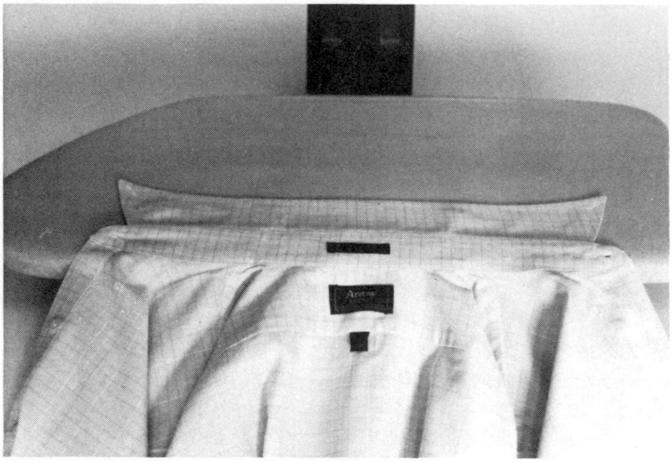

FIG. 12.5 Place collar so neckline seam is even with the edge of the board.

FIG. 12.6 Press cuffs simultaneously.

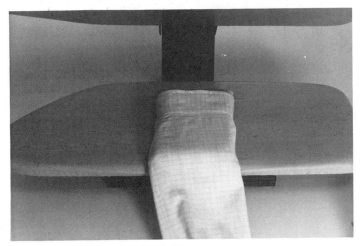

FIG. 12.7 Slide small pressing cushion up to where the pleats begin and press with half pressure.

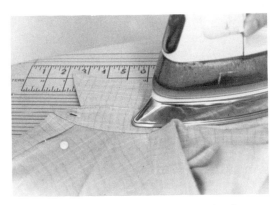

FIG. 12.8 Iron collar on the wrong side, then the right side, from the points in.

5. Pull shirt toward you and to the left, snugging the back shoulder up to the right end of the board (Fig. 12.4). Press.

6. Continue around the rest of the shirt, pulling it toward you, and press.

7. Pull shirt off press. Place collar on the board so collar stand is on press and neckline seam is even with the edge of the board (Fig. 12.5). Press. Remove collar.

8. Press cuffs at the same time by sliding them on the two free ends of the press (Fig. 12.6). Press.

9. Button shirt and press the rest of the shirttail.

10. For a better finish on pleated cuffs, slide the small pressing cushion up to where pleats begin and press with partial pressure (Fig. 12.7). To finish the wristband opening, open cuff and slide it on the right end of the board; press with full pressure. Repeat for other side, using the left end of the board.

With the Hand Iron

For permanent-press fabrics, steam from the hand iron is usually sufficient for touching up a dress shirt. For other fabrics, evenly dampen the shirt or blouse with warm water before ironing. If you are not going to press an item immediately after it has been dampened, roll it up and store in a plastic bag in the refrigerator to prevent mildew.

HINT: An easy way to fill your iron is to pour the distilled water into an old clear plastic ketchup or mustard bottle. I've also filled my iron using a funnel.

1. Iron collar on the wrong side first, from the points in. Repeat, ironing collar on the right side (Fig. 12.8).

2. Next, iron cuffs on the wrong side, then the right side.

3. Fold sleeve on the seamline and iron along the seam first (Fig. 12.9). Then iron

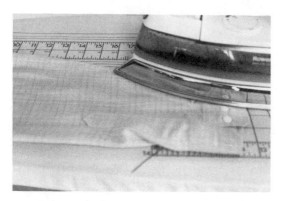

FIG. 12.9   Iron along sleeve seamline first.

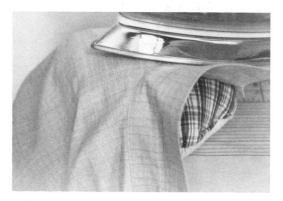

FIG. 12.10   Iron shoulder area, using ham or seam roll.

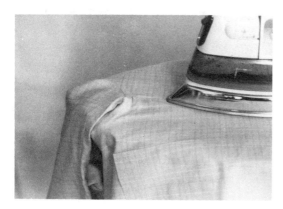

FIG. 12.11   Snug narrow end of board up under the armhole.

out to the fold. For a blouse, iron sleeve on a sleeve board or seam roll to prevent creasing.

4. Iron back and/or front yoke next, following the grainline. Iron shoulder area using appropriate pressing cushion, ham, or seam roll when necessary (Fig. 12.10).

5. Iron wrong side of front tab, then the right side.

6. Place shirt on ironing board to iron the front.

7. With one hand, pull the shirt partially off the board and toward you, centering the side seam in the center of the board. Snug the narrow end of the board up under the armhole (Fig. 12.11). Iron side of shirt, smoothing the side seam and following the lengthwise grain.

8. Pull the shirt toward you, then snug the narrow end up to the collar and press the back in two or three steps. If there is a pleat in the center back, center pleat on the board, pin or hold the pleat in shape, and iron.

9. Finish ironing the other side and front by pulling the shirt toward you, snugging the narrow end of the board up to the underarm or neckline.

10. To press around buttons, press shirt on the wrong side so buttons imbed themselves in the padded surface of the ironing board. Then top press around each button.

PRESSING A BLOUSE

With the Press

Generally, a blouse is pressed/ironed the same way as a shirt, but pressing cushions are used to press and freshen up areas with puffs and gathers.

1. Place blouse on press doubled from the underarm seam to the bottom of the armhole (Fig. 12.12). Press.

2. Press fronts from closure to armholes, using both ends of the board (Fig. 12.13).

3. If there are slight gathers at the shoulder line, slip the small cushion under gathers and press with half pressure (Fig. 12.14).

4. For a yoke with a gathered bodice, slip the small cushion on your hand so that the

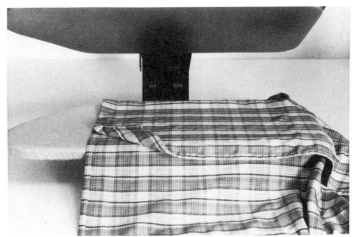

FIG. 12.12 Place blouse on press, doubled from the underarm seam to the bottom of the armhole.

FIG. 12.13 Press fronts from closure to armholes, using both ends of the board.

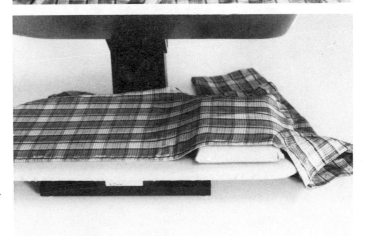

FIG. 12.14 Slip small cushion under gathers at the shoulders or neckline opening and press with half pressure.

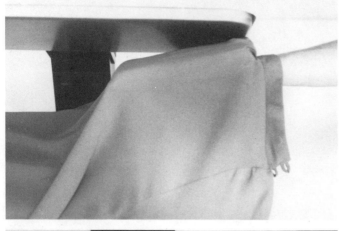

FIG. 12.15 With the cushion over the back of your hand, touch gathers against the heating shoe.

FIG. 12.16 With hand holding cushion inside the sleeve, touch gathers gently against the heating shoe.

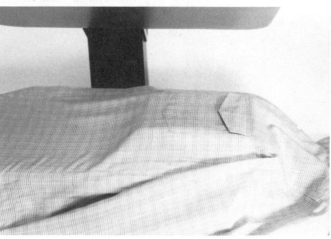

FIG. 12.17 Place small cushion under pocket and flap. Press with half pressure.

cushion is over the back of your hand. Touch the gathers against the heating shoe (Fig. 12.15).

With the Hand Iron

Iron blouse wrong side out. Iron seams open, darts to the appropriate side, then finish in the following sequence: collar, sleeves, shoulders, facings, front, side, back, side, and front.

Sleeves and Pockets

With the Press

1. To press a sleeve gathered at the wrist, button the cuff. Push the long sleeve cushion in the sleeve from the shoulder, snugging it into the gathers at the wrist. Press cushioned gathers by touching them lightly against the heating shoe.

2. To press a puffed sleeve, stuff small cushion into puff, smoothing gathers. Dampen sleeve. With hand inside the sleeve and holding the cushion, touch gathers gently against the heating shoe (Fig. 12.16).

3. To press shirts with patch pockets and/or flaps, place small pressing cushion under pocket, including flap, and press with half pressure (Fig. 12.17). Remove cushion and finish pressing as for a dress shirt.

With the Hand Iron

1. To press a sleeve gathered at the wrist, press the wrong side, then the right side of the cuff. Slip the sleeve over a sleeve board, so cuff is on the narrow end. Hold the cuff taut and lift it slightly with one hand while pushing the point of the iron into the gathers with the other (Fig. 12.18).

2. To press a puffed sleeve, dampen it, and press the sleeve band on the wrong side, then on the right side. Slide it on a sleeve board, and hold one end taut while working the tip of the iron into the gathers on the other. For larger sleeves, stuff pressing mitt into the puff and press.

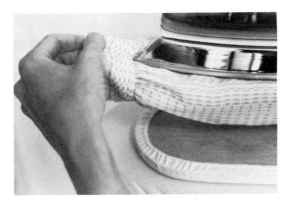

FIG. 12.18 Hold cuff taut and lift it slightly while pushing point of the iron into gathers.

FIG. 12.19 Press puffed sleeve from wrong side, working the curves of puff iron into the gathers.

HINT: If you have a puff iron, press sleeve from the wrong side, working the curves of the puff iron into the gathers (Fig. 12.19 and 12.20).

3. To press shirts with patch pockets and/or flaps, dampen shirt and press flaps first on the wrong side, then on the right side. With flap out of the way, place a pressing pad under and press cloth over the pocket, then press it so the stitching is smooth (Fig. 12.21). If you don't have a pressing pad, place a folded towel under and press cloth over the pocket to press pocket smooth. Iron the rest of the shirt as described above.

FIG. 12.20 Use puff iron to press puffed sleeve.

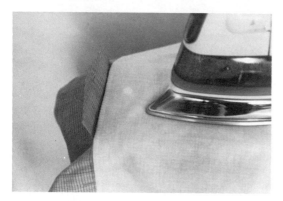

FIG. 12.21 Using a press cloth, press pocket over pressing pad.

PRESSING PANTS

With the Press

For wool and other more delicate fabrics, top press using a press cloth.

1. Press pocket linings flat. Because of the 100 pounds (45 kg) of pressure, you need to press linings only on one side.

2. Place small pressing cushion at the right end of the board. Place waist end of pants over cushion, and dampen fabric or press cloth slightly. Press around waistband and over zipper, bringing the heating shoe down and pressing with half pressure (Fig. 12.22).

3. Press each leg in four steps. Starting with the left leg, place it so the crotch is up and at the left end of the board and the inseam is even with the front of the board (Fig. 12.23). Press.

4. Slide leg down and press from the knee down, again positioning the inseam even with the front of the board.

5. Pull bottom of pants leg toward the back of the press, positioning the inseam even with the back of the board. Press.

6. Grab the leg at the crotch between the index and middle finger of your left hand and flip it over to finish the back half.

7. Start on the back half of the right leg first. Place it so crotch is up, at the right end

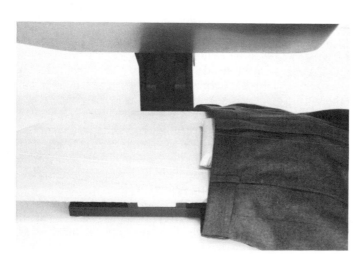

FIG. 12.22 With small pressing cushion underneath, press around waistband and over zipper, using half pressure.

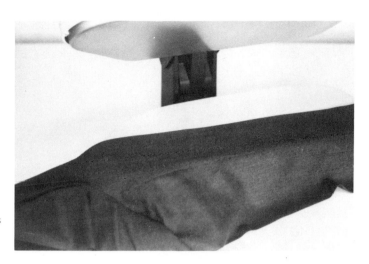

FIG. 12.23 Place left leg so crotch is at the left end and inseam is even with the front of the board.

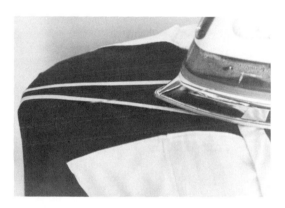

FIG. 12.24 From the wrong side, iron center front and center back seams open.

of the board, and the inseam is even with the front of the board. Press.

8. Slide leg down and press the back leg from the knee down.

9. Pull bottom of pants leg toward the back of the press and press from the knee down.

10. Flip leg over as before and finish pressing right leg.

HINT: For touch-ups, I press front and back creases by pressing pants legs together in the four steps. Position legs so creases are in the center of the board and inseams and outside seams are even with the front of the board.

Press back creases in two steps from the crotch to the hems; repeat for front creases.

For jeans, straighten out inseams and outside seams by folding pant legs in half at the seams. Dampen seam and/or press with steam. While press is closed, pull on either end of the seam to flatten it out. After seams are flattened, press jeans as you would any other pair of pants.

With the Hand Iron
Use a press cloth for top pressing to prevent shine on any fabric.

1. Turn pants to wrong side and iron pocket linings on each side.

2. With the wrong side out, place top of pants over the narrow end of the board and iron the inside of the waistband. Iron center front and center back seams open to the crotch (Fig. 12.24).

3. Press darts or pleats from the waistline down. Close zipper and press zipper area from the wrong side, being careful not to press zipper coil with the iron.

4. Turn pants right side out. Hold pants legs together, matching inseam with outer seam of each leg. Lay pants on ironing board, one leg over the other and press out any bagginess in the knee with steam or dampened press cloth.

177

5. Fold top leg back across the waist and iron under leg from bottom of crotch to hemline. Iron front and back creases. Turn leg over and iron outer leg from crotch down. Again, iron front and back creases. Repeat for other leg.

6. To freshen up a pair of pants, hold pant legs together, matching inseams, outer seams, and creases of each leg. Lay pants on ironing board so one leg is on top of the other. Press creases from crotch to hem on front legs. Repeat for back legs.

PRESSING A SKIRT

When I got my press, I wanted to press everything in my laundry basket with it. Although I wouldn't trade it for anything, I find I also need an iron and ironing board for some items of clothing, one of which is a skirt. I am tall and like longer length skirts. For me, pressing all the way around a long, full skirt with a waistline zipper or elastic waistband is more trouble than it's worth on the press. However, for pressing shorter skirts, children's skirts, straight skirts, wraparounds, or those that button or zip down the front or back, the press is ideal.

With the Press

1. Turn skirt inside out. If the skirt is lined or has pocket linings, press lining inside out. Press seams open or to one side with travel iron. Then position lining on the board so the rest of the skirt is on your lap. Press lining.

2. Turn skirt right side out. Place small pressing cushion on the right end of the board and press around waistline, using half pressure to press darts and tucks and over zipper.

For short, straight skirts or children's skirts, press around the top, and finish the rest of the skirt on the right end of the board (Fig. 12.25).

For a longer, straight skirt, press the kick pleat in two steps, using one end of the board for one side and the other end of the board for the other side of the pleat.

HINT: If kick pleat has two or three layers, press over small pressing cushion using half pressure. Press around the bottom of skirt the width of the kick pleat to the hem. If skirt is lined, pull lining out, then press.

For a wraparound skirt, or one that buttons up the front or back and is unlined, press from the wrong side (Fig. 12.26). If the skirt is lined, top press using a press cloth where necessary. Press the wrong side of waistband first. Then place skirt on board so the waistband is to the right and the bulk of the skirt is behind the board and to the back of the press. Pull skirt toward you, positioning it so the waistline seam is at the right edge of the board. Press. Pull skirt toward you and press again. Continue until skirt is finished.

For short, pleated skirts, open zipper and slip waistline over right end of the board, positioning pleats carefully. Turn skirt around and press the bottom. If necessary, pin pleats down to the padded pressing surface (Fig. 12.27).

For a skirt with a ruffle on the bottom, place ruffle on the left end of the board, so the seam is even with the edge of the board (Fig. 12.28). Dampen ruffle or use steam. Close the press, and gently pull ruffle up so the gathers are pressed open against the edge of the heating shoe.

HINT: To smooth gathers at the seamline, snug gathers up on the left end of heating shoe and pull ruffle from side to side over curve (Fig. 12.29).

With the Hand Iron

Since my day at the dry cleaners, I always press a skirt with a hand iron on the wrong side. It's easier to press and smooth seams, I rarely use a press cloth because I don't worry about shine, and the results are very good. Yes, this is somewhat unorthodox, but it works. The procedure for pressing a skirt with the hand iron is almost the same, regardless of the size or style.

HINT: The following techniques are for woven fabrics only. If pressing a knit, the procedure for laying the garment on the board is the same;

FIG. 12.25 For short, straight skirts, press around top and finish the rest of the skirt on the right end of the board.

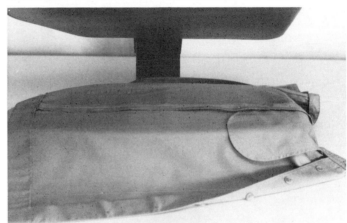

FIG. 12.26 Press skirt from wrong side. Pull skirt toward you and press.

FIG. 12.27 For pleated skirts, pin pleats down to padded pressing surface.

FIG. 12.28 Place ruffle on left end of board, seam even with edge.

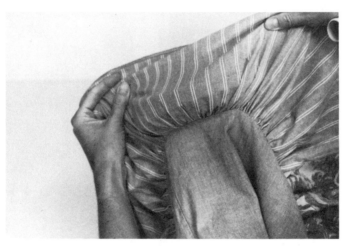

FIG. 12.29 Snug gathers up on left end of heating shoe, and pull ruffle back and forth by hand.

however, the iron must be used in an up and down pressing motion, so you do not distort the fabric.

1. Open zipper or button closure. Turn skirt inside out. Iron the inside, then the outside of waistband flat. If skirt is lined, iron wrong side of lining, smoothing seams open or to one side, depending on how the skirt is made.

2. Iron pocket linings first on one side, then the other.

3. With wrong side out, place skirt so the waistband is on the narrow end of the board.

Iron seams open or to one side, depending on how the skirt is constructed. Iron skirt on the lengthwise grain from hemline to waistline.

For children's skirts, iron from the wrong side, using a sleeve board.

For a longer, straight skirt, top press in two steps. First, place skirt on the board and press top part of kick pleat using steam and/or a dampened press cloth (Fig. 12.30). Next, fold top part of pleat back and press the under pleat (Fig. 12.31). Finish ironing skirt from the wrong side.

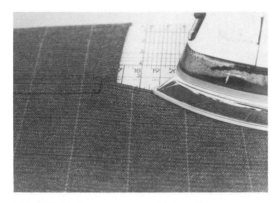

FIG. 12.30 Press top part of pleat first.

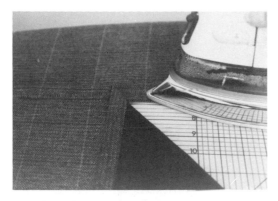

FIG. 12.31 Press under pleat next.

FIG. 12.32 Lift waistband slightly and work the point of the iron into the gathers.

For a wraparound skirt or one that buttons up the front or back and is unlined, iron from the wrong side. If skirt is lined, iron fashion fabric from the wrong side, separately from the lining. Iron pocket linings first on one side, then the other. Place skirt so the waistband is positioned on the narrow end of the board and the majority of the skirt is hanging behind the board. Iron seams open or to one side, and smooth the rest of the skirt on the lengthwise grain, ironing from hemline to waistline. Pull skirt toward you and iron a section at a time until you're finished.

For a pleated skirt with pressed-down pleats, iron seams open or to one side. Iron pocket linings first on one side, then the other. Open zipper and slip waistline over narrow end of the board, right side up. Position pleats carefully, pinning hem edge to the padded ironing board if necessary. Top press the pleats, using a dampened press cloth. Iron on the lengthwise grain from hemline to waistline. Remove pins, reposition skirt on board, pin, and iron again until finished.

For a gathered skirt or ruffle, open zipper and place skirt on board wrong side up, with waistband at the narrow end. Iron seams open or to one side on the lengthwise grain from hemline to waistline. Lift waistband slightly and work point of the iron into the gathers (Fig. 12.32). Then pull skirt toward you, and iron a section at a time until you're finished.

PRESSING A DRESS

I press shirtwaist and T-shirt dresses on my press. Other, more intricately constructed dresses I usually press with a hand iron.

Shirtwaist Dress

With the Press

1. Follow the same procedure for pressing a dress shirt, pressing the sleeves first. For an uncreased sleeve, slide the sleeve cushion into the sleeve so the wider end is to the back. Press with half pressure (Fig. 12.33).

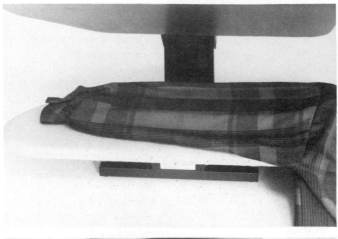

FIG. 12.33 For an uncreased sleeve, slide sleeve cushion into the sleeve so the wider end is to the back; press with half pressure.

FIG. 12.34 Press around the bodice, pulling the fabric toward you.

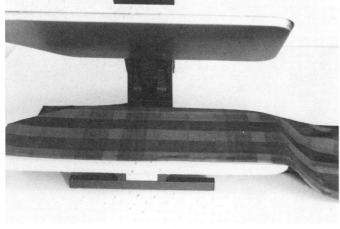

FIG. 12.35 Press the extra length around the bottom to the hemline.

2. Next press the bodice, using the same procedure to position the dress on the press as you do for a dress shirt. Press a section at a time, pulling the fabric toward you (Fig. 12.34).

3. To press the extra length at the bottom, put dress back on board so the pressed area is to the right as shown (Fig. 12.35). Press around the bottom to the hemline.

4. Finish by pressing collar and cuffs as you would when pressing a dress shirt.

With the Hand Iron

1. Using a press cloth, iron collar on the wrong side, then the right side, from the points in. If the collar is contoured, top press over a ham or pressing mitt using a press cloth.

2. Iron sleeves over a seam roll or small end of a sleeve board to avoid creases. Top press shoulder line and sleeve cap over a ham or mitt.

3. On areas with double thicknesses, such as facings, cuffs, front tabs, pockets, bands, and buttonhole areas, press from the wrong side first; then top press over a ham on the right side to avoid pressing in ridges (Fig. 12.36). Remember to press with the grain.

4. Turn dress inside out and iron the bodice so that darts, seams, and tucks are pressed in the same direction they were during construc-

tion. Press and shape the curved areas over a ham or mitt.

5. Press skirt from hemline to waistline following the lengthwise grain.

HINT: For a dress with a zipper, iron zipper area over a seam roll. Top press along each side of zipper with point of iron, using a dampened press cloth. Press again on the wrong side without ironing over zipper coil (it may melt or scratch your iron).

T-shirt Dress

With the Press

1. Place both sleeves on the board at the same time; then remove the top sleeve to the left side (Fig. 12.37). Press one sleeve, pull it off the board toward you, and place it in front of the press. Put other sleeve on board and press.

2. If the dress has a front tab, unbutton it and slip one side on the left end of the board and press (Fig. 12.38).

HINT: To press the tab flat, gently pull on it when the press is closed.

Remove pressed side from the press, place the other side on the right end of the board, and press.

3. If dress has a collar, press it next in two steps, pressing half the collar on one end of

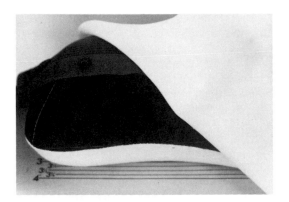

FIG. 12.36 On areas with double thicknesses, iron the wrong side, then top press over a ham on the right side to avoid pressing in ridges.

FIG. 12.37 Place both sleeves on the board at the same time, then remove the top sleeve to the left side.

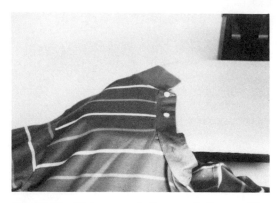

FIG. 12.38 Unbutton tab front and slip one side on the left end of the board and press. Repeat for other side.

FIG. 12.39 Press collar using both ends of the press.

the press and the other half on the other end of the press (Fig. 12.39).

4. Position the dress on the board so the neckline is toward you and the edge of the board is just below the front tab (Fig. 12.40). Press a section, pull the dress toward you, press another section and another, until the dress is pressed to the hemline.

With the Hand Iron

If you have a press and an iron, press knits with the press. Because the press works with-

out the heating shoe moving over the fabric, the fabric does not stretch or become distorted. If you must use a hand iron to press your knits, use an up and down pressing motion.

1. Press collar on the wrong side, then the right side, pressing from the points in. Turn dress inside out and press seams, darts, or tucks open or to one side. Press facings on wrong side, then right side.

2. Unbutton front tab and press it on the wrong side, then right side. Press over ham to prevent ridges. Press shoulders, pressing contours over the ham.

3. Turn dress right side out and press sleeves on a seam roll or sleeve board.

HINT: If I'm in a hurry, I press each sleeve flat on the ironing board, first pressing one side, then the other.

4. Put dress on ironing board so the neckline is at the narrow end. With an up and down pressing motion, press dress with a lot of steam, following the lengthwise grain and doing a section at a time. Let most of the steam evaporate while the dress is on the board. Otherwise, the wrinkles have a tendency to stay in the fabric.

PRESSING A BLAZER

Press a blazer from the right side, being careful not to overpress.

With the Press

1. Place small pressing cushion or mitt in shoulder and press with a series of short touches on the heating shoe.

2. Stuff long sleeve cushion in sleeve, snugging it into the contours of the armhole seam. Press with half pressure (Fig. 12.41). Repeat for other sleeve.

3. Put blazer into the press so collar is to the right, hem edge to the left, the body of the blazer is at the back of the press, and the sleeves are straight behind and to the right so they won't wrinkle (Fig. 12.42).

FIG. 12.40 Position so neckline is toward you and edge of board is just below the front tab.

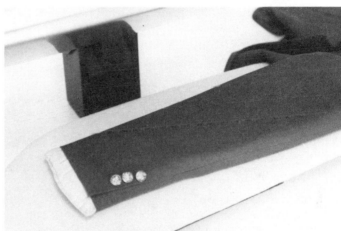

FIG. 12.41 Press sleeve stuffed with sleeve cushion on half pressure.

FIG. 12.42 Place blazer on press so collar is to the right, hem edge to the left, body of blazer is at the back, and sleeves are straight behind and to the right.

4. Pull blazer over pressing board, snugging the shoulder up into the right end of the board. If there are pockets, slip small pressing cushion under them and press with half pressure. Remove cushion and press blazer front with half pressure and steam. If blazer is wool, brush steam away and freshen the nap with a draftsman's brush.

5. Pull blazer to the right and toward you to press the side from the bottom of the armhole to the hem, centering the side seam on the board. Continue around the rest of the blazer, pulling it toward you, and press.

6. Pull blazer off press and press lapel and collar in two steps from the wrong side, as shown (Fig. 12.43). Leave some moisture in the fabric. Hang blazer on a dress form or hanger, and fold the lapel and collar back, shaping them with your hands.

With the Hand Iron

To press a blazer, top press with steam and a press cloth. Notice I said press, not iron. To avoid overpressing, use a lot of steam and let the garment hang and dry completely before wearing.

1. Press sleeves over a seam roll or sleeve board.

HINT: To press the lower hem edge of a sleeve in a blazer or jacket, slip several soft-cover magazines rolled in muslin into the sleeve and let the magazines adjust to the diameter.

2. Top press shoulder, using steam and a press cloth, and pressing over a ham.

3. Place blazer on the ironing board so the collar is at the narrow end and the front is right side up. Press front. If there are pockets, press pockets over a pressing pad or folded towel.

HINT: For a crisp edge where the facing and jacket front join, steam the edge and hold a wooden clapper or your tailor board over the seam to hold in the steam and flatten the edge.

4. Pull blazer toward you, so the narrow end of the board is under the bottom of the armhole seam and press the side. Pull blazer

Nancy Zieman

Beaver Dam, Wisconsin

Nancy Zieman hosts "Sewing with Nancy," the longest running sewing program on cable network television in the country. (It is also shown on public television.) She has produced and hosted 26 hours of "Sewing with Nancy" videos. Her 106-page mail-order catalog, "Nancy's Notons," contains specialty sewing books, notions, videos, and fabrics, reaching over 300,000 home sewers twice a year. Despite all this, she is about the most humble person I know.

Nancy started sewing at age ten through the 4-H program and took all the sewing she could. "Mom was the 4-H leader, so that really helped." She got her B.S. in home

Nancy Zieman

economics from the University of Wisconsin, Stout. After graduation, she gave seminars on pattern fitting and eventually started free-lancing. At the seminars she passed out 8½" × 11" fliers advertising her mail-order notions.

"TV started as a fluke. A local cable producer asked me to be a guest on his sewing program, and I did four segments. It was received well, and he asked if I wanted to do eleven more shows. After the eleventh show, he ran into financial difficuties and asked me if I'd like to produce them myself. I innocently said yes.

"The big break for the program, though, was after the time slot changed to Saturday morning. The working women were home, and everything really turned around."

Her husband quit his job a few years ago and manages the day-to-day business. She has recently built a new facility, employs forty people, and was named the 1988 Entrepreneurial Woman of the Year by the Wisconsin Entrepreneurs Association.

I asked her if she has any siblings who sew and she said, "I have an eighteen-year-old sister. None of her friends sew, but the other day she was talking to my mother and me and said she was going to try the 'S' word. She should have all the help she needs to sew successfully, don't you think?"

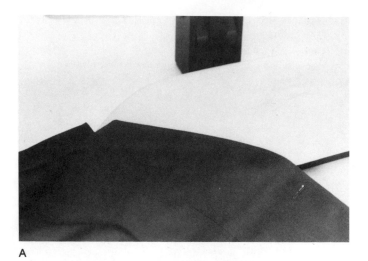

A

B

FIG. 12.43 *A* and *B* Press blazer collar in two steps from the wrong side.

toward you again, so the narrow end snugs up into the back shoulder area, and press. If there is a vent or back pleat, press it in two steps, first pressing the under part of the pleat, folding it under, then pressing the top part of the pleat. Continue to press and pull the blazer toward you until you have pressed around the body.

5. Top press the collar and lapel over a ham using a press cloth. Hang blazer on dress form

or hanger to shape the collar and lapel and to finish drying before wearing.

PRESSING KNITWEAR

Who says knits don't wrinkle? I press every knit garment I wear. It looks like new and stays cleaner longer. Why? Pressing compacts the fibers, so dirt has a difficult time penetrating a piece of fabric. Also, the more a garment is pressed, the less pressing is necessary after it comes out of the dryer.

There are many styles of knit garments today. The techniques above have shown you the proper way to position any garment, knit or woven, on the press or ironing board. However, knits do require special care, so the following information will help you achieve a better finish press to your knits.

With the Press

I usually press knits on the press doubled because the combination of heat and pressure is enough to press through both sides at once. Besides, it's fast and easy.

Press silk-screened T-shirts so that the art is against the board rather than the heating shoe. Otherwise you run the risk of melting the design.

Press dark colors on the wrong side. As with other uneven surfaces such as pockets, pleats, etc., place the small pressing cushion under the area and press with steam and half pressure.

To press sweaters, lightly dampen or steam, and pat the heating shoe on the surface of the sweater a few times without applying pressure.

To straighten or block a knitwear item, dampen it lightly with warm water, or set your press for steam. Place the sweater on the board, push it into shape by hand, and pat the heating shoe on the surface. Lightly brush steam away with the drafting brush. Fold and hang on a protected hanger as you would a pair of pants.

With the Hand Iron

After my tour of the dry cleaners, I learned to steam-press my knits rather than iron them. To do this:

1. Hold the steam iron $\frac{1}{2}"$–$1"$ (1.3 cm–2.5 cm) above the fabric so the steam penetrates the fabric.

2. Gently press the iron over the areas that need pressing without dragging the iron across the fabric. Allow fabric to dry before wearing.

PRESSING FLAT PIECES— NAPKINS, TOWELS, SHEETS, TABLECLOTHS

With the Press

Napkins

If the edge of a napkin or handkerchief is curling, straighten the edges before pressing by sliding them by hand along the edge of the heating shoe. Press the rest of the napkin by placing it flat on the board, wrong side up, and pressing with steam or while damp. Fold napkin on the board after pressing.

Towels

Dampen towel or set the press for steam. Center the towel on the board and press. Fold long edges in and press again (Fig. 12.44). Fold towel on the board after pressing.

Sheets or Tablecloths

1. Dampen sheet (or tablecloth). Fold it in half the long way.

2. Place one end on the board and pleat it into 4"–5" (10 cm–12.5 cm) pleats. Stack pleats behind the board (Fig. 12.45).

3. Begin pressing by pulling the fabric toward you. *Note:* Because of the 100 pounds (45 kg) of pressure, you can press two or more layers flat at the same time. Try to press as much moisture out of the fabric as possible for a permanent press.

4. The press can help you fold. Turn the press off, and let it cool. Fold sheet in half the long way. Place one end in the press while holding the other end yourself (Fig. 12.46). Fold sheet toward press. Release the press, anchor both ends in the press, and fold again. It's like having another person on the other end to help you.

With the Hand Iron

Napkins

Use the tip of your iron to press curled edges. Iron napkin or handkerchief from the

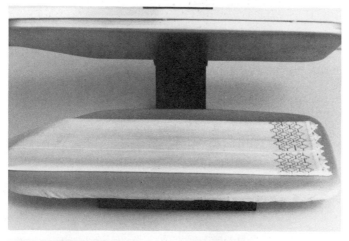

FIG. 12.44 Fold towel edges in and press again.

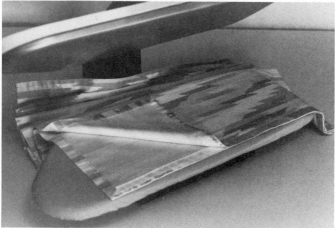

FIG. 12.45 Place tablecloth on one end and pleat. Stack pleats behind the board.

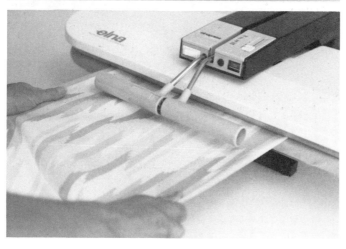

FIG. 12.46 The press can help you fold.

center out, ironing out as much moisture as possible. Fold and put away.

Towels

Center towel on the ironing board. Iron flat following the lengthwise grain. Fold long edges into the center and iron again until most of the moisture has evaporated. Fold and put away.

Sheets or Tablecloths

If you don't have a press, I recommend that you use permanent-press sheets and send your large tablecloths to the cleaner for cleaning and pressing. If you must use a hand iron, however, this is the way to do it.

1. Thoroughly dampen the tablecloth by spritzing warm water on it and rolling it up, so the moisture is evenly distributed.

2. Set ironing board up on a clean floor or place a large sheet under the board, so the tablecloth rests on a clean surface. Fold tablecloth in half the long way and place it on the ironing board so fold and hem edges are parallel to the long edges of the board and the length of the tablecloth is draped on the square end of the board. Begin by straightening the hem edges. Then iron fabric flat on the lengthwise grain.

3. Pull fabric toward the narrow end and iron again, a section at a time. Turn tablecloth over and iron as described above on the other side. Iron as much of the moisture out of the fabric as possible. Hang cloth on a protected hanger until all moisture has evaporated before folding and putting it away.

PRESSING APPLIQUÉD OR EMBROIDERED PIECES AND NAPPED FABRICS

With the Press
Press appliquéd or embroidered areas before pressing the rest of the garment. To do this, place the stitchery right side down, and press with full pressure so that stitchery is imbedded in the padded surface.

To press napped fabric, set your press for steam or dampen a bristled or woolen press cloth. Place the nap side up. If your press has steam, let steam penetrate the fabric. If your press doesn't have steam, place the press cloth on the fabric. Bring the heating shoe to the surface of the napped fabric, but do not put any pressure on it. Hold the heating shoe on the fabric for a few seconds until most of the moisture has evaporated. Repeat if necessary.

With the Hand Iron
Press appliquéd or embroidered areas before pressing the rest of the garment. To do this, place the stitchery face down on a pressing pad or a lofty terry cloth towel. Press iron over stitchery so that all the fabric around it is pressed flat (Fig. 12.47).

To press napped fabric, use a needle board or Velvaboard. Place napped side against the surface of needle or Velvaboard. Hold iron above the fabric, letting steam penetrate, and press with gentle pressure, lifting the iron and moving it from section to section.

HINT: If you are not pressing a lot of napped fabrics, make a press cloth of the same fabric as the garment and press so the napped surfaces are against one another.

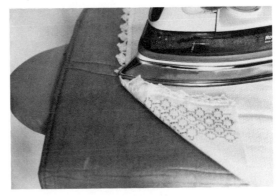

FIG. 12.47 Press iron over stitchery so all the fabric around it is pressed flat.

BLOCKING HAND-KNIT PIECES AND NEEDLEPOINT

Knit Pieces

The principles for blocking a hand-knit piece with a press and hand iron are the same.

1. Block each knitted piece before construction. Use a dry iron on wool setting, with a soft, dampened press cloth.

2. Lay knitted piece on the board, wrong side up. Place press cloth on top. Iron seams straight with slight pressure.

3. Lay blocked piece flat on a cutting board or dryer until it is completely dry. If the piece is curling, pin it to the board with rustproof pins.

HINT: Wool and some cottons can be adjusted and made larger with the use of steam and by pushing into shape by hand. Acrylics and some blends cannot be stretched or shrunk after knitting.

Needlepoint

1. Pin needlepoint to board with rustproof pins, right side down.

2. Set your press or iron for steam. If you don't have the steam setting on your press, lightly dampen a press cloth and place it over the work. Press needlepoint with slight pressure, straightening it as necessary. Don't move the piece until the moisture has evaporated completely. *Note:* Depending on the stitch used, some needlepoint must be stretched and shaped vigorously to block it into the appropriate shape.

PRESSING QUILT BLOCKS

Robbie Fanning, co-author with her husband, Tony, of *The Complete Book of Machine Quilting,* says "The usual advice on pressing seams in pieced work is to press them toward the lighter-weight fabric." She further explains, "I suspect this advice has been handed down from early quilting when seams were handpieced and could not stand up to the strain of having the seams pressed open. But we now use modern threads so strong they are apt to last longer than the fabric. Our machine stitches can be as even and as close as we wish. So why not press open machine-pieced seams?"

With the Press

Place quilt block wrong side up. Press seam open with the tip of your travel iron. Bring heating shoe down to the quilt block and press with full pressure. If the block has been distorted in the sewing process, pin it to the padded board and use the steam setting or a dampened press cloth to square it.

HINT: If you have a puff iron, open narrow seams with it, then press the block flat as described.

With the Hand Iron

Place quilt block wrong side up. Open seam with the tip of your iron, using steam. Press seams flat with firm pressure on your iron. Move iron to the next section and press again. If the block has been distorted in the sewing process, pin it to the padded ironing board to press. Let all the moisture evaporate before moving it.

CLEANING YOUR PRESS AND IRON

We've used a lot of fusibles to construct your blazer and, chances are, you may have some "gunk" on the heating shoe of your press or soleplate of your iron. To prevent scorching, shine, and the gunk from pressing onto your ironing board cover and finished projects, clean pressing surfaces as described.

The Press

Turn press upside down. Heat press to the cotton setting, and be sure to clean it in a well-ventilated room. Use a soft cloth folded into enough layers that you don't burn your

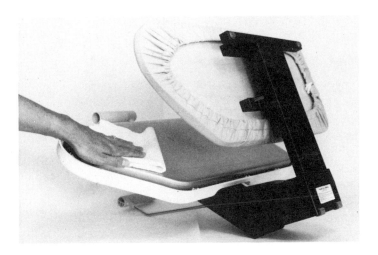

FIG. 12.48 Cleaning the press.

hand when using it. Squeeze hot iron cleaner (available at your local fabric store) on soft cloth and rub it over the hot heating shoe until all adhesive has been removed (Fig. 12.48). This may take two or more treatments, depending on how much residue has built up on the press. To clean spray starch off the press, use Formula 409® on a paper towel to dissolve it.

To prevent water marks and color distortion on your fashion fabric, wash the ironing board cover frequently.

HINT: If you have used your press as much as Sara Bunje of San Mateo, California, the pressing pad under the ironing board cover may be flattened too much to do any good. Therefore, remove the old pad, use it as a pattern, and cut a new one from an old army blanket, as she did.

The fabric used to make the pressing board covers is specially treated to withstand the heat of the press. Therefore I recommend purchasing a new cover from your local press dealer. If you choose to make a replacement cover, use your old cover as a pattern, and make it from preshrunk, unbleached muslin.

Because the muslin is not treated to withstand a lot of heat, you may have to replace it more often.

The Hand Iron

If you use a Teflon soleplate, you probably won't have to clean your iron as frequently because the Teflon helps repel fusible adhesive. When you do clean your iron, do so in a well-ventilated room. Place newspapers down so the cleaner will not drip off the soleplate and soil the surface you are working on. Heat iron to the cotton setting. Use a soft cloth folded in enough layers that you don't burn your hand when using it. Squeeze a small amount of hot iron cleaner (available at your local fabric store) on the soft cloth and rub it over the soleplate of the iron until all adhesive has been removed. You may have to repeat this a couple of times.

Replace ironing board cover and pad when they are worn or not doing the job for you. Pads mat down after a while. A new pad can help eliminate pressing ridges, creases, and other unwanted marks in a piece of fabric.

Afterword

How do you like your speed-tailored jacket, your notebook of stitch samples, and your beautifully pressed wardrobe? If you've done nothing else than gain confidence in trying new techniques and products designed to make your sewing faster, easier, and more interesting, then the time we spent together has been worth it. Continue to look for ideas, to experiment and perfect your own techniques, then escape to your Ultimate Sewing Center: put it all together and create your own couture originals.

Presser Foot Chart

Note: This chart shows Viking feet and their respective lettered designations; nomenclature will be different for other brands, but presser foot configurations are similar.

Standard Feet with Machine Purchase

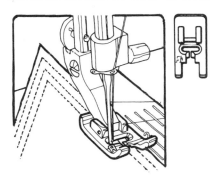

A. *Standard (topstitch) foot*

B. *Utility foot*

C. *Buttonhole foot*

D. *Blind hem foot*

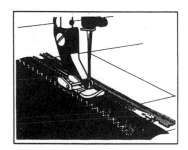

E. *Zipper foot*

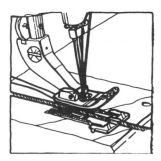

F. *Raised seam foot & guide*

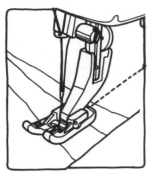

H. Teflon foot

J. Overcast
(edging) foot

Button reed/clearance plate

Edge guide

Transparent appliqué foot

Extra Feet and Attachments

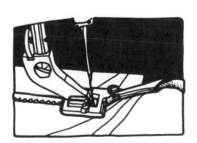

Bias binder

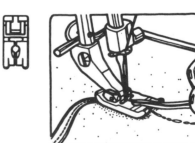

Braiding foot & guide

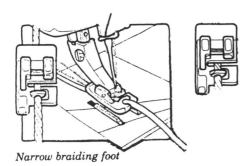

Narrow braiding foot

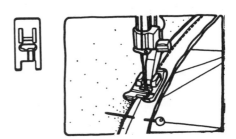

Piping foot

Roller presser

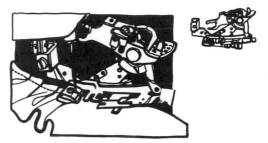

Ruffler

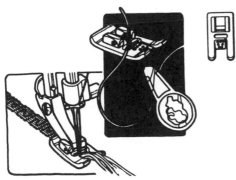

Seven-hole cording foot & threader

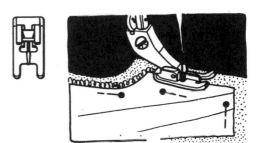

Special marking foot

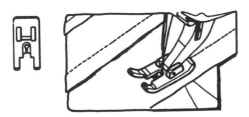

Straight stitch foot

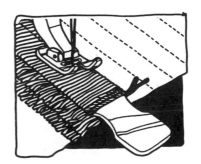

Weaver's reed

Buttonholer

Circular sewing attachment

Darning foot

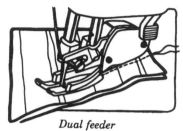

Dual feeder

Eyelet plate (4mm)

Gathering foot

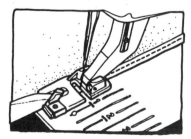

Hemmer (2mm)

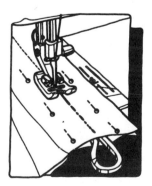

Hemstitch fork

198

Sources of Supply

SEWING MACHINE, SERGER, AND FURNITURE COMPANIES

Archer-Finesse
Melex USA, Inc.
1200 Front St.
Raleigh, NC 27609

Bernina of America
534 W. Chestnut
Hinsdale, IL 60521

Brother Sewing Machine Co.
8th Corporation Pl.
Piscataway, NJ 08854

Elna, Inc.
7642 Washington Ave. South
Minneapolis, MN 55344

Kenmore
Sears Tower
Chicago, IL 60607

Necchi Logica/Allyn International
1075 Santa Fe Dr.
Denver, CO 80203

Nelco
164 W. 25th St.
New York, NY 10001

New Home Sewing Machine Co.
171 Commerce Dr.
Carlstadt, NJ 07072

J.C. Penney Co., Inc.
1301 Avenue of the Americas
New York, NY 10019

Pfaff American Sales Corp.
610 Winters Ave.
Paramus, NJ 07653

Riccar America Co.
14281 Franklin Ave.
Tustin, CA 92680

Simplicity/Tacony Corp.
4421 Ridgewood Ave.
St. Louis, MO 63116

Singer Co.
135 Raritan Center Pkwy.
Edison, NJ 08837

Viking White Sewing
11760 Berea Rd.
Cleveland, OH 44111

Ward's (Montgomery Ward)
PO Box 8339
Chicago, IL 60680

PRESSING EQUIPMENT

Presses

Bernina of America
534 W. Chestnut
Hinsdale, IL 60521
   Bernette Press

Elna, Inc.
7642 Washington Ave. South
Minneapolis, MN 55344
   ElnaPress

Singer Co.
135 Raritan Center Pkwy.
Edison, NJ 08837
   Singer Press

Viking White Sewing
11760 Berea Rd.
Cleveland, OH 44111
   Husky Press
   Supra Press

Commercial Irons and Pressing Aids

Hi-Steam Corp.
610 Washington Ave.
Carlstadt, NJ 07072
   Naomoto HYS-5 iron
   Press'N Dry PND-2000 Vacuum Ironing
   Board

Rowenta, Inc.
281 Albany St.
Cambridge, MA 02139
    Irons, garment steam brushes

June Tailor, Inc.
2861 Highway 175
Richfield, WI 53076
    Tailor board, hams, mitts, press cloths, etc.
    Color catalog

Sussman Automatic Steam Products Corp.
43-20 34th St.
Long Island City, NY 11101
or
6659 Peachtree Industrial Blvd.
Suite M
Norcross, GA 30092
    Pressmaster gravity-feed irons, ironing boards
    with sleever, Pressmate Vacuum Pressing
    System (vacuum ironing board)

(NOTE: The following listings were adapted with permission from *The Complete Book of Machine Embroidery* by Robbie and Tony Fanning [Chilton, 1986].)

THREADS

NOTE: Ask your local retailer or send a pread-dressed, stamped envelope to the companies below to find out where to buy their threads.

Extra-fine

Assorted threads
    Robison-Anton Textile Co.
    175 Bergen Blvd.
    Fairview, NJ 07022

DMC 100% cotton, Sizes 30 and 50
    The DMC Corp.
    107 Trumbull St.
    Elizabeth, NJ 07206

Dual-Duty Plus Extra-fine, cotton-wrapped
polyester
    J&PCoats/Coats & Clark
    PO Box 6044
    Norwalk, CT 06852

Iris 100% rayon
    Art Sales
    4801 W. Jefferson
    Los Angeles, CA 90016

Iris 100% silk—*see* Zwicky

Madeira threads
    Madeira Co.
    56 Primrose Drive
    O'Shea Industrial Park
    Laconia, NH 03246

Mettler Metrosene Fine Machine Embroidery
cotton, Size 60/2
    Swiss-Metrosene, Inc.
    7780 Quincy St.
    Willowbrook, IL 60521

Natesh 100% rayon, lightweight
    Aardvark Adventures
    PO Box 2449
    Livermore, CA 94550

Paradise 100% rayon
    D&E Distributing
    199 N. El Camino Real #F-242
    Encinitas, CA 92024

Sulky 100% rayon, Sizes 30 and 40
    Speed Stitch, Inc.
    PO Box 3472
    Port Charlotte, FL 33949

Zwicky 100% cotton, Size 30/2
    Viking White Sewing
    11760 Berea Rd.
    Cleveland, OH 44111

Zwicky 100% silk
    Viking White Sewing
    11760 Berea Rd.
    Cleveland, OH 44111

Ordinary

Dual-Duty Plus, cotton-wrapped polyester—*see*
Dual-Duty Plus Extra-fine

Also Natesh heavyweight, Zwicky in cotton and polyester, Mettler Metrosene in 30/2, 40/3, 50/3, and 30/3, and Metrosene Plus

Metallic

YLI Corp.
45 West 300 North
Provo, UT 84601

Troy Thread & Textile Corp.
2300 W. Diversey Ave.
Chicago, IL 60647
    Free catalog

MACHINE-EMBROIDERY SUPPLIES

(hoops, threads, patterns, books, etc.)

Aardvark Adventures
PO Box 2449
Livermore, CA 94550
    Also publishes "Aardvark Territorial
    Enterprise"

Clotilde, Inc.
1909 SW First Ave.
Ft Lauderdale, FL 33315

Craft Gallery Ltd.
PO Box 8319
Salem, MA 01971

D&E Distributing
199 N. El Camino Real #F-242
Encinitas, CA 92024

Verna Holt's Machine Stitchery
PO Box 236
Hurricane, UT 84734

Nancy's Notions
PO Box 683
Beaver Dam, WI 53916
    Catalog $.60 in stamps

Patty Lou Creations
Rt 2, Box 90-A
Elgin, OR 97827

Sew-Art International
PO Box 550
Bountiful, UT 84010
    Catalog $2

Speed Stitch, Inc.
PO Box 3472
Port Charlotte, FL 33952
    Catalog $2

SewCraft
Box 1869
Warsaw, IN 46580
    Also publishes newsletter/catalog

Treadleart
25834 Narbonne Ave.
Lomita, CA 90717

SEWING MACHINE SUPPLIES

The Button Shop
PO Box 1065
Oak Park, IL 60304
    Presser feet

Sewing Emporium
1087 Third Ave.
Chula Vista, CA 92010
    Presser feet, accessories

MISCELLANEOUS

Applications
871 Fourth Ave.
Sacramento, CA 95818
    Release paper for appliqué

Berman Leathercraft
145 South St.
Boston, MA 02111
    Leather

Boycan's Craft and Art Supplies
PO Box 897
Sharon, PA 16146
    Plastic needlepoint canvas

Cabin Fever Calicoes
PO Box 54
Center Sandwich, NH 03227

Clearbrook Woolen Shop
PO Box 8
Clearbrook, VA 22624
    Ultrasuede scraps

The Fabric Carr
170 State St.
Los Altos, CA 94022
    Sewing gadgets

Folkwear
Box 3798
San Rafael, CA 94912
   Timeless fashion patterns—$1 catalog

The Green Pepper Inc.
941 Olive St.
Eugene, OR 97401
   Outdoor fabrics, patterns—$1 catalog

Home-Sew
Bethlehem, PA 18018
   Lace—$.25 catalog

Libby's Creations
PO Box 16800, Ste. 180
Mesa, AZ 85202
   Horizontal spool holder

LJ Originals, Inc.
516 Sumac Pl.
DeSoto, TX 75115
   TransGraph

Lore Lingerie
3745 Overland Ave.
Los Angeles, CA 90034
   1 lb. of silk remnants, $9.45

Osage Country Quilt Factory
400 Walnut
Overbrook, KS 66524
   Washable fabric spray glue

The Pellon Company
119 West 40th St.
New York, NY 10018
   Machine appliqué supplies and interfacings

The Perfect Notion
115 Maple St.
Toms River, NJ 08753
   Sewing supplies

Salem Industries, Inc.
PO Box 43027
Atlanta, GA 30336
   Olfa cutters, rulers

Solar-Kist Corp.
PO Box 273
LaGrange, IL 60525
   Teflon pressing sheet

Summa Design
Box 24404
Dayton, OH 45424
   Charted designs for knitting needle machine
   sewing

Susan of Newport
Box 3107
Newport Beach, CA 92663
   Ribbons and laces

Tandy Leather Co.
PO Box 791
Ft. Worth, TX 76101
   Leather

Theta's School of Sewing
2508 NW 39th St.
Oklahoma City, OK 73112
   Charted designs for knitting needle machine
   sewing, smocking directions and supplies for
   the machine

MAGAZINES

(write for rates)

Aardvark Territorial Enterprise
PO Box 2449
Livermore, CA 94550
   Newspaper jammed with information about
   all kinds of embroidery, design, and things to
   order.

disPatch
1042 E. Baseline
Tempe, AZ 85283
    Newspaper about quilting and machine arts

Fiberarts
50 College St.
Asheville, NC 28801
    Gallery of the best fiber artists, including
    those who work in machine stitchery.

Needlecraft for Today
4949 Byers
Ft. Worth, TX 76109
    Creative uses of the sewing machine

SewCraft
Box 1869
Warsaw, IN 46580
    Newspaper and catalog combination
    containing machine embroidery articles,
    designs, and supplies.

Sew It Seams
PO Box 2698
Kirkland, WA 98083-2698

Sew News
PO Box 1790
Peoria, IL 61656
    Monthly tabloid, mostly about garment
    sewing

Threads
Box 355
Newton, CT 06470
    Magazine on all fiber crafts

Treadleart
25834 Narbonne Ave.
Lomita, CA 90717
    Bimonthly about machine embroidery

Update Newsletters
2269 Chestnut, Suite 269
San Francisco, CA 94123

VIDEO TAPES

Betzina, Sandra. "Power Sewing" (BETA or VHS).
Write Power Sewing, P.O. Box 2702, San Francisco, CA 94126.

Clotilde, Inc. Clotilde's TV Teaching Segments Series numbers 1 through 6 (BETA or VHS). For
more information write Clotilde, Inc., 1909 SW
First Ave., Ft. Lauderdale, FL 33315.

——. Clotilde's Seminar Videos: "Sew Smart for
the $500 Look," "Smart Tailoring," "Ultra-
suede and Other Leather-like Fabrics" (BETA
or VHS).

Salyers, Donna. "Sew a Wardrobe in a Weekend,"
"Re-Do a Room in a Weekend," "Super Time-
Saving Sewing Tips," "Craft and Gift Ideas."
For further information, write Congress Video
Group, 10 East 53rd St., New York, NY 10022.

Tailor, June. "Pressing Matters." Write June
Tailor, P.O. Box 208, Richfield, WI 53076.

Zieman, Nancy. Five pages of her current catalog
are devoted to available video tapes, which are
too numerous to list here. For more information, write Nancy's Notions, P.O. Box 683, 333
Beichl Ave., Beaver Dam, WI 53919.

Bibliography

Ambuter, Carolyn, *The Open Canvas,* Workman Publishing, New York, 1982.

Betzina, Sandra, *Power Sewing,* Sandra Betzina, San Francisco, 1985.

Bishop, Edna Bryte, and Marjorie Stotler Arch, *The Bishop Method,* W & W Publishing, Memphis, 1966.

Brown, Gail, and Pati Palmer, *The Complete Handbook for Overlock Sewing,* Palmer/Pletsch, Inc., Portland, OR, 1985.

Coffin, David Page, *The Custom Shirt Book,* David Page Coffin, c/o Threads Magazine, Newtown, CT, 1985.

Dodson, Jackie, *Know Your Bernina,* Chilton Book Co., Radnor, PA, 1987.

——, *Know Your Sewing Machine,* Chilton Book Co., Radnor, PA, 1988.

Fanning, Robbie and Tony, *The Complete Book of Machine Embroidery,* Chilton, Radnor, PA, 1986.

Habeeb, Virginia, *Ladies' Home Journal Art of Homemaking,* Simon & Schuster, New York, 1973.

Jabenis, Elaine, *The Fashion Director,* John Wiley & Sons, New York, 1972.

O'Connell, Barbara Weiland, *Shaping Fashion: A Guide to Today's Interfacing,* Update Newsletters, San Francisco, 1988.

Palmer, Pati, Gail Brown, and Sue Green, *Creative Serging Illustrated,* Chilton Book Co., Radnor, PA, 1987.

Reader's Digest Complete Guide to Sewing, Reader's Digest Association, Pleasantville, NY, 1976.

Saunders, Janice S., *Illustrated Speed Sewing: 103 Machine Shortcuts,* Speed Sewing Ltd., Centerline, MI, 1985.

Shaeffer, Claire B., *The Complete Book of Sewing Shortcuts,* Sterling Publishing, New York, 1984.

Simplicity, *New Simplicity Sewing Book,* Simplicity Pattern Co., New York, 1979.

Simplicity's Simply the Best Sewing Book, Simplicity Pattern Co., New York, 1988.

Singer, *Singer Sewing Update 1988,* Cy DeCosse Inc., Minnetonka, MN, 1988.

Vogue, *The New Vogue Sewing Book,* Butterick Publishing, New York, 1980.

Index